PC
QuickSteps
Second Edition

Bath & North East Somerset	
1 9 0016797 4	
Askews	08-Jan-2009
004.16	£9.99

GUY HART-DAVIS

McGraw Hill

New York Chicago San Francisco
Lisbon London Madrid Mexico City
Milan New Delhi San Juan
Seoul Singapore Sydney Toronto

The *McGraw·Hill* Companies

Library of Congress Cataloging-in-Publication Data

Hart-Davis, Guy.
   PC quicksteps / Guy Hart-Davis.—2nd ed.
      p. cm.
   Includes index.
   ISBN 978-0-07-159983-2 (alk. paper)
   1. Microcomputers. I. Title.
QA76.5.H3727 2008
004.16—dc22

                     2008036317

PC QUICKSTEPS, SECOND EDITION

ISBN   978-0-07-159983-2
MHID   0-07-159983-5

SPONSORING EDITOR / Roger Stewart

EDITORIAL SUPERVISOR / Patty Mon

PROJECT MANAGER / Vasundhara Sawhney (International Typesetting and Composition)

SERIES CREATORS AND EDITORS / Marty and Carole Matthews

ACQUISITIONS COORDINATOR / Carly Stapleton

TECHNICAL EDITOR / Curt Simmons

COPY EDITOR / Sally Engelfried

PROOFREADER / Divya Kapoor

INDEXER / Karin Arrigoni

PRODUCTION SUPERVISOR / Jean Bodeaux

COMPOSITION / International Typesetting and Composition

ILLUSTRATION / International Typesetting and Composition

SERIES DESIGN / Bailey Cunningham

ART DIRECTOR, COVER / Jeff Weeks

COVER DESIGN / Pattie Lee

COVER ILLUSTRATION / Tom Willis

To Rhonda and Teddy

About the Author

Guy Hart-Davis is the author of *How to Do Everything: iPod & iTunes, Fourth Edition*, *How to Do Everything: Microsoft Office Word 2007*, *How to Do Everything: Microsoft Office Excel 2007*, and *Mac OS X Leopard QuickSteps*.

About the Technical Editor

Curt Simmons is the author of more than 50 technology books, including such titles as *How to Do Everything with Windows Vista*, *How to Do Everything with Your BlackBerry*, and *How to Do Everything with Windows XP*.

Contents at a Glance

Contents

3   Chapter 3   **Connecting to and Using the Internet** 53

4   Chapter 4   **Installing and Using Programs** 81

Chapter 5 Installing and Using Audio and Video Hardware 99

Chapter 6 Upgrading, Installing, and Configuring Hardware 125

Chapter 7 Securing Your PC 139

Chapter 8 Setting Up a Home Network 163

Acknowledgments

My thanks go to the following people, who put in a huge amount of work on this book:

- Marty Matthews, series editor and technical editor, developed the first edition of the book and made countless suggestions for improvements throughout.

- Curt Simmons, technical editor, reviewed the second edition for technical accuracy and contributed many helpful suggestions.

- Sally Engelfried, editor, edited the book skillfully and with good humor.

- Patty Mon, editorial supervisor, and Vasundhara Sawhney, project manager, kept the book project moving and the author under control.

- Divya Kapoor, proofreader, caught widely varied inconsistencies.

- Roger Stewart, Editorial Director and Grand Hierophant at McGraw-Hill, helped create the series and pulled strings in the background throughout the process.

Two PCs were harmed during the creation of this book.

Introduction

QuickSteps books are recipe books for computer users. They answer the question "how do I…" by providing a quick set of steps to accomplish the most common tasks with a particular operating system or application.

The sets of steps are the central focus of the book. QuickSteps sidebars show how to quickly perform many small functions or tasks that support the primary functions. QuickFacts sidebars supply information that you need to know about a subject. Notes, Tips, and Cautions augment the steps, presented in a separate column to not interrupt the flow of the steps. The introductions are minimal rather than narrative, and numerous illustrations and figures, many with callouts, support the steps.

QuickSteps books are organized by function and the tasks needed to perform that function. Each function is a chapter. Each task, or "How To," contains the steps needed for accomplishing the function along with the relevant Notes, Tips, Cautions, and screenshots. You can easily find the tasks you need through:

- The Table of Contents, which lists the functional areas (chapters) and tasks in the order they are presented

- A How To list of tasks on the opening page of each chapter

- The index, which provides an alphabetical list of the terms that are used to describe the functions and tasks

- Color-coded tabs for each chapter or functional area with an index to the tabs in the Contents at a Glance (just before the Table of Contents)

Conventions Used in This Book

PC QuickSteps uses several conventions designed to make the book easier for you to follow. Among these are

- A ⊕ in the table of contents and in the How To list in each chapter references a QuickSteps sidebar in a chapter, and a ⬤ references a QuickFacts sidebar.

- WINDOWS KEY represents the key or keys on the keyboard that bear the Windows logo. (Some keyboards don't have this key.)

- **Bold type** is used for words or objects on the screen that you are to do something with—for example, "click **Start**, and then click **Computer**."

- *Italic type* is used for a word or phrase that is being defined or otherwise deserves special emphasis.

- Underlined type is used for text that you are to type from the keyboard.

- SMALL CAPITAL LETTERS are used for keys on the keyboard such as ENTER and SHIFT.

- When you are expected to enter a command, you are told to "press" the key or keys. If you are to enter text or numbers, you are told to "type" them.

How to...

Chapter 1
Getting to Know Your PC

PCs are indispensable to many people, are a source of daily frustration to other people, and are both to many people. This book shows you how to get a PC that suits you and make it do the things you need it to do.

This chapter explains what a PC is and what it does, advises you on how to choose a PC and operating system that meets your needs, shows you how to set up the PC, and tells you how to start the PC and shut it down.

Understand What a PC Is and Does

PC is the abbreviation for *personal computer*, a computer designed to be used by an individual rather than by a department or a company as a whole. PCs come in various sizes, formats, and capabilities (Figure 1-1 shows examples), but the term is generally used to mean an IBM-compatible personal computer that can run the Windows operating system. By contrast, the computers made by Apple Computer, Inc. are generally referred to as Macintoshes, or Macs, after the name Apple uses on its predominant line of computers.

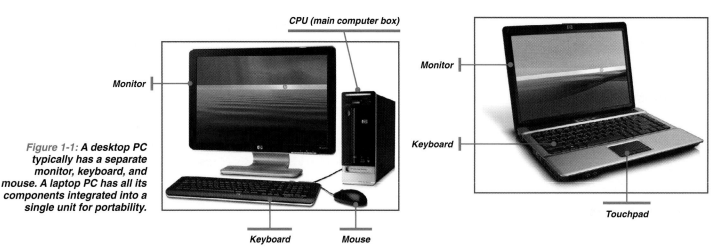

CPU (main computer box)

Monitor

Monitor

Keyboard

Figure 1-1: A desktop PC typically has a separate monitor, keyboard, and mouse. A laptop PC has all its components integrated into a single unit for portability.

Touchpad

Keyboard

Mouse

A PC's purpose is to manipulate information in the ways you tell it to, but most people find it easier to think of a PC's purpose in terms of what they can do with it. For example, with the right software, you can

- Create a memo, letter, or spreadsheet
- Edit a digital picture
- Send and receive e-mail
- Record and play back digital audio files
- Edit video files and burn CDs and DVDs

You can use a PC by itself if you choose, but you can gain access to vast amounts of information (or data) by connecting your PC to the Internet, the worldwide computer network. At home or at work, you can connect your PC to other PCs using a local area network (LAN) so that it can share data, services, and hardware resources with other computers.

Understand Desktops and Laptops

The two main types of PCs are desktops and laptops (see Figure 1-1).

- A *desktop* is a PC designed for use in a static location, typically a desk. Most desktop PCs consist of several separate parts: the CPU (central processing unit), or main computer box; the monitor; and a separate mouse and keyboard.

- A *laptop* is an all-in-one PC with an integrated keyboard, pointing device (such as a touchpad or a pointing stick), and monitor (in a lid that folds shut for protection).

NOTE

Some PC designs blur the differences between desktops and laptops. For instance, some laptops include detachable monitors; and some desktops have most of the components (except for the keyboard and mouse) built into the monitor housing.

QUICK**FACTS**

UNDERSTANDING 32-BIT AND 64-BIT PROCESSORS

One of the most confusing terms in personal computing is the number of bits for a processor. These days, most PCs use either 32-bit processors or 64-bit processors.

Here, the "bit" measurement tells you how much data the processor can handle at once. 32-bit means that there are 32 data wires running in parallel, allowing the PC to manipulate 32 bits of data at once. By historical standards, this is a large amount of data, but 64-bit processors (with 64 wires running in parallel) are now becoming widespread. The 64-bit processors can handle far more data at once than 32-bit processors, but they require 64-bit operating systems and programs for best performance.

To make things more complicated, most 64-bit processors (such as AMD's Athlon 64) can also run 32-bit programs at nearly full speed. Most consumer versions of Windows Vista are 32-bit, so even if the PC you buy has a 64-bit processor, it is probably operating in 32-bit mode when running Windows Vista.

Identify the Components of a PC

Most PCs consist of a number of standard components, although these components may look different or be physically different in different PCs. This section explains those components. You don't need to understand the components of a PC in order to use it, but having a basic understanding of the components usually helps when you're planning to buy a PC (so that you can evaluate PC specifications) and when you need to troubleshoot problems (see Chapter 10).

CPU

The *central processing unit*, or *CPU*, technically refers to the PC's processor, but also tends to be used as a general term for the main box of a desktop computer—the box that contains the PC's motherboard (or main circuit board), processor, memory, hard drive, and other components. You can see a CPU box in Figure 1-1.

The CPU contains most of the components of a desktop PC: the processor and memory; the hard drive, optical drive, and floppy drive (if the PC includes one); the graphics, sound, and network cards; the power supply; and all the cables that connect these components together. On a typical desktop PC, the CPU is usually a rectangular box designed to lie flat on your desk or stand on end, either on your desk or on the floor; a minitower or larger tower box designed to stand upright on the floor; or a miniature unit designed to fit unobtrusively where there's space. In a laptop PC, the CPU typically lies under the keyboard and the other surface of the lower part of the PC, together with most of the components of the PC apart from the monitor.

PROCESSOR

The processor, or microprocessor, is the main chip in the PC. This is where the bulk of the computing gets done. Your PC runs Windows courtesy of the

TIP

Processor speeds, or *clock speeds*, are confusing because different processor designs perform different numbers of actions per processor cycle. For example, Intel's Core 2 Duo processors perform more actions per cycle than Intel's Pentium IV processors, even though their clock speeds are lower. Similarly, a processor that has a 64-bit data path can perform many more actions, even at a lower clock speed, than a processor with a 32-bit data path. To get an idea of how different processors compare, look at processor benchmarks on a site such as Tom's Hardware (go to www.tomshardware.co.uk and look for the Charts section).

QUICK**FACTS**

CHOOSING A PROCESSOR

Most desktop PCs use processors made by either Intel Corporation or AMD (Advanced Micro Devices, Inc.).

All current desktop processors are more than fast enough to run Windows Vista.

- **Core 2 Duo** is Intel's main line of processors for desktop computers and notebook computers. Intel also makes higher-powered processors, such as the Core 2 Quad (for multimedia enthusiasts) and Core 2 Extreme (for gamers and those with money to burn), but most people do not need these.

- **Celeron** is Intel's less expensive and less capable processor family.

- **Athlon** is AMD's answer to Intel's high-end processors. Athlon 64 is a family of 64-bit versions of Athlon that can also run 32-bit applications.

- **Sempron** is AMD's less expensive and less capable processor family.

Continued . . .

microprocessor performing millions of calculations per second. Windows Vista requires a 600MHz Pentium or faster processor, which is ancient and slow by today's standards.

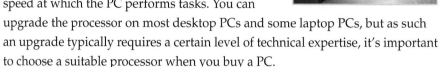

The processor is one of the main influences on the speed at which the PC performs tasks. You can upgrade the processor on most desktop PCs and some laptop PCs, but as such an upgrade typically requires a certain level of technical expertise, it's important to choose a suitable processor when you buy a PC.

Historically, processor speeds have been measured in megahertz (MHz; millions of cycles per second) and gigahertz (GHz; billions of cycles per second). Faster processor speeds, or *clock speeds*, have typically meant faster performance. All other things being equal, a 3GHz processor performs ten times more calculations per second than a 300MHz processor and will deliver better performance.

HARD DRIVE

The *hard drive*, or *hard disk*, is the device on which your PC stores most of your information. For example, in almost all PCs, the operating system is stored on the hard drive. If you create a file in a word processor (such as Microsoft Word), you usually store it on your hard drive so that you can access it again later. (In a business situation, you will often store your files on a network drive rather than on your PC's hard drive.)

If your PC's hard drive fails, you can lose some or all of your data, so it's important to back up (store outside your computer) any data that you can't easily recover from other sources. See Chapter 7 for instructions on backing up your data.

QUICK**FACTS**

CHOOSING A PROCESSOR *(Continued)*

Most laptop PCs use processors specifically designed for laptops because they're smaller, consume less power, and produce less heat. However, some larger, performance-oriented laptops use desktop processors, usually at the expense of battery life. All current laptop processors are fast enough to run Windows Vista. Choose a processor to meet your needs and your budget.

- **Desktop-replacement laptops** use processors designed for desktop PCs or modified processors, such as Core 2 Duo and Mobile Athlon 64 X2. These processors provide impressive speed at an affordable price but may overheat if used for a long period of time. You may need to use a fan under the PC to prevent it from becoming too hot. Battery life in these laptops varies from short to disappointing.

- **Economy laptops** use lower-specification desktop processors (such as Intel Celeron processors or AMD Mobile Sempron processors). These processors provide adequate speed at a low price, produce a fair amount of heat (but less than high-specification desktop processors), and deliver modest battery life.

- **High-performance laptops** use processors designed for laptop PCs, such as Intel's mobile Core 2 Duo processors and AMD's Turion 64 X2 processors. These processors deliver impressive performance, along with modest heat and long battery life, but are expensive. Some processor packages include built-in wireless network capabilities, but even those that don't are compatible with widely available wireless network modules.

Most PCs have one hard drive, but many desktop PCs and a few laptop PCs have space for additional internal hard drives. You can also attach external hard drives to a desktop or a laptop PC using a Universal Serial Bus (USB) or FireWire connection.

MEMORY (RAM)

Random access memory, generally referred to simply as "memory" or by its acronym *RAM*, is one or more chips that your PC uses to temporarily store information while it is performing calculations and manipulating data. The more RAM you have (up to your PC's upper limit), the better Windows Vista will run.

Note the words "temporarily store" in the definition of RAM. When power is removed from a PC, the contents of RAM are lost. When you shut down Windows using its normal procedure, it will prompt you to save any unsaved data in your documents that are in RAM before the power is shut off and the contents of RAM are lost. To prevent a power failure from causing a loss of RAM contents and other problems, you may need an uninterruptible power supply (UPS), which is described in Chapter 7.

Windows Vista requires a theoretical minimum of 512MB of RAM to run at all; 1GB (1024MB) is a practical minimum for light use of Windows Vista; 2GB is a good idea for standard use with multiple users; and 3GB or 4GB or more is recommended for heavy use. If Windows Vista runs too slowly on your PC, adding memory is likely to be the most effective way of boosting performance.

How much RAM you can put in your PC depends on the number of memory sockets on the motherboard and the capacity of the memory chips you buy. Many PC motherboards have two memory sockets, each of which can hold

CHOOSING A HARD DRIVE

Hard drives for PCs come with different rotation speeds (measured in revolutions per minute, or rpm), buffers (measured in megabytes, or MB), seek times (measured in milliseconds, or ms), and capacities (measured in gigabytes, or GB).

- A faster rotational speed usually gives better performance, but the drive may be noisier and will definitely be more expensive. For a desktop computer, get a 7200rpm drive, or even a 10,000rpm drive, rather than a 5400rpm drive. Most laptop drives run at 5400rpm or 4200rpm, but 7200rpm models provide better performance (not to mention more heat).

- A bigger buffer improves performance.

- A lower seek time (smaller number)—the average time to access data—is better than a higher seek time.

- Buy as large a drive as you can reasonably afford. Multimedia data (such as audio and video files) take up a huge amount of space. For a desktop PC, you may be able to get more space for your buck, and maybe increased reliability, by buying two or more medium-sized drives than one colossal drive.

- Commodity hard drives—those not intended for professional use—typically last for several years, but you should always back up your data (see Chapter 7) in case of trouble. Any hard drive can fail at any time without warning.

Conventional hard disks consist of one or more platters that rotate at high speed. Newer hard disks consist instead of memory chips. These are called *solid-state devices* or SSDs.

Continued . . .

a 512MB, 1GB, or 2GB memory chip, giving up to 4GB total. Motherboards for heavier-duty computers, such as video workstations and servers, have more memory slots and so can take more RAM. At this writing, 1GB chips offer the best value for money; 2GB chips are proportionally much more expensive.

For technical reasons, 4GB is the upper limit for most 32-bit PCs—and because the PC takes some memory to manage its internal devices, you cannot actually have 4GB available. If you install 4GB of memory chips, you usually get 3GB to 3.5GB available. (This is enough for most uses.)

Some older computers include a 3½-inch floppy disk drive for backward compatibility. Most recent and current computers do not have these drives, because the disks' low capacity makes them of little use compared to modern alternatives, such as USB memory keys and recordable CDs and DVDs. If you have data stored on floppy drives, but your PC doesn't have a drive, either use a friend's PC to transfer the data to another medium, or buy or borrow a USB-connected external floppy drive.

OPTICAL DRIVES

An optical drive is a drive that works with an optical disc, such as a CD or DVD, as opposed to a magnetic disk. Most PCs have a single optical drive, usually one that can both read data and burn it to CDs and DVDs. Some burners can write data to a CD or DVD only

once, but others (called rewriters) can write data, erase it, and write again. To rewrite data, you must use rewritable optical discs.

Speeds for burning DVDs and CDs are denoted with 1X, 2X, and so on. 1X for CDs is 150KBps, while 1X for DVDs is 1.32MBps—about nine times as fast. This is why a DVD drive can burn DVDs at "only" 16X, but burn CDs at 52X or more—the measurements are of different speeds. At 1X, burning a DVD takes about 55 minutes; at 4X, 15 minutes; at 10X, 6 minutes; and at 16X, 4 minutes. Burning a CD at any speed over 32X takes only a couple of minutes, so higher-speed CD burning is largely irrelevant—you're not likely to notice the difference.

CHOOSING A HARD DRIVE *(Continued)*

At this writing, SSDs have smaller capacities than conventional hard drives, are far more expensive, and are not widely used—but capacity is increasing, prices are descending, and usage is going up. SSDs provide good performance, use less energy, and run quieter and cooler, making them good for mobile PCs.

CHOOSING MEMORY

Memory comes in a bewildering variety of types that use different memory technologies, different speeds, and different physical formats. These days, most memory comes in pieces called dual inline memory modules, or DIMMs. Older PCs used single inline memory modules, or SIMMs.

When choosing memory, you must get not only exactly the right type of chip for your PC, but also the right kind of chip to complement your existing chips. If you don't know what type that is, use a program such as CPU-Z (freeware; www.cpuid.com/cpuz.php); visit an automatic memory configuration utility, such as that found at Crucial Technology (www.crucial.com) or Kingston Technology (www.kingston.com); talk to an expert at an online store; or have your local computer store examine your computer and tell you what you need.

SOUND CARD

The *sound card* enables your PC to output sound to your speakers, headphones, or receiver and receive sound input from a line input or microphone. With a sound card, you can use your PC to play music and record audio. On many desktop PCs and almost all laptop PCs, the sound card is built into the motherboard, so you don't get a choice of sound card. If, however, that sound card doesn't produce the quality of sound you need, you can replace it with an internal sound card (on a desktop PC) or an external USB sound card (on either a desktop or a laptop PC) and bypass the built-in sound card.

Standard sound cards typically produce good enough sound for listening to music or general audio. If you plan to use your PC to produce music, ask your musician friends for recommendations for a high-quality sound card.

GRAPHICS CARD

In order to display images on your monitor, your PC needs a *graphics card* (also called a *graphics adapter*, *video card*, or *video adapter*). A laptop's graphics card routes its output directly to the laptop's built-in monitor, but many laptops also include a graphics connector that lets you usually connect a supplementary external monitor. A desktop PC's graphics card has a connector to which you connect the monitor's cable.

The graphics card is built into many desktop PCs and almost all laptop PCs. On a desktop PC, you can install another graphics card and use it either in tandem with or instead of the built-in graphics card. On a laptop PC, you can seldom change the built-in graphics card.

NETWORK CARD

The *network card* enables your PC to connect to a network so that it can share data with or receive data from other PCs. There are two main types of network cards: wired network cards that you use with a cabled network, and wireless network cards that create a network across the airwaves. Chapter 8 discusses how to choose hardware for wired and wireless networks, including network cards.

CHOOSING AN OPTICAL DRIVE

DVDs are great for backing up large amounts of data. The DVD–R standard is 4.7GB, while a CD holds only 700MB (0.7GB). A dual-layer DVD holds twice as much data: 9.4GB. When choosing an optical drive, first consider a DVD rewriter—a DVD drive that can write and erase and rewrite to both DVDs and CDs and can play both DVDs and CDs.

There are six different recordable DVD standards: DVD+RW, DVD-RW, DVD+R, DVD-RAM, DVD-R for General, and DVD-R for Authoring. The two you should focus on are DVD+RW and DVD-RW.

- DVD+RW can write data to a disc multiple times, and it looks like this is becoming the dominant format for rewritable DVDs.

- DVD-RW can write data to a disc multiple times but is now less widely used than DVD+RW. DVD-RW and DVD+RW use different technologies to perform the same tasks, much as VHS and Betamax VCRs used different technologies.

For greatest flexibility, get a combination drive that can handle DVD+RW and DVD-RW. These drives are sometimes described as DVD±RW drives.

Most PC users find DVD burning useful. However, if you are certain you will never need to burn DVDs on your PC, you can save a little money by buying a combination DVD/CD-RW drive—a drive that can play DVDs and write and rewrite CDs.

MONITOR

The *monitor*, sometimes called the *display* or *screen*, is the device on which your PC displays information for you to see. The amount of data that the monitor displays at any one time is called the *resolution* and is described by the number of *pixels* (picture elements, or dots) used across the screen and the number used down the screen. For example, the resolution 1024×768 means the monitor uses 1024 pixels across the screen and 768 pixels down it.

Monitors come in two main types:

- *CRT* (cathode-ray tube) monitors are the larger type of monitor, like a standard TV set. CRTs can display a variety of resolutions, but none of them is perfectly sharp. Also, CRTs take a lot of desk or table space and are heavy.

- *LCD* (liquid crystal display) monitors are the slimmer type of monitor. Most LCDs can display only one resolution sharply; this is called the LCD's *native resolution* and matches the pixel count of the screen. Other resolutions require the LCD to split display information across pixels, which makes for a blocky and hard-to-read effect.

Both CRTs and LCDs come in a variety of sizes and resolutions. Laptop PCs have a built-in LCD display that you can't change without major surgery. In almost all desktop PCs, the monitor connects via a cable to the CPU, so you can use various types of monitors.

When choosing a monitor, choose one that provides the resolution you need and a picture you like. LCDs deliver a sharper, more stable picture and take up less room on the desktop, while CRTs are less expensive and can usually display a wide variety of resolutions.

MOUSE

Mouse is the generic term for the pointing device used with the PC. The mouse is a small, usually curved box that you put your hand on and move on a flat surface, such as a mouse pad, to indicate where you want the mouse pointer on the screen to move.

Mice (some people say *mouses*) are widely used, but you can also use many other pointing devices, such as the following:

CHOOSING A GRAPHICS CARD

Even economy PCs come with adequate graphics cards for most normal use. However, you may need to upgrade your graphics card if:

- You play action games on your PC.
- You want to watch or record TV on your PC.
- You work extensively with video.
- You need to use a huge monitor (or several huge monitors).

CHOOSING A MONITOR, MOUSE, AND KEYBOARD

The monitor, mouse, and keyboard—and to a lesser extent the sound card and speakers—form the user interface of your PC. Having a good, easily visible monitor that displays enough data and a mouse and keyboard that you find comfortable and easy to use make more difference to your computing experience than having a fast processor, colossal hard drive, or high-end graphics card.

When buying a PC, pay the most attention to these interface components because they'll make or break your enjoyment of using the PC. It's like buying a car: having comfortable seats and easy steering are almost always preferable to being able to go from 0 to 60 in four seconds in searing discomfort.

Most manufacturers supply moderate monitors and basic keyboards, mice, and speakers with their desktop PCs. Consider upgrading the monitor when you purchase

Continued . . .

- A *trackball* is a stationary device in which you roll a ball with your fingers or hand to move the mouse pointer. Because you don't move the whole trackball, you can use it in a smaller space than a mouse, which is good for small or crowded desks, and some people find them easier for moving the pointer precisely.

- A *touchpad* is a touch-sensitive surface on which you drag your finger to move the mouse pointer. Touchpads are widely used on laptop PCs (see the laptop in Figure 1-1), but you can get them for desktop PCs as well. (You can also get desktop keyboards that have a touchpad built in.)

- A *pointing stick* is a pressure-sensitive button embedded between the G, H, and B keys. You move the mouse pointer by pressing the pointing stick. (Pointing sticks are normally used on laptops, but you can get desktop keyboards with a pointing stick built in.)

A laptop PC typically has a touchpad, a pointing stick, or a trackball built in. Some laptop PCs have both a touchpad and a pointing stick built in.

KEYBOARD

Almost every PC comes with a keyboard, but most manufacturers supply inexpensive, basic keyboards with their desktop PCs unless you choose to pay for a more expensive model. A basic keyboard works fine for light PC usage, but if you use your PC extensively, consider buying a custom keyboard. A wide variety of models are available, from standard models featuring different keyboard "feels" to ergonomic one-handed and two-handed keyboards featuring exotic key layouts.

QUICK**FACTS**

CHOOSING A MONITOR, MOUSE, AND KEYBOARD *(Continued)*

your PC and replacing the other components with your preferred input and output devices.

In a laptop PC, the monitor, keyboard, and pointing device are built-in and are almost impossible to replace, so be sure to test each laptop PC you're thinking of buying. While you can supplement these devices with external devices easily at your desk (for example, you can plug in a different pointing device to replace the built-in pointing device), you'll probably need to use the built-in devices when working with the laptop PC on the move.

When evaluating PCs, consider also how much noise they make. Many PCs have fans and hard drives loud enough to be distracting. If peace is important to you, consider buying an especially quieted PC.

NOTE

If you have an older PC, its USB ports may meet only the much slower USB 1.*x* standard. USB 1.*x* is adequate for devices such as keyboards and mice, which need to transfer only a small amount of data, but for devices such as hard disks and optical discs (CDs and DVDs), which need to transfer large amounts of data quickly, USB 2.0 is essential. If your PC has only USB 1.*x*, you may be able to add USB 2.0 ports via a PCI card (on a desktop) or a PC Card or ExpressCard (on a laptop).

On a laptop PC, the keyboard is important. For desktop use, you can plug in any standard desktop keyboard instead of using the built-in keyboard. If you take your laptop PC traveling, however, lugging an extra keyboard is usually not practical, so you'll want to get the best laptop keyboard you can.

TECHNOLOGIES FOR CONNECTING PERIPHERALS

PCs use several types of technologies for connecting peripheral devices. Which technologies you need depends on which types of devices you plan to attach to your PC.

- **USB**   Universal Serial Bus, or USB, is a technology for connecting external drives and peripheral devices to your PC. USB can be used for connecting anything from a keyboard, mouse, or other input device to connecting external hard drives or optical drives. All recent and current PCs have one or more USB ports that meet the fast USB 2.0 standard. If you need to connect more USB devices than your PC has ports, you can connect a *hub*, a device that provides extra ports.

- **Serial Ports**   Serial ports are used for connecting older devices such as mice, some organizers, external modems, and some uninterruptible power supplies (UPSes). Most recent and current PCs no longer have serial ports.

- **Parallel Ports**   Parallel ports are used primarily for connecting older printers. Most recent and current PCs no longer have parallel ports.

- **FireWire**   FireWire is a high-speed connection technology for connecting external drives and peripheral devices to your PC. Usually, only high-end PCs have FireWire built in. If you need to import video footage from a digital video camera, you may need FireWire on your PC. You can add FireWire to a desktop PC by installing a PCI card and to a laptop PC by inserting a PC Card or ExpressCard.

Get Started with Your PC

To get started with your PC, you may need to choose and install an operating system, set up your PC, and then be able to turn it on and shut it down.

Choose Your Operating System

To make your hardware do anything useful, you need software. The first essential is an operating system, or OS. The OS is the software that makes the

CHOOSING BETWEEN A DESKTOP AND A LAPTOP PC

If you're planning to buy a PC, your first key choice is between a desktop PC and a laptop PC. Consider your priorities carefully when making this choice because you'll probably want to use your PC for years to come. At this writing (June 2008), laptop PCs outsell desktop PCs by a small margin.

HOW YOU'LL USE YOUR PC

If you need to be able to take your PC with you wherever you go (within reason or without), buy a laptop PC. Most desktop PCs aren't portable by conventional standards: once you've got a desktop PC set up and working, you're unlikely to want to move it unless you move your home or office. Similarly, if you want to be able to do your computing from the living room couch or kitchen table as easily as from your desk, get a laptop PC. (You'll probably also want a wireless network so that you can access your Internet connection from wherever you're using your PC. See Chapter 8.)

If you plan to do all your computing in the same location (for example, your desk), a desktop PC may be a better bet. If, however, you want to be able to slip your PC into a drawer to get it out of the way of your social life, toddler, or mastiff, a laptop PC may have the edge over a desktop PC.

COST

Until early 2003, laptop PCs cost so much more than desktop PCs that you had to have a strong reason for preferring a laptop to pay the price premium. These days, the prices are much closer, and it's worth considering a laptop PC even if you plan to use it mostly in a single location.

Continued . . .

PC operate and enables programs to communicate with hardware components as necessary. Programs, or *applications*, are the software that run on the operating system and that you use to get most of your work done. For example, a word processor (such as Microsoft Word) is a program, as is an e-mail program (such as the Windows Mail program included with Windows Vista).

The vast majority of PCs in the world run a version of Microsoft Windows, either Windows Vista (the latest version of Windows) or an earlier version, such as Windows XP. If you're choosing an operating system for your PC, Windows Vista is probably the best choice.

DIFFERENT EDITIONS OF WINDOWS VISTA

There are four main versions of Windows Vista:

- Windows Vista Home Basic is meant for economical home PCs that don't need features such as TV playback and recording.
- Windows Vista Home Premium is intended for full-powered home PCs (including TV playback and recording).
- Windows Vista Business Edition is configured for business use, most notably connecting to a domain-based network running on Windows servers. (A *domain* provides central administration for a larger network.)
- Windows Vista Ultimate Edition is designed to provide all the business features of Windows Vista, together with home-oriented features (such as TV playback and recording).

LINUX

Windows is not the only OS you can run on a PC, but it's by far the most popular. The next most widely used OS for PCs is Linux. (Macs—computers made by Apple Corporation—run Mac OS, which doesn't run on PCs. Macs can run Windows but typically don't.) Figure 1-2 shows Xandros, a version of Linux aimed at consumers (rather than at businesses).

One main motivation for choosing Linux is to reduce the total cost of your PC. If you already have a PC with an Internet connection, you can download several versions of Linux for free. Others cost a few dollars on CD. Full-packaged versions of Linux typically cost between $30 and $100, but many include a wide selection of programs, so you're less likely to need to spend additional money

CHOOSING BETWEEN A DESKTOP AND A LAPTOP PC *(Continued)*

With the same capabilities, laptop PCs still cost more than desktop PCs for a couple of reasons. First, most laptop PCs use custom parts, from the case to many of the innards. Second, all laptop PCs include a built-in monitor, whereas many desktop PCs are sold without a monitor (or with a monitor as an option).

CAPABILITY

Laptop PCs have improved so substantially that they offer nearly the same performance as desktop PCs. Even better, PC hardware has improved faster than PC software's demands have grown, so even more modestly configured desktop PCs and laptop PCs can easily run all widely used programs.

ERGONOMICS

Because laptop PCs are less configurable than desktop PCs, they tend to be less ergonomic (comfortably and safely usable by a human). If you're choosing a laptop PC, make sure that its ergonomics are at least adequate for the uses you're planning.

When you're at your desk, you can attach an external keyboard, mouse, and monitor to make your laptop PC easier to use. When you're on the road, you probably will not want to carry extras beyond an external mouse.

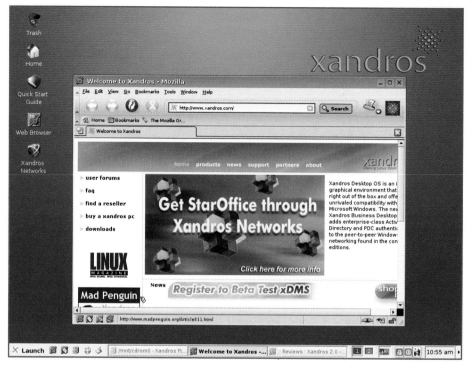

*Figure 1-2: **Linux is a low-cost alternative to Windows and provides many similar features. Linux can run some Windows programs, typically by using additional software.***

on programs. Many packaged versions of Linux are licensed for installation on multiple PCs, so if you're equipping a home or an office with several PCs, this can save you a lot of money on software.

Another main motivation for using Linux is that you are allowed to modify the software yourself—assuming you have the technical skills to do so.

Generally speaking, Linux is not quite as easy to use as Windows Vista and is better suited to advanced computer users who need the additional features and security that Linux offers. Out of the box, few versions of Linux can run Windows programs, so if you're used to Windows programs, you'll need to learn new ones. Some versions of Linux, however, include Crossover Office, which enables you to run Microsoft Office and some other widely used Windows programs on Linux.

Another drawback to Linux is that, despite the coding efforts of the Linux community, Linux supports only some of the most widely used hardware devices.

Set Up Your PC

If you've just bought a PC, unpack it from its box, and follow the instructions that came with it to put it together.

- For a desktop PC, you'll need to plug several cables into the CPU—at a minimum, cables for the keyboard, mouse, monitor, and power supply, and perhaps also a network connection. Figure 1-3 shows a typical desktop PC with the connections labeled.

- For a laptop PC, you'll need to connect the power supply, any cables required for your network or Internet connections, and external devices (for example, speakers). You may need to charge your laptop's battery fully before switching it on.

If you need to install Windows Vista on your PC, see "Install Windows Vista," later in this chapter. If your PC won't start as described in this section, see Chapter 10 for suggestions.

Start Your PC

To start a desktop PC, press the power button on the CPU and the power button on the monitor. To start a laptop PC, press the power button or slide the power switch, depending on the model. If you have a printer connected to your PC, switch that on, too.

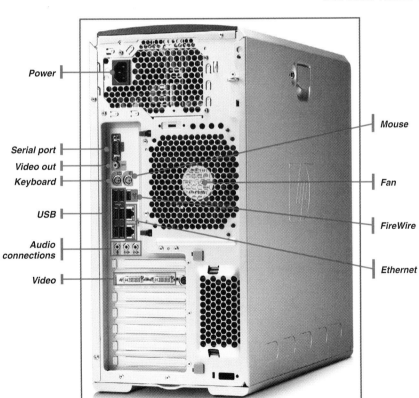

Power
Serial port
Video out
Keyboard
USB
Audio connections
Video
Mouse
Fan
FireWire
Ethernet

Figure 1-3: **Connections available on the back of the CPU of a recent desktop PC**

```
AMIBIOS(C)2001 American Megatrends, Inc.
BIOS Date: 02/22/06 20:54:49  Ver: 08.00.02

Press DEL to run Setup
Checking NVRAM..

512MB OK
Auto-Detecting Pri Channel (0)...IDE Hard Disk
Auto-Detecting Pri Channel (1)...Not Detected
Auto-Detecting Sec Channel (0)...CDROM
Auto-Detecting Sec Channel (1)...
```

Your PC displays startup information as it starts (as shown here). Most of this is just information about the hardware it discovers, but you'll also see a message telling you which key (usually **DELETE** or **F2**) to press to enter the Setup routine. Assuming your PC was set up correctly by whomever assembled it, you shouldn't need to use this Setup routine unless you change your PC's hardware configuration—or unless something goes wrong with your PC.

You'll then see the Windows Vista logo as Windows loads, until the logon screen is displayed.

If your PC is set up for multiple people to use, Windows Vista displays the logon screen shown in Figure 1-4. Click your username to log on, type your password, and press **ENTER**. Windows Vista displays the desktop.

If your PC is set up for just you to use, Windows Vista may be set to log you on automatically using a password you've saved. In this case, Windows Vista goes straight through the logon process and displays the desktop.

QUICK**FACTS**

SUPPLYING POWER TO A DESKTOP PC

The main points for supplying power to a desktop PC are

* Most desktop PCs have separate power cables for the CPU and the monitor. If you have a printer or other external component, it will probably have its own power supply.

* Most laser printers draw a lot of electricity and need to be plugged into a wall socket rather than into a power strip.

* Unless your house or office is well supplied with electrical sockets, use a power strip to provide enough sockets to power all your hardware at once. Any power strip with adequate capacity will do, but power strips designed for PC use tend to offer more space for each socket. This makes it easier to plug large power adapters into the sockets without blocking other sockets. Also, power strips designed for PCs often provide protection from power surges.

* To keep your PC running through brownouts (dips in the power supply, so-called because they make electric lights look brown) and outages, use an uninterruptible power supply (UPS). See Chapter 8 for more details.

Figure 1-4: *On the logon screen, click your user account and enter your password.*

NAVIGATE THE DESKTOP

The Windows Vista desktop (see Figure 1-5) normally displays a picture as wallpaper in the background, which can change its look completely.

The mouse is the primary means of navigating the Windows desktop:

- Move the mouse or other pointing device so that the mouse pointer is over the object you want to affect.

- Click an object to select it.

- Double-click an object (click twice in quick succession) to open it.

- Right-click an object to display a context menu, or shortcut menu, of commands related to the object.

USE THE START MENU

Click the **Start** button to display the Start menu (see Figure 1-6), which provides access to most of the programs on your PC and to essential commands (such as turning off your PC). The six icons on the middle-left area of the Start menu are programs Windows thinks you might want to use (at first). After you've used Windows for a while, these icons change to reflect the programs you've used most frequently.

To access other programs on the Start menu, click **All Programs**, click the menu that contains the program you want, and then click the program.

Start menu, used to start programs and access control functions, folders, and other menus.

Recycle Bin, opens a folder of deleted items

Mouse pointer, used to indicate and select objects

Desktop, holds windows, dialog boxes, and icons; the background is a picture you can change

Start button, opens the Start menu

Taskbar, shows a button for each open program or document

ScreenTip, shows information about the object the mouse pointer is pointing to

Notification area, holds the system clock and icons for frequently used programs

Figure 1-5: **The Windows desktop is highly customizable, but this is its basic look.**

QUICK**FACTS**

BUYING A NEW PC OR UPGRADING AN OLDER ONE

If you have an older PC (for example, a hand-me-down), you may need to decide between upgrading your clunker to run Windows Vista or buying a new PC. Windows Vista requires at least a 600MHz processor, 512MB of RAM, and 16GB of hard drive space—absolute minimum.

Normally, it's best to buy a new PC. But if your older PC comfortably exceeds these requirements, you may choose to try running Windows Vista on it. With computer prices continuing to drop as faster and more capable hardware is released, however, it makes less and less sense to spend money upgrading an older PC unless you have a compelling reason to do so. (At this writing, you can buy Vista-capable computers from $500 upward.) Even if you upgrade essential components that are not up to scratch, you may not be able to get Vista running quickly and smoothly enough to be worth the cost and effort.

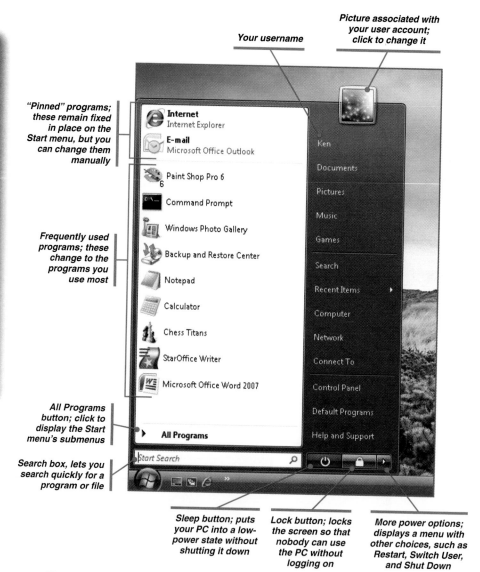

Your username

Picture associated with your user account; click to change it

"Pinned" programs; these remain fixed in place on the Start menu, but you can change them manually

Frequently used programs; these change to the programs you use most

All Programs button; click to display the Start menu's submenus

Search box, lets you search quickly for a program or file

Sleep button; puts your PC into a low-power state without shutting it down

Lock button; locks the screen so that nobody can use the PC without logging on

More power options; displays a menu with other choices, such as Restart, Switch User, and Shut Down

Figure 1-6: **The Start menu gives you access to the programs and folders on your PC.**

Install Windows Vista

Three normal ways to install Windows Vista are

- Have your computer manufacturer install Windows Vista for you.
- Upgrade Windows XP to Windows Vista.
- Install Windows Vista on a computer that doesn't have Windows XP installed, or install Windows Vista alongside your existing version of Windows.

GET WINDOWS VISTA PREINSTALLED

If you decide to get Windows Vista as the operating system for your new PC, your best bet is to have the OS preinstalled by the PC manufacturer. Buying Windows Vista preinstalled is much less expensive than buying a boxed copy of Windows Vista, but be sure that the manufacturer includes a Windows Vista DVD with the PC so that you can reinstall the OS if necessary. (Some manufacturers include the Windows Vista installation files on the PC's hard drive. From here, you can burn them to a DVD manually, but it's easy to forget to do so. If your PC suffers severe problems and you haven't yet burned a Windows Vista DVD, it may be too late to do so.)

UPGRADE TO WINDOWS VISTA

If your PC has Windows XP installed, you can upgrade to Windows Vista. Upgrading preserves your applications and settings, so you don't need to reinstall them or reconfigure Windows after the upgrade.

To begin the upgrade, start Windows XP. When Windows has completed loading, insert the Windows Vista DVD. The Install Windows window should open automatically; if not, double-click **My Computer** to open the My Computer window, right-click the icon for your PC's optical drive, and click **AutoPlay**. The Install Windows window opens. Click the **Install Now** button. On the Get Important Updates For Installation screen, click the **Go Online To Get The Latest Updates For Installation** button if your PC is connected to the Internet via a broadband connection; if not, click the **Do Not Get The Latest Updates For Installation** button, but be aware that the installation may not be successful and that your PC will not be fully protected against the latest security threats.

> **NOTE**
>
> Upgrade versions of Windows Vista are less expensive than full, new versions but work only if you have a supported version of Windows: Windows XP Home Edition for Windows Vista Home Basic Edition or Windows Vista Home Premium Edition; Windows XP Professional for Windows Vista Business Edition or Windows Vista Ultimate Edition.

On the Type Your Product Key For Activation screen, type the product key (the 25-character sequence on the Windows DVD's packaging). Clear the **Automatically Activate Windows When I'm Online** check box, because it's best to check that all your hardware is working before you activate Windows (which you can do easily using a manual process). Then click **Next**.

On the next screen, read the license, select the **I Accept The License Terms** check box, and click **Next**. On the Which Type Of Installation Do You Want? screen (shown here), click the **Upgrade** button, and then follow through the rest of the upgrade process.

INSTALL WINDOWS VISTA YOURSELF

Perhaps the least likely scenario is that you need to install a full version of Windows Vista on a PC that has no operating system installed. In this case, you need to pay for a full version of Windows Vista:

- For a full-featured home PC, choose Windows Vista Home Premium Edition.
- For a budget home PC, choose Windows Vista Home Basic Edition.
- For a standard business PC, choose Windows Vista Business Edition.
- For a full-featured home-and-work PC (for example, a powerful laptop), choose Windows Vista Ultimate Edition.

Put the DVD in the optical drive, and restart your PC. Press **SPACEBAR** to boot from the DVD when your PC prompts you to do so.

The Windows Vista installation process is as straightforward as Microsoft was able to make it and usually takes less than an hour, depending on the speed of your PC. On the Which Type Of Installation Do You Want? screen, the installer makes the Upgrade button unavailable, leaving only the Custom button for you to choose. After that, the first point at which you must really pay attention is choosing the physical disk and partition on which to install Windows Vista.

NOTE

You may need to configure your PC's BIOS (Basic Input/Output System) to start from the optical drive. To do so, press the key mentioned in the startup message (usually **DELETE** or **F2**) to access the BIOS. The names of boot options vary depending on the BIOS and version, but look for an option such as Boot Sequence or Boot Device Priority. Use the options to make your optical drive a boot device before the hard drive, and then exit the BIOS configuration screen, saving your changes. When your PC restarts, it will offer to boot from the DVD.

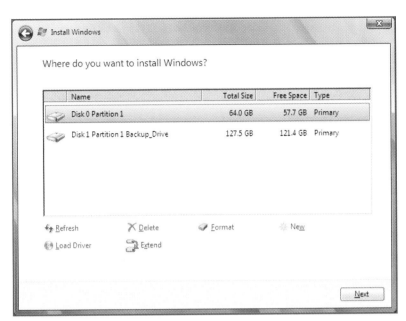

Figure 1-7: **On the partitioning screen, select the disk and partition on which you want to install Windows Vista. You can format an existing partition to remove all its contents, clearing the space for Windows Vista.**

Figure 1-7 shows an example of the partitioning screen, from which you can delete existing partitions and create new partitions.

● Deleting a disk partition deletes all the data it contains. Delete a partition only if it contains no data you want to keep.

● Windows Vista requires a partition of at least 16GB; a much bigger partition is better.

● Windows Vista's efficient NTFS file system makes it reasonable to partition each hard drive as a single partition.

After choosing a partition, click the **Next** button. The installer then installs Windows Vista, rebooting your PC several times in the process. At the end of the process, the Set Up Windows Wizard starts and walks you through several steps to create a user account and choose essential settings. These are the main steps:

● On the Choose A User Name And Picture screen (shown here), type a username and password for your user account, and click the picture you want to use as your icon. Click the **Next** button.

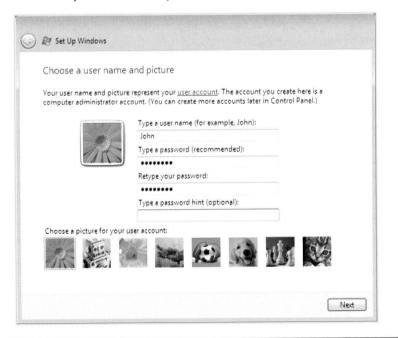

Set Up Windows

Select your computer's current location

Windows has detected that this computer is connected to a network. Windows will automatically apply the correct network settings for the location.

Home
Choose this for a home or similar location. Your computer is discoverable and you can see other computers and devices.

Work
Choose this for a workplace or similar location. Your computer is discoverable and you can see other computers and devices.

Public location
Choose this for airports, coffee shops, and other public places or if you are directly connected to the Internet. Discovery of other computers and devices is limited.

If you aren't sure, select Public location.

CAUTION

Always close Windows from the Start menu rather than pressing the power button on your PC. Pressing the power button when Windows is running can lose information in RAM, corrupt vital files on the hard drive, and cause Windows problems when you try to restart it.

TIP

You can configure the actions Windows takes when you press the power button or sleep button on your PC. See Chapter 9 for more information. (This applies to both desktops and laptops.)

- On the Help Protect Windows Automatically screen, click the **Use Recommended Settings** button to give your PC maximum protection against Internet threats.

- On the Review Your Time And Date Settings screen, choose your time zone and set the date and time.

- On the Select Your Computer's Current Location screen (shown here), click the **Home** button if your PC is connected to a home network. Click the **Work** button if the network is at a workplace. Click the **Public Location** button if the network is in a public place—for example, a coffee shop.

- When the Set Up Windows Wizard displays the Thank You screen, click the **Start** button on it. The wizard closes, and Windows displays your desktop.

Shut Down Your PC

After you finish working in Windows, you can close Windows and shut down your PC as follows:

1. Close all the programs you have been running. If you are prompted to save files with unsaved changes, decide whether to save the changes or discard them.

2. Click the **Start** button, click or highlight the right-arrow button in the Start menu's lower-right corner, and click **Shut Down**.

Alternatives to Shutting Down

Instead of shutting down your PC, you can lock your PC, log off, switch users, put your PC to sleep, or restart your PC.

LOCK YOUR PC

To keep your programs running but lock the PC so that nobody else can use them without logging on, you can lock your PC. Click the **Start** button, and then click the **Lock This Computer** button (the button with the lock icon) in the lower-right corner of the Start menu.

To lock your PC quickly using the keyboard, press WINDOWS-l.

LOG OFF

Log off to end your user session, close all your applications, and display the logon screen so that someone else can log on.

To log off, click the **Start** button, click or highlight the right-arrow button in the Start menu's lower-right corner, and then click **Log Off**.

SWITCH USERS

Switching users keeps your user session active and your applications open but displays the logon screen so that someone else can log on. Your user session keeps running in the background. When you log on again, your applications are as you left them.

To switch users, click the **Start** button, click or highlight the right-arrow button in the Start menu's lower-right corner, and then click **Switch User**.

PUT YOUR PC TO SLEEP

When you don't need to use your PC for a while, but you want to be able to resume using it quickly, you can put it to sleep.

To put your PC to sleep, click the **Start** button, and then click the **Power** icon at the bottom of the Start menu.

RESTART YOUR PC

You usually need to restart your PC only if Windows has become unstable or programs have crashed. You also need to restart Windows after installing certain updates or software, but these items usually offer to restart Windows automatically.

To restart your PC, click the **Start** button, click or highlight the right-arrow button in the Start menu's lower-right corner, and then click **Restart**.

Chapter 2
Working with Windows Vista

In this chapter you'll learn the essentials of working with Windows. First, you'll learn to work with the major components of the Windows interface: windows, dialog boxes, menus, and toolbars. After that you'll learn to customize your Windows desktop for speed, comfort, and aesthetics. You'll then see how to manage files and folders using Windows Explorer and how to burn CDs or DVDs to back up or transfer files.

Use the Windows Interface

The major components of the Windows interface are the desktop, windows, and dialog boxes. You'll need to use these components to take almost any action in Windows.

TIP

This chapter (and the rest of the book) discusses Windows Vista, but most of the information applies to earlier versions of Windows as well.

Work with the Desktop

The desktop (see Figure 2-1) takes up most of the screen and is the background against which you do your work.

- When you open a program, it appears in a window on the desktop; you can resize the window so that it takes up more or less space, and you can adjust its position relative to other open windows.

Dialog box ⎯⎯⎯⎯⎯⎯⎯ **Windows**

Figure 2-1: Windows and dialog boxes appear on the desktop. You can drag them to different positions—for example, so that you can see the items you need to see.

Start button · **Taskbar** · **Desktop**

- When you open a dialog box, it appears in a rectangular area on the desktop, usually in front of the program to which it refers.

- The taskbar (which contains the Start button) appears at the bottom of the desktop by default. You can drag it to the other three edges of the desktop if you prefer.

- You can position icons for files and folders on the desktop so that you can access them quickly.

Work with Windows

A window represents a running application or an open document in a running application. Almost all windows have menus that enable you to take actions using the mouse or the keyboard, and almost all windows can be resized by dragging their sizing handles in the lower-right corner or by dragging one of their borders. Figure 2-2 shows you the key components of a typical window and explains how to use them.

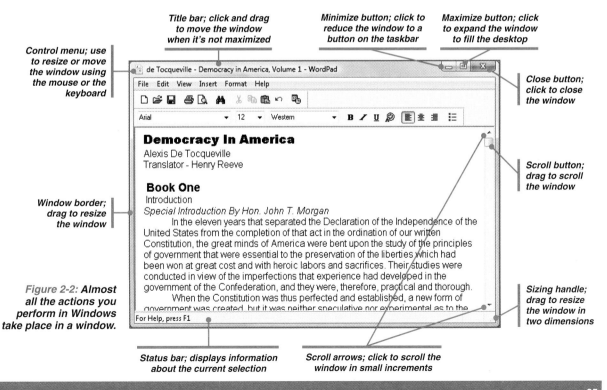

Title bar; click and drag to move the window when it's not maximized

Minimize button; click to reduce the window to a button on the taskbar

Maximize button; click to expand the window to fill the desktop

Control menu; use to resize or move the window using the mouse or the keyboard

Close button; click to close the window

Scroll button; drag to scroll the window

Window border; drag to resize the window

Figure 2-2: Almost all the actions you perform in Windows take place in a window.

Sizing handle; drag to resize the window in two dimensions

Status bar; displays information about the current selection

Scroll arrows; click to scroll the window in small increments

1

3

4

5

6

7

8

9

10

QUICKSTEPS

SWITCHING AMONG WINDOWS USING THE KEYBOARD

Windows lets you switch among open windows quickly using the keyboard:

- Hold down **WINDOWS KEY** and press **TAB** to display your open windows in a rotating stack. Still holding down **WINDOWS KEY**, press **TAB** to bring the window you want to the front, and then release **WINDOWS KEY**. This technique works only on the Windows Aero interface, the more graphical interface that Windows Vista provides.

- Hold down **WINDOWS KEY-CTRL** and press **TAB** to display the rotating stack of open windows. You can then release **WINDOWS KEY-CTRL** and simply press **TAB** (or click) to select the window you want.

- Hold down **ALT** and press **TAB** to display a panel containing an icon for each open window. Still holding down **ALT**, press **TAB** to bring the window you want to the front, and then release **ALT**.

- Hold down **ALT-CTRL** and press **TAB** to display panel of open windows. You can then release **ALT-CTRL** and simply press **TAB** (or click) to select the window you want.

CHANGE A WINDOW'S STATE

A window can be in one of three states:

- A **maximized** window occupies the whole of your desktop except for the taskbar area. To maximize a window, click the **Maximize** button.

Maximize/Restore Down button

Minimize button   *Close button*

- A **normal** window can be any size to which you drag it using the sizing handle or any of its borders. To change a maximized window to a normal window, click the **Restore Down** button that replaces the Maximize button when you maximize the window.

- A **minimized** window is a window shrunk down to a button on the taskbar. In a normal or maximized window, click the **Minimize** button to minimize the window. Click the button on the taskbar to restore the window to its previous size.

ARRANGE MULTIPLE WINDOWS

You can open multiple windows at once and arrange them on the desktop as you need by dragging them manually or by right-clicking the system clock or open space in the taskbar and choosing the appropriate command from the shortcut menu:

- **Cascade Windows** arranges the windows so that you can see the title bar of each.

- **Show Windows Stacked** arranges the nonminimized windows in a horizontal arrangement so that all of them are visible and each occupies roughly the same amount of space.

- **Show Windows Side By Side** arranges the nonminimized windows in a vertical arrangement so that all of them are visible and each occupies roughly the same amount of space.

- **Show The Desktop** hides all open windows and dialog boxes so that you can see the desktop. Right-click the system clock or open space in the taskbar, and choose **Show Open Windows** to restore the windows to their previous arrangement.

MAKE A WINDOW ACTIVE

Only one window can be active at any given time. The active window receives the keystrokes you type using the keyboard. To make a window active, click it or click its taskbar button. The active window has a different color than other windows; the color depends on the Windows color scheme you're using, but it's usually darker so that it stands out. The taskbar button for the active window is also a different color than the other taskbar buttons.

CLOSE A WINDOW

To close a window, click its **Close** button, or open the **File** menu and click either **Close** or **Exit** (depending on the application to which the window belongs).

Work with Dialog Boxes

A dialog box is a rectangle of more or less fixed size that contains features called *controls* for taking actions or setting preferences. Figure 2-3 shows a dialog box that uses many of the standard Windows controls.

The common controls in dialog boxes are

- The **title bar** contains the name of the dialog box and is used to drag the dialog box around the desktop. (You may need to move a dialog box so that you can see the part of the window or desktop that it is obscuring.)

- **Tabs** let you select from among several pages of controls in a dialog box.

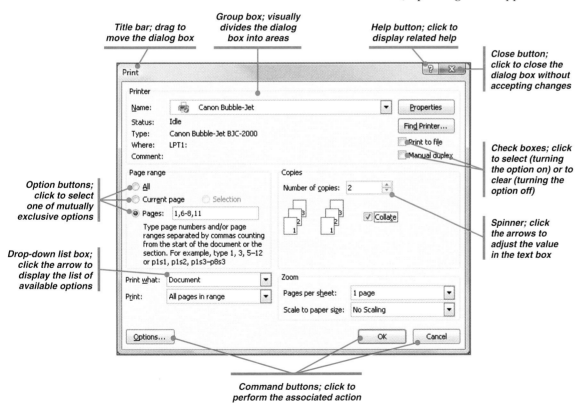

Title bar; drag to move the dialog box

Group box; visually divides the dialog box into areas

Help button; click to display related help

Close button; click to close the dialog box without accepting changes

Check boxes; click to select (turning the option on) or to clear (turning the option off)

Option buttons; click to select one of mutually exclusive options

Spinner; click the arrows to adjust the value in the text box

Drop-down list box; click the arrow to display the list of available options

Command buttons; click to perform the associated action

Figure 2-3: *Dialog boxes are used for many different purposes, including printing documents (as shown here), saving files, and formatting text.*

- A **drop-down list box** opens a list from which you can choose one item that will be displayed when the list is closed.

- **Option buttons**, also called *radio buttons* (because only one can be selected at a time, like the station buttons on a radio), let you select one from among mutually exclusive options.

- A **text box** lets you enter and edit text.

- **Command buttons** perform functions such as closing the dialog box and accepting changes to the settings (the OK button), or closing the dialog box and discarding the changes (the Cancel button).

- A **spinner** lets you select from a sequential series of numbers.

- A **slider** lets you select from several values.

- **Check boxes** let you turn features or options on (by *selecting* the check box, placing a check mark in it) or off (by *clearing* the check box, removing the check mark from it).

- **Group boxes** are lines used to separate distinct parts of the dialog box—for example, to group related controls.

- The **Help button** displays related Help content. (Help is available for only some items in dialog boxes.)

Some dialog boxes include an Apply button that you can click to make the changes you've chosen so far take effect without closing the dialog box.

Work with Menus and Toolbars

The main way to issue commands in Windows is to use menus and toolbars. Menus normally appear on the menu bar at the top of a window. To use a menu:

- Click the menu name using the mouse so that the menu appears, and then click the appropriate command on it.

  –Or–

- Press **ALT** and then press the menu's underlined letter to display the menu. You can then press **DOWN ARROW** to select an item from the menu and press **ENTER** to invoke it, or simply press the underlined letter (if there is one) to select the menu item and invoke it.

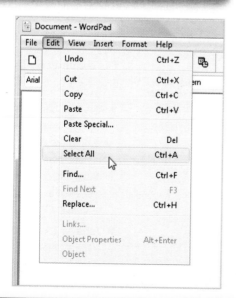

NOTE

Complex programs may have dozens or even scores of toolbars. In most programs, you can toggle the display of a toolbar by clicking the **View** menu, clicking **Toolbars**, and then clicking the name of the toolbar on the submenu. You may also be able to toggle the display of a toolbar by right-clicking any toolbar that's displayed, and then clicking the toolbar name on the resulting menu.

A toolbar typically appears at the top of a window, just below the menu bar, but can often be dragged to another edge of the window or dragged into the window so that it floats freely. To use a toolbar, click the button that represents the action you want to take. If the toolbar button is graphical, you can often display a ScreenTip containing information about it by hovering the mouse pointer over the button for a moment without clicking, as shown here.

In Windows Vista, Windows Explorer has a toolbar that combines command buttons and menus (see Figure 2-4). The toolbar changes the controls it displays to suit the current folder or object.

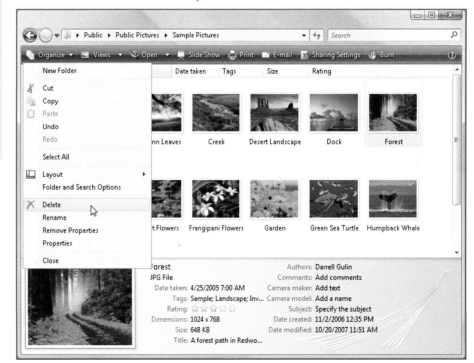

Figure 2-4: **The toolbar in Windows Explorer displays menus and command buttons related to the folder you've opened or the object you've selected. Here, a picture file is selected, so Windows Explorer displays picture-related commands on the toolbar.**

The main programs in Microsoft Office 2007—the word processor Microsoft Word, the spreadsheet program Microsoft Excel, and the presentations program Microsoft PowerPoint—use a different type of interface called the Ribbon. The Ribbon (see Figure 2-5) appears at the top of the program window and consists of a series of tabs that contain related commands. You click a tab to display its contents, and then click the command you want.

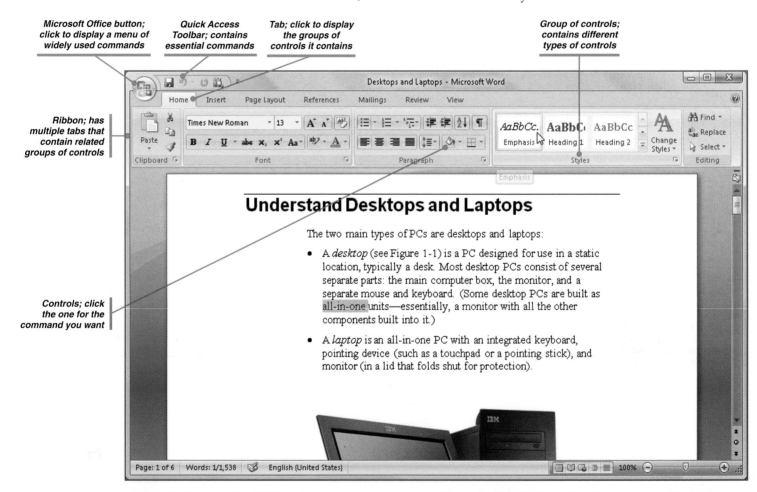

Microsoft Office button; click to display a menu of widely used commands

Quick Access Toolbar; contains essential commands

Tab; click to display the groups of controls it contains

Group of controls; contains different types of controls

Ribbon; has multiple tabs that contain related groups of controls

Controls; click the one for the command you want

Desktops and Laptops - Microsoft Word

Home   Insert   Page Layout   References   Mailings   Review   View

Clipboard   Font   Paragraph   Styles   Editing

Understand Desktops and Laptops

The two main types of PCs are desktops and laptops:

- A *desktop* (see Figure 1-1) is a PC designed for use in a static location, typically a desk. Most desktop PCs consist of several separate parts: the main computer box, the monitor, and a separate mouse and keyboard. (Some desktop PCs are built as all-in-one units—essentially, a monitor with all the other components built into it.)

- A *laptop* is an all-in-one PC with an integrated keyboard, pointing device (such as a touchpad or a pointing stick), and monitor (in a lid that folds shut for protection).

Page: 1 of 6   Words: 1/1,538   English (United States)   100%

Figure 2-5: Microsoft Word 2007 and the other main programs in Microsoft Office 2007 use the Ribbon to present related controls in a graphical way.

Customize Windows Vista

Windows Vista lets you customize many different aspects of its look and behavior. This book shows the default look you get when you install a fresh copy of Windows Vista onto a computer. If your computer's manufacturer installed Windows Vista for you, or if you upgraded from another version of Windows, Windows Vista may look different.

To configure Windows Vista quickly to suit you, follow the steps in this section.

Change How Your Screen Looks

The look of your screen should be both pleasing and easy for you to read. There are three major areas that you can change: the screen resolution and color quality, the desktop background and icons, and the screen saver.

CHANGE THE RESOLUTION AND COLOR QUALITY

First, set the resolution and color qualities that work best with your monitor.

1. Right-click open space on the desktop, and click **Properties**. The Personalization window appears.

2. Click the **Display Settings** button to open the Display Settings dialog box (see Figure 2-6).

3. If you have two or more monitors, click the icon for the monitor you want to affect first.

4. Drag the **Resolution** slider to adjust the resolution, and then click **Apply** to test the resolution. In the small Display Settings dialog box (shown here), click **Yes** or **No** as appropriate.

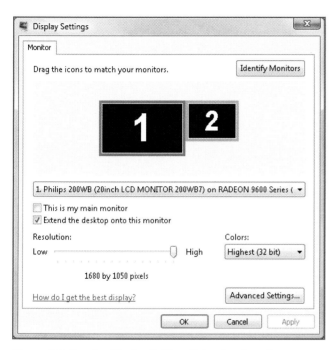

Figure 2-6: *Use the Display Setting dialog box to set a comfortable resolution and color depth. If your PC has multiple monitors (like the PC shown here), you can set a different resolution and color depth for each monitor.*

TIP

After changing the resolution and color depth, you may need to adjust a CRT (cathode-ray tube) monitor so that the picture appears as large as possible without overlapping any edges.

TIP

You can set a picture as your desktop background from Windows Explorer by right-clicking it and clicking **Set As Desktop Background**.

TIP

To choose a picture in another folder, click **Browse** and use the Browse dialog box to select the picture.

Figure 2-7: *The Desktop Icon Settings dialog box lets you choose which items to display on the desktop— Computer, User's Files, Network, Recycle Bin, or Control Panel—and choose which icons to use for them.*

5. To adjust the color quality, open the **Colors** drop-down list, and select the quality that's best for you (probably the highest available for the resolution you picked). Click **Apply** and make your choice in the Monitor Settings dialog box again.

6. If you have a CRT (cathode-ray tube) monitor that is flickering, increase the refresh rate: click **Advanced Settings**, click the **Monitor** tab, choose a higher refresh rate in the **Screen Refresh Rate** drop-down list, and click **Apply**. Click **OK** to close the Advanced Monitor And Display Adapter dialog box.

7. Click **OK** to close the Display Settings dialog box. Leave the Personalization window open so that you can continue to use it.

CHANGE THE DESKTOP BACKGROUND AND ICONS

With the Personalization window still open, choose a desktop background and the icons that appear on it.

1. Click **Desktop Background** to display the Desktop Background window.

2. Open the **Picture Location** drop-down list and choose the category of background you want: **Windows Wallpapers** (the backgrounds included with Windows), **Pictures** (in your Pictures folder), **Sample Pictures** (samples included with Windows), **Public Pictures** (pictures in the Public Pictures folder), or **Solid Colors** (such as white, blue, or black).

3. In the How Should The Picture Be Positioned area, select the **Fit To Screen** option button, the **Tile** option button, or the **Center** option button.

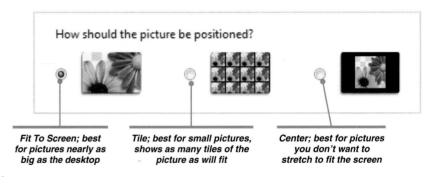

Fit To Screen; best for pictures nearly as big as the desktop

Tile; best for small pictures, shows as many tiles of the picture as will fit

Center; best for pictures you don't want to stretch to fit the screen

4. Click **OK** to return to the Personalization window.

5. In the Tasks list on the left, click **Change Desktop Icons** to display the Desktop Icon Settings dialog box (see Figure 2-7).

6. Select or clear the check boxes in the Desktop Items area to control whether icons for Computer, User's Files (your user folder—the one with your name), Network, Control Panel, and Recycle Bin appear on your desktop.

7. If you want to change the icon for one of the desktop items, click its icon in the main box. Click the **Change Icon** button to display the Change Icon dialog box, click the icon you want, and then click **OK**.

8. Click **OK** to close the Desktop Icon Settings dialog box.

SET UP A SCREEN SAVER

A screen saver is a changing pattern that hides the onscreen display when you leave your PC unused for a specified length of time. Screen savers used to be needed to prevent static text images from burning into a CRT screen (hence the name), but are now mostly used for security or entertainment, as they aren't needed to prevent harm to LCDs or to modern CRTs.

To change the screen saver:

1. In the Personalization window, click **Screen Saver** to open the Screen Saver Settings dialog box (see Figure 2-8).

2. Select a screen saver in the **Screen Saver** drop-down list box.

3. Click **Preview** to see the screen saver full-screen. Move the mouse to cancel the preview.

4. Click **Settings** and use the resulting dialog box to set any configurable options in the screen saver.

5. Change the **Wait** text box to specify how many minutes of inactivity Windows Vista should allow before starting the screen saver.

6. Select the **On Resume, Display Logon Screen** check box if you want Windows Vista to show the logon screen when someone interrupts the screen saver. Using this setting means that your PC is password protected from when the screen saver starts (but not until then).

7. Click **OK** to close the Screen Saver Settings dialog box.

Figure 2-8: *Configure a screen saver to hide your screen after a specified interval.*

Change How Objects Look

With Windows you can change not only how the screen looks, but also how objects and icons look on the screen.

NOTE

If you have Windows Vista Home Basic, the Aero interface with its transparency effects is not available. All the other major versions of Windows Vista do have the Aero interface. However, if you are using an older PC with underpowered graphics, it may not be able to run the Aero interface. In this case, Aero will not be available.

CHANGE THE APPEARANCE OF OBJECTS

You can change the appearance of Windows objects by applying a different theme or by changing the window color and appearance.

The theme changes the overall look of Windows. To change the theme:

1. Click **Theme** in the Personalization window to open the Theme Settings dialog box.

2. If you've modified your current theme by changing the desktop background, and you want to be able to return to this theme, save it by clicking **Save As** and specifying a name.

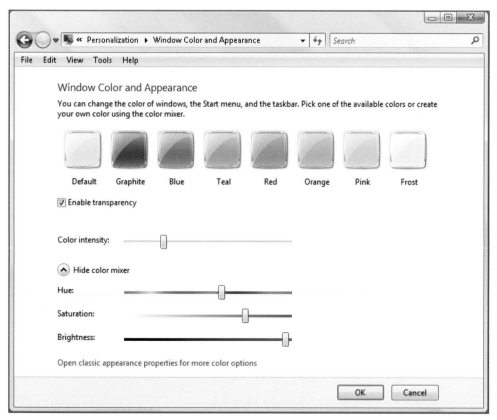

Figure 2-9: *To customize the overall look of the Vista Aero user interface, work in the Window Color And Appearance window.*

3. Open the **Theme** drop-down list box and choose the theme you want. For example, choose **Windows Classic** to apply the look used for Windows 98, Me, and 2000 instead of the Windows Vista theme.

4. Click **OK** to close the Theme Settings dialog box.

Changing the window color and appearance lets you make smaller adjustments. To change the window color and appearance:

1. Click **Window Color And Appearance** in the Personalization window to open the Window Color And Appearance window (see Figure 2-9).

2. Use the controls to change the overall color, transparency (whether what's behind a window shows through its title bar and frame), and color intensity.

3. If you want to change the hue, saturation, and brightness, click the **Show Color Mixer** button to reveal the extra controls at the bottom of the window.

4. If you want to make further adjustments, click **Open Classic Appearance Properties For More Color Options** to open the Appearance Settings dialog box (see Figure 2-10).

Figure 2-10: **The Appearance Settings dialog box lets you apply the less-graphical Windows Vista Basic user interface or the older-looking Windows Standard or Windows Classic interfaces.**

NOTE

The Windows Vista Basic item in the Color Scheme list in the Appearance Settings dialog box lets you switch Windows to the less-graphical Vista Basic user interface or the even less graphical Windows Standard or Windows Classic interfaces. If you select Windows Classic, you can then click **Advanced** and use the Advanced Appearance dialog box to adjust the look of specific items—for example, changing the font in the menu bar, or increasing the thickness of a window border. After you turn on one of these interfaces, clicking **Window Color And Appearance** in the Personalization window opens the Appearance Settings dialog box rather than the Window Color And Appearance window.

5. In the Color Scheme list box, click the color scheme you want to use. View the preview to help decide which scheme you want.

6. To choose visual effects, click the Effects button, choose settings in the Effects dialog box, and then click **OK**.

- Select the **Use The Following Method To Smooth Edges Of Screen Fonts** check box if you want to use font-smoothing to make fonts look less jagged and easier to read. Choose **ClearType** or **Standard** in the drop-down list. Try ClearType first, as it applies more smoothing than Standard.

- Select the **Show Shadows Under Menus** check box if you want Windows to display shadows under menus you open. This is pure "eye candy" and has no practical use.

- Select the **Show Window Contents When Dragging** check box if you want Windows to show the contents of a window while you move it. Clear this check box if you're content to see only the window frame (which requires much less redrawing of the screen).

7. Click **OK** to close the Appearance Settings dialog box.

8. Click **OK** to close the Personalization window.

ORGANIZE THE ICONS ON YOUR DESKTOP

To organize the icons on your desktop:

1. Right-click your desktop to open the context menu, click the **View** submenu, and then choose **Large Icons**, **Medium Icons**, or **Classic Icons**.

NOTE

Whether and how you organize the icons on your desktop is entirely up to you. Some people use desktop icons as a major means of navigation in Windows Vista. Other people prefer to open their program windows full-screen, which makes the desktop inaccessible. If you do this, you may prefer to keep your icons on the Start menu or on the Quick Launch toolbar rather than on the desktop.

2. Right-click the desktop again, click **View**, and choose other options as needed:
   - To arrange icons automatically, select **Auto Arrange** (putting a check mark next to it). Right-click again, click **Sort By**, and choose **Name**, **Size**, **Type**, or **Date Modified** to specify the arrangement.
   - To arrange icons aligned to an invisible grid, select **Align To Grid** (putting a check mark next to it).
   - If you need to turn off the display of desktop icons altogether, click **Show Desktop Icons** (removing the check mark from next to it).
   - To arrange icons manually, clear **Auto Arrange**, redisplay the submenu, and clear **Align To Grid**. Then drag the icons to where you want them.

Customize the Start Menu and the Taskbar

The two primary controls in Windows are the Start menu and the taskbar (including the notification area, also called the *system tray*). There are several customization steps you can take with both of these controls.

CUSTOMIZE THE START MENU

To make the Start menu as useful as possible, configure it so it shows what you need.

1. Right-click the **Start** button, and click **Properties** to open the Taskbar And Start Menu Properties dialog box.

2. Click the top **Customize** button to open the Customize Start Menu dialog box (see Figure 2-11).

3. Use the options in the main list box to control how the Start menu behaves, which items appear on it, and how they appear. For example, you can display Computer as a menu appearing off the Start menu rather than as a link that opens a Computer window.

4. Set the **Number Of Recent Programs To Display** setting to control how tall the Start menu is. For example, if you have a laptop with a small screen, choose a small number here.

5. In the Show On Start Menu area, choose whether to show an **Internet Link** and an **E-mail Link** on the Start menu. In the drop-down list, choose the program associated with each of these links.

6. Click **OK** to close the Customize Start Menu dialog box. Leave the Taskbar And Start Menu Properties dialog box open so that you can customize the taskbar, as discussed next.

Figure 2-11: Use the Customize Start Menu dialog box to put the items you need on the Start menu—and remove any items that you don't find useful.

QUICKSTEPS

CUSTOMIZING THE TASKBAR FROM THE DESKTOP

You can customize the taskbar from the desktop.

1. Right-click the notification area or open space on the taskbar, and click **Lock The Taskbar** to turn locking on or off.

2. With locking off, move the mouse pointer over the border between the taskbar and the desktop so that the mouse pointer turns into a two-headed arrow. Drag up to increase the number of rows of taskbar buttons; drag down to decrease it.

3. With locking off, drag from open space in the taskbar to a different edge of the desktop to move the taskbar there.

4. To set the date or time, click the clock in the notification area, and then click **Change Date And Time Settings** in the clock panel that appears. On the Date And Time tab of the Date And Time dialog box, click the **Change Date And Time** button, go through User Account Control for the Date And Time feature, and then use the Date And Time Settings dialog box to set the date and time. To synchronize your PC's time automatically with a time server on the Internet, click the **Internet Time** tab, click the **Change Settings** button, and go through User Account Control for the Date And Time feature. In the Internet Time Settings dialog box, select the **Synchronize With An Internet Time Server** check box, open the **Server** drop-down list and choose the server to use, and then click **OK**.

CUSTOMIZE THE TASKBAR AND NOTIFICATION AREA

You can also customize the taskbar and notification area.

1. Click the **Taskbar** tab in the Taskbar And Start Menu Properties dialog box (see Figure 2-12).

2. In the Taskbar Appearance area, choose whether to:
   - **Lock The Taskbar** so that you can't move it by accident.
   - **Auto-Hide The Taskbar** when you're not using it. (This frees up desktop space for program windows. To summon the taskbar, move the mouse pointer to the edge of the screen where the taskbar is hiding.)
   - **Keep The Taskbar On Top Of Other Windows** rather than letting other windows hide it.
   - **Group Similar Taskbar Buttons** to reduce the number of buttons.
   - **Show Quick Launch**, the toolbar that contains icons for launching programs.
   - **Show Window Previews (Thumbnails)**, the preview windows that Windows displays when you hover the mouse pointer over the buttons on the taskbar.

3. To customize the notification area, click the **Notification Area** tab, and choose whether to:
   - **Show Clock**, **Volume**, **Network**, and **Power**. Most people find these icons useful for quick access to these essential functions. The Power check box is available only on laptops and other PCs that can run from batteries.
   - **Hide Inactive Icons**. To manage icon behavior, click **Customize**, use the options in the Customize Notification Icons dialog box, and then click **OK**.

4. Click **OK** to close the Taskbar And Start Menu Properties dialog box.

Figure 2-12: *Customize the taskbar so that it behaves in your preferred way.*

QUICKFACTS

UNDERSTANDING FOLDERS

All the data stored on your hard drive is kept in files, which are contained in folders. A folder is a special type of file that acts as a container for files or other folders. Folder is another term for *directory*, a term used in older, nongraphical operating systems, such as DOS and UNIX.

ROOT FOLDERS, FOLDERS, AND SUBFOLDERS

The *root folder* is the master folder on a drive and contains all the files and other folders stored on that drive. The other folders are contained within and can be said to "branch off" the root folder in the form of an inverted tree. Windows represents the root folder as a drive icon and encourages you to think of it as a drive. For clarity, this book follows that convention.

A *subfolder*, or *child folder*, is a folder stored inside another folder (its *parent folder*, or *containing folder*). Usually, these terms are used only when precision is required; plain "folder" is the normal description.

SYSTEM FOLDERS

Windows Vista includes many system folders to keep its programs, functions, and data organized. To discourage you from disturbing these files and perhaps causing problems in Windows, Windows Vista hides most of its system files from you. Windows Vista stores most of its files in the Windows folder on the *boot drive*, the drive from which your PC starts (typically the C: drive). Windows Vista stores other vital files in the root folder of the boot drive. Windows Vista stores programs in the Program Files folder.

Your PC manufacturer may also have stored vital files on your hard drive. For example, many manufacturers put a folder (often with a name such as i386) containing the Windows Vista installation files on the hard drive rather than supplying a Windows Vista DVD.

Continued . . .

Manage Files and Folders Using Windows Explorer

When you use a program in Windows, the program uses your PC's memory (RAM) to store the data temporarily so that it can manipulate it. Memory stores data only while you're working with it and only while the PC is running. For example, if you open the WordPad program that comes with Windows Vista and use it to write a letter, the data is stored in memory. When you close WordPad, the data is removed from the memory so that the memory can be used to store other data. When you shut down your PC, all the data is removed from the memory.

If you want to store data permanently so that you can use it later, you *save* it to the hard disk or another disk. So, normally, after writing a letter in WordPad, you'll save it to a disk so that you can keep it rather than losing it when you close WordPad.

When you save information to a disk, you save it in a named *file* that you place within a folder. (See the QuickFacts "Understanding Folders" for details on folders.)

To manage files and folders in Windows, you use the program called Windows Explorer. Windows Explorer usually manifests itself as a window, but it also runs the desktop, which functions as a special-purpose Windows Explorer window.

Use the Computer Window

The Computer window is a special view in Windows Explorer that displays the drives and major hardware (such as scanners and cameras) attached to your PC.

1. Click the **Start** button. The Start menu is displayed.
2. Click **Computer**. The Computer window opens.

Figure 2-13 shows an example of the Computer window. The Computer window for your PC will have different contents depending on the drives and hardware attached to the PC.

QUICKFACTS

UNDERSTANDING FOLDERS (Continued)

USER FOLDERS

Windows Vista provides a set of folders for each user (see "Manage Files and Folders Using Windows Explorer" in this chapter) along with links for easily accessing these folders.

USE THE FAVORITE LINKS AREA, THE FOLDERS BAR, AND THE DETAILS PANE

On the left of the window, Windows Explorer displays the Favorite Links area and the Folders bar. At the bottom of the window, Windows Explorer displays the Details pane.

- The Favorite Links area contains links to other folders you may want to access from this folder. If there's a More link, you can click it to display further favorite links that won't fit into the area at its current size.

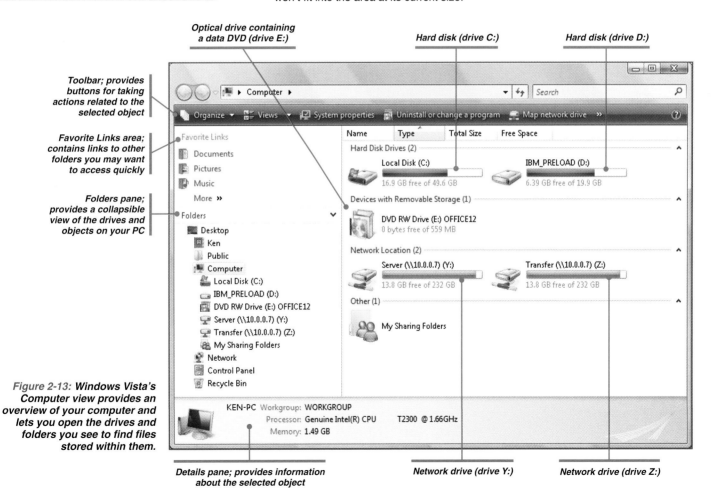

Optical drive containing a data DVD (drive E:)

Hard disk (drive C:)

Hard disk (drive D:)

Toolbar; provides buttons for taking actions related to the selected object

Favorite Links area; contains links to other folders you may want to access quickly

Folders pane; provides a collapsible view of the drives and objects on your PC

Figure 2-13: **Windows Vista's Computer view provides an overview of your computer and lets you open the drives and folders you see to find files stored within them.**

Details pane; provides information about the selected object

Network drive (drive Y:)

Network drive (drive Z:)

TIP

You can expand or collapse the Folders bar by clicking the title bar. Some people find the Folders bar handy as a means of navigation, because it shows where drives and folders are in relation to each other.

NOTE

The Computer's default view is to display the drives and folders broken up into categories: Hard Disk Drives, Devices With Removable Storage, Network Location (if you have any), Other (such as Windows Messenger's My Sharing Folders), and Scanners And Cameras (if you have a scanner or camera attached).

NOTE

Many hardware manuals assume that your optical drive is drive D:. If your optical drive has another letter assigned, you'll need to substitute that letter when following such instructions. If you need to check which drive is which, open the **Computer** window and read the descriptions.

TIP

Many CDs and DVDs include a file that runs automatically when you double-click the drive that contains the disc—for example, to install a program that the disc contains. To view the contents of a disc rather than launch the installation routine, right-click the drive and choose **Explore**.

- The Folders bar contains a collapsible list of drives and folders. Once you've expanded a drive, click a + sign next to a folder to expand the folders under it. Click the – sign that replaces the + sign to collapse the expanded folders again.
- The Details pane at the bottom displays information about the selected object.

IDENTIFY LOCAL DRIVES

As you can see in Figure 2-13 (earlier in this chapter), each drive is assigned a drive letter, which is designated as a capital letter followed by a colon.

- Drive A: is the floppy drive (if the PC has one; most modern PCs don't).
- Drive C: is the PC's first hard drive. Subsequent hard drives are assigned the letters D:, E:, and so on. The PC shown has two hard drives, C: and D:.
- Drive D: is usually the PC's first optical drive (CD or DVD). If the PC has two or more hard drives, the first optical drive gets the next letter (for example, E: if there are hard drives C: and D:) rather than getting D:.
- Drive E: is the PC's second optical drive (if it has one).

IDENTIFY NETWORK DRIVES

Beyond these local drives and devices, your PC may have network drives attached, as the PC in Figure 2-13 does. Windows Vista by default automatically assigns drive letters to network drives, starting with Z: and working backward through the alphabet.

Your PC may also have other local drives attached, such as a removable memory drive (for example, an SD card, a CompactFlash drive, or Memory Stick drive. Such drives are assigned letters after the last optical drive. For example, in the PC shown in Figure 2-13, such a drive would be assigned the letter F.

To see what a drive contains, double-click it. Figure 2-14 shows an example of the contents of a CD. From here, you can double-click one of the folders or files to open it, or simply click the **Back** button to move back up to the Computer window.

1
2
3
4
5
6
7
8
9
10

Computer ▸ DVD RW Drive (E:) OFFICE12 ▸   Search

Organize ▾   Views ▾   Burn to disc

Favorite Links

Documents
Pictures
Music
More »

Folders

Desktop
    Ken
    Public
    Computer
        Local Disk (C:)
        IBM_PRELOAD (D:)
        DVD RW Drive (E:) OFFICE12
        Server (\\10.0.0.7) (Y:)
        Transfer (\\10.0.0.7) (Z:)
        My Sharing Folders
    Network
    Control Panel
    Recycle Bin

| Name | Size | Type | Date modified | Location |

Files Currently on the Disc (20)

Access.en-us   Admin
File Folder   File Folder

Catalog   Enterprise.WW
File Folder   File Folder

Excel.en-us   Groove.en-us
File Folder   File Folder

InfoPath.en-us   Office.en-us
File Folder   File Folder

Office64.en-us   OneNote.en-us
File Folder   File Folder

Outlook.en-us   PowerPoint.en-us
File Folder   File Folder

Proofing.en-us   Publisher.en-us
File Folder   File Folder

20 items

*Figure 2-14: **Double-click a drive to display its contents. If the drive contains a file that runs automatically when you double-click, right-click the drive and choose Explore instead.***

TIP

From the Properties dialog box for a drive, you can change the drive's name by typing in the text box at the top. You can also verify which file system the drive is using by looking at the File System readout. Windows Vista's standard file system for local hard drives is NTFS (NT File System). Removable drives may use the FAT32 file system, which can be read by Windows 98 and Windows Me (these OSes cannot read NTFS).

Check the Amount of Space on a Drive

You can see a quick readout of a drive's size and its amount of free space by using the Tiles view in a Computer window, as shown in Figure 2-13 (earlier in this chapter). To see more detail:

1. Click the **Start** button, and click **Computer** to open the Computer window.

2. Right-click the drive (move the mouse pointer over the drive's icon or name, and click the right mouse button), and click **Properties** from the context menu. The Properties dialog box for the drive appears. Figure 2-15 shows an example of the Properties dialog box for a hard drive.

3. Examine the Used Space and Free Space readouts and the pie chart that shows the proportion of used space and free space.

4. Click **OK** to close the Properties dialog box.

*Figure 2-15: **Use the Properties dialog box for a drive to check how much space is available on it. The Previous Versions tab appears only in Windows Vista Business Edition and Windows Vista Ultimate Edition.***

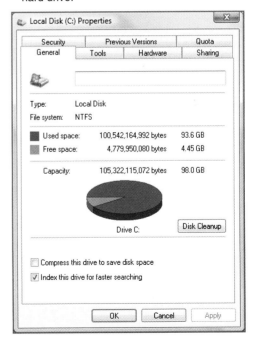

Local Disk (C:) Properties

| Security | Previous Versions | Quota |
| General | Tools | Hardware | Sharing |

Type: Local Disk
File system: NTFS

Used space: 100,542,164,992 bytes   93.6 GB
Free space: 4,779,950,080 bytes   4.45 GB

Capacity: 105,322,115,072 bytes   98.0 GB

Drive C:

Disk Cleanup

☐ Compress this drive to save disk space
☑ Index this drive for faster searching

OK   Cancel   Apply

NOTE

Each user who has a separate user account on a PC has separate folders of his or her own. The Documents, Pictures, and Music links on the Start menu display the folders for the user who is currently logged on to the PC.

QUICKSTEPS

USING DISK CLEANUP TO FREE UP DISK SPACE

These days, the hard drives on new PCs are large enough to hold impressive quantities of files. If you store a lot of graphics, music files, and video files on your hard drive, however, you may fill it up. Files that you delete take up space in your Recycle Bin until you empty it.

Apart from the files that you create, Windows and its accessory programs need a fair amount of space on your hard drive. Windows needs between 8 and 10GB for permanently storing its files and several gigabytes of space to use as *virtual memory*, temporary storage space for data that won't fit in RAM. Internet Explorer, the Web browser, needs space to store temporary files—files containing data you've downloaded and that you may need again.

The easiest way to free up space is to remove files that you've created and that you no longer need. For example, after creating and finishing a movie, you might back up all its files to a DVD and then remove the originals from your hard disk to make space.

Windows also offers an automated tool called Disk Cleanup that can remove certain types of old files for you. To free up space:

1. Click the **Start** button, click **All Programs**, and then click **Accessories**. Click **System Tools**, and click

Continued . . .

Use Files and Folders

The files and folders on a hard drive store the information that you work with and want to keep. To use your PC quickly and easily, you need to be able to navigate smoothly through the structure of folders and files. You also need to know how to create, select, rename, and search files and folders.

NAVIGATE WINDOWS VISTA'S FOLDER STRUCTURE

To help you manage your files and folders, Windows Vista automatically builds a structure of folders for you to keep your files and folders in. The key folders have links on your Start menu by default so that you can access them quickly.

- **Documents** is the default folder for saving documents that aren't pictures, music, or videos. For example, if you save a file in the WordPad word processing program that comes with Windows Vista, WordPad suggests using the Documents folder.
- **Music** is the default folder for saving music files. For example, the Windows Media Player program (usually included with Windows) uses this folder.
- **Pictures** is the default folder for saving picture files—anything from photographs to pictures you create using the Paint program that comes with Windows Vista.
- **Videos** is the default folder for saving video files you create (for example, by using the Windows Movie Maker program usually included with Windows Vista). This folder doesn't have a link on the Start menu unless you choose to add it manually.

To open one of these folders, click the **Start** button, and click the appropriate link.

CREATE A FOLDER

You can create folders within these folders (or within other folders) as needed so that you have convenient places to store and organize your files. To create a folder:

1. In a Windows Explorer window, open the folder in which you want to create the new folder.

2. Open the **Organize** menu, and then click **New Folder**. A new folder is displayed with its default name highlighted.

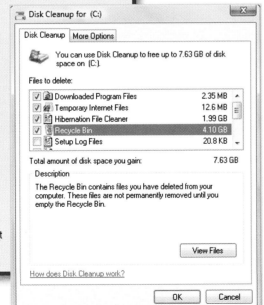

USING DISK CLEANUP TO FREE UP DISK SPACE (Continued)

Disk Cleanup. The Disk Cleanup Options dialog box appears.

2. If you are an administrator and want to clear as much space as possible, click the **Files From All Users On This Computer** button, and then go through User Account Control for the Disk Space Cleanup Manager For Windows program. Otherwise, click the **My Files Only** button (for which you do not need to go through User Account Control).

3. If the Disk Cleanup: Drive Selection dialog box appears, select the drive, and click **OK**.

4. The Disk Cleanup dialog box appears.

5. Select the check boxes for the items you want to delete.

6. Click **OK**.

If you need to free up more space, click the **More Options** tab, and choose to remove optional Windows components or installed programs you don't use, or remove all System Restore data (see Chapter 10) except for the last restore point.

3. Type a name for the folder.

4. Press **ENTER** to apply the name. Double-click the folder to open it.

CHANGE THE FOLDER VIEW

Depending on the contents of the folder, Windows Explorer offers up to seven different views. You can change the view using the Views button on the toolbar.

- The four icon views—**Extra Large Icons**, **Large Icons**, **Medium Icons**, and **Small Icons**—display an icon preview for each item. Extra Large Icons view is useful for identifying graphics and videos quickly by eye. You can drag the slider to set the balance between the icon size and the number of icons displayed in the available space.

- **List** view shows a tiny icon and the name for each object. List view is best for browsing folders that contain many objects.

- **Details** view shows columns of information, such as the name, size, type, and date modified. You can sort the files by clicking a column heading; click again to reverse the sort order.

- **Tiles** view displays a medium-sized icon for each object.

Usually, the best way to change the folder view is to click the **Views** button on the toolbar, and then choose the view you want from the menu. However, you can cycle through the views by simply clicking the Views button. Click once to switch to the next view; click again to switch to the view after that; and so on.

SELECT FILES OR FOLDERS

You can select files and folders by clicking and dragging.

- To select a single file or folder, click it.
- To select multiple contiguous files or folders, drag a selection rectangle around them, as shown here. Alternatively, click the first file or folder, hold down **SHIFT**, and click the last file or folder.
- To select multiple noncontiguous files or folders, click the first file or folder, hold down **CTRL**, and click each of the other files or folders you want to select.

RENAME A FILE OR FOLDER

To rename a file or folder that's not selected:

- Click the name once, pause, and click again (don't double-click). Type the new name, and press **ENTER**.

  –Or–

- Right-click the name, choose **Rename**, type the new name, and press **ENTER**.

  –Or–

- Click the name, open the **Organize** menu, choose **Rename**, type the new name, and press **ENTER**.

SEARCH FOR FILES AND FOLDERS

When your PC contains many files and folders, you may have to search to find the one you need.

1. Click the **Start** button, and click **Search**. The Search Results window opens.
2. To search quickly for all kinds of items matching the terms you type, type in the Search box in the upper-right corner. Windows displays matching results (see Figure 2-16).
3. If you want to restrict the search to only particular file types, click the **E-mail** button, the **Document** button, the **Picture** button, the **Music** button, or the **Other** button in the Show Only bar. To return to displaying all file types, click the **All** button.
4. Double-click the file or folder you want to open, or right-click a result and click **Open File Location** to open the folder that contains the result.

TIP

To select all the files in a folder, open the **Organize** menu, and click **Select All**; or press **CTRL-A**. To select all the files in a folder except one, select that file, press **ALT**, open the **Edit** menu, and choose **Invert Selection**.

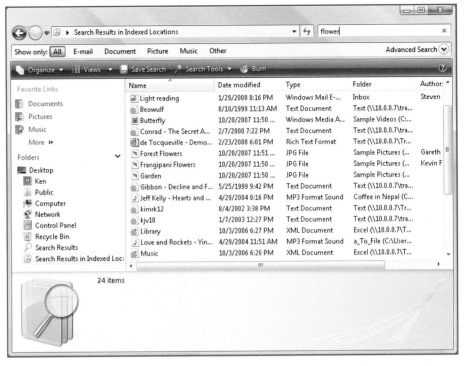

QUICKSTEPS

DELETING FILES AND FOLDERS

When you don't need a file or folder any more, delete it. Windows places objects you delete in the Recycle Bin, a special folder, in case you need to recover them.

If the Recycle Bin becomes full, Windows automatically deletes the oldest objects without consulting you. To keep this from happening, you should empty the Recycle Bin from time to time.

DELETE A FILE OR FOLDER

With the file or folder in view:

- Click the icon to select it, press **DELETE**, and click **Yes** to confirm the deletion.

  –Or–

- Right-click the icon, click **Delete**, and click **Yes** to confirm the deletion.

RECOVER A DELETED FILE OR FOLDER

If you just deleted a file or folder using Windows Explorer, open **Edit** and click **Undo Delete**.

If you deleted the file or folder a while ago:

1. Double-click the **Recycle Bin** on the desktop. The Recycle Bin is displayed.

2. Click the icon for the file or folder, and click **Restore This Item** on the toolbar.

Recycle Bin

PERMANENTLY DELETE A FILE OR FOLDER

If you're sure you want to delete a file or folder permanently:

- Click the icon, hold down **SHIFT** while you press **DELETE**, and click **Yes** to confirm the deletion.

  –Or–

Continued . . .

Figure 2-16: *Use Windows Vista's Search feature to find files or folders. You can use the buttons on the Show Only bar to display only the results for certain file types.*

You can also perform an advanced search using more complex criteria:

1. Click the **Start** button, and click **Search**. The Search Results window opens.

2. Click the **Advanced Search** button to display the Advanced Search controls (shown here).

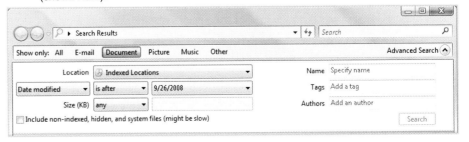

QUICKSTEPS

DELETING FILES AND FOLDERS
(Continued)

- Double-click the **Recycle Bin** on the desktop to open it, right-click the icon for the file or folder, click **Delete**, and click **Yes** to confirm the deletion.

EMPTY THE RECYCLE BIN

1. Double-click the **Recycle Bin** on the desktop. The Recycle Bin windows opens.

2. On the toolbar, click **Empty The Recycle Bin**. The Delete Multiple Items dialog box appears.

3. Click **Yes**.

   –Or–

   Right-click the **Recycle Bin** on the desktop, and click **Empty Recycle Bin** on the shortcut menu.

CONFIGURE THE RECYCLE BIN

To change the amount of space the Recycle Bin takes up:

1. Right-click the **Recycle Bin** on the desktop, and click **Properties**. The Recycle Bin Properties dialog box appears.

2. Click the drive you want to affect, go to the Settings For Selected Location box, select the **Custom Size** option button, and set your desired size in the Maximum Size (MB) box. Select the **Do Not Move Files To The Recycle Bin. Remove Files Immediately When Deleted**

Continued . . .

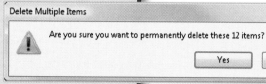

Delete Multiple Items

Are you sure you want to permanently delete these 12 items?

Yes   No

Recycle Bin Properties

General

Recycle Bin Location | Space Available
IBM_PRELOAD ... | 19.9 GB
Local Disk (C:) | 49.6 GB

Settings for selected location
- Custom size:
  Maximum size (MB):   2047
- Do not move files to the Recycle Bin. Remove files immediately when deleted.

☑ Display delete confirmation dialog

OK   Cancel   Apply

3. Open the **Location** drop-down list and choose the location you want to search:

- **Indexed Locations**   Searches all the locations that Windows Vista indexes. See the QuickSteps "Changing the Indexed Locations for Searching" for details on indexing.
- **Computer**   Searches the whole PC.
- **Local Hard Drives**   Searches the PC's hard drives—for example, C: and D:.
- **[drive letter]**   Searches the drive you select.
- **Choose Search Locations**   Opens the Choose Search Locations dialog box, which lets you select the folder you want to search.

4. If appropriate, specify a date criterion. In the first drop-down list, choose **Date**, **Date Modified**, or **Date Created**. Then in the second drop-down list, choose **Is**, **Is Before**, or **Is After**. (Choosing **Any** in the second drop-down list turns off date matching.) Then open the third drop-down list and choose the date.

5. If you want to search by file size, choose **Equals**, **Is Less Than**, or **Is Greater Than** in the drop-down list next to Size, and then specify the size. For example, choose **Is Greater Than 5MB** to find only larger files.

6. To search by name, type the name or part of it in the Name box.

7. To search by tags (additional information added to a file), type a tag word in the Tags box.

8. To search by author, type a name in the Authors box.

9. If you want to search through all your files rather than just the ones that Windows Vista indexes for searching, select the **Include Non-Indexed, Hidden, And System Files** check box. Your searches will then take longer.

10. Click the **Search** button to start searching.

11. Double-click a search result to open it, or right-click a result and click **Open File Location** to open the folder that contains the result.

QUICKSTEPS

DELETING FILES AND FOLDERS

(Continued)

option button only if you are certain you do not want to use the Recycle Bin for a drive. (This is strongly discouraged because it enables you to delete files instantly even when you've made a mistake.)

3. If you don't want to see deletion confirmation messages, clear the **Display Delete Confirmation Dialog** check box. Normally, this confirmation is helpful.

4. Repeat steps 2 and 3 for each other drive.

5. Click **OK** to close the Recycle Bin Properties dialog box.

QUICKSTEPS

CHANGING THE INDEXED LOCATIONS FOR SEARCHING

To make searches quicker, Windows Vista automatically indexes key folders on your PC, going through them and building a list of file names and keywords. When you search, Windows Vista returns results from the index almost instantly rather than searching through the folders again (which would take much longer).

KNOW WHICH FOLDERS WINDOWS VISTA AUTOMATICALLY INDEXES

Windows Vista automatically indexes:

- The files in your user folders
- Folders in the Start menu
- Any offline files you have

Continued . . .

After you finish searching, open the **Organize** menu, and click **Close** to close the Search Results window.

Control What Happens When You Insert a Removable Disk

Windows' AutoPlay feature can automatically take a specified action when you insert a removable disk (for example, a CD or a memory card). To configure AutoPlay:

1. Click the **Start** button, and click **Control Panel** to open a Control Panel window.

2. If a dot appears next to Control Panel Home in the upper-left corner of the window, click **Classic View** to switch to Classic view.

3. Double-click the **AutoPlay** icon to open the AutoPlay window (see Figure 2-17).

4. Make sure the **Use AutoPlay For All Media And Devices** check box is selected. (If you clear this check box, you turn AutoPlay off.)

5. In the Media area, choose the action you want for each media type. For example, open the **Audio CD** drop-down list and choose the action for audio CDs, such as **Play Audio CD Using Windows Media Player**. The choices vary depending on the programs installed on your PC.

6. When you have finished choosing actions, click the **Save** button.

7. Click the **Close** button (the × button) to close the Control Panel window.

Once you've done this, Windows will take the action you specified when you insert a removable disk in the drive. If you told Windows to ask you what to do, a dialog box appears that offers you a choice of actions.

If you want to choose which action to take for a particular content type each time you insert a disk, select the **Ask Me Every Time** item in the corresponding drop-down list. If you want to insert a removable disk without Windows reacting, select **Take No Action**.

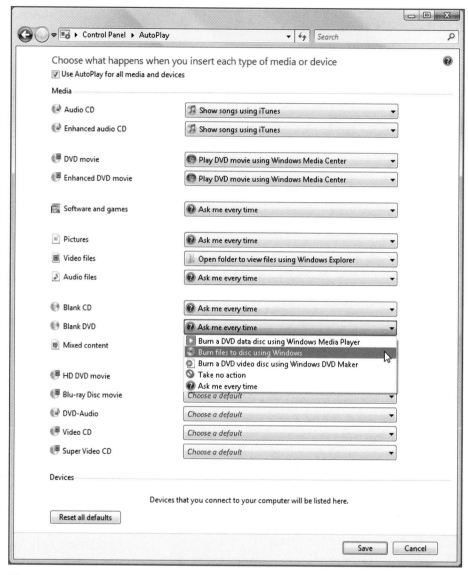

QUICKSTEPS

CHANGING THE INDEXED LOCATIONS FOR SEARCHING
(Continued)

ADD OTHER FOLDERS TO THE INDEX

If you keep your documents in other folders, add them to the index:

1. Click the **Start** button, and click **Control Panel** to open a Control Panel window.

2. If a dot appears next to Control Panel Home in the upper-left corner of the window, click **Classic View** to switch to Classic view.

3. Double-click the **Indexing Options** icon to open the Indexing Options dialog box.

4. Click the **Modify** button to open the Indexed Locations dialog box.

5. Click the **Show All Locations** button and go through User Account Control for the Common Indexed Locations Settings program. The Indexed Locations dialog box opens.

6. In the Change Selected Locations list box, expand the drive that contains the folder.

7. Select the check box for the folder. Windows adds the folder to the Summary Of Selected Locations list box.

8. When you've finished adding folders, click **OK**.

9. Click **Close** to close the Indexing Options dialog box.

Keep your index small by indexing only the most important folders. If you try to index your whole PC, Windows will spend a lot of time indexing, and the index will be too large to function effectively.

Figure 2-17: *By configuring AutoPlay, you can tell Windows how to handle different types of removable media.*

![Clock icon] **UICK**STEPS

COPYING AND MOVING FILES AND FOLDERS

Windows Vista offers several ways to copy and move files and folders. The following are the most consistent and easiest ways of copying and moving.

COPY FILES OR FOLDERS

1. Select the files or folders you want to copy.

2. Press **ALT**, open the **Edit** menu, and click **Copy To Folder**. The Copy Items dialog box appears.

3. Navigate to the destination folder by double-clicking each drive and folder. If necessary, you can create a new folder inside the current folder by clicking **Make New Folder** and typing the name for the new folder.

4. Click **Copy**. The dialog box closes, and the files or folders are copied.

MOVE FILES OR FOLDERS

1. Select the files or folders you want to move.

2. Press **ALT**, click the **Edit** menu, and click **Move To Folder**. The Move Items dialog box appears. This dialog box is functionally the same as the Copy Items dialog box, except that it moves the files or folders instead of copying them.

3. Navigate to the destination folder. If necessary, you can create a new folder inside the current folder by clicking **Make New Folder**, typing the name for the new folder, and pressing **ENTER**.

4. Click **Move**. The dialog box closes, and the files or folders are moved.

Continued . . .

Create Shortcuts

Shortcuts allow you to quickly access files or folders from places other than where the files or folders are stored. For example, you can start a program from the desktop even though the actual program file is stored in another folder.

To create a shortcut, right-click and drag any file or folder to a different folder, and then choose **Create Shortcuts Here** from the shortcut menu.

After creating the shortcut, you can rename it as you would any other object.

The icon for a shortcut has an upward-pointing arrow in its lower-left corner:

Create Data CDs and DVDs

If your PC has a CD or DVD recorder (often called a CD or DVD *burner*), you can use Windows Vista's features for burning CDs and DVDs. Windows Vista can create audio CDs that you can play in almost any CD player, and both data CDs and data DVDs that you can use for archiving data or transferring data from one PC to another. Depending on the version of Windows Vista you have, you may also be able to create video DVDs.

Prepare to Record a CD or DVD

To create your own CDs or DVDs, you need recordable CDs or DVDs, and you must select the files or music you want to put on the discs.

QUICKSTEPS

COPYING AND MOVING FILES AND FOLDERS *(Continued)*

COPY FILES OR FOLDERS TO A REMOVABLE DISK

1. Connect a removable disk to your PC. For example, plug a USB key drive into a USB port.

2. Select the files or folders you want to copy.

3. Press **ALT**, click the **File** menu, click **Send To**, and then click the letter for the removable disk. The files or folders are copied to it.

TIP

Use recordable discs when you want to create a permanent CD or DVD—for example, an audio CD or a data archive DVD. Use rewritable discs when you want to store data temporarily and then replace it. For example, you might use seven rewritable discs for backup, one for each day of the week, erasing and overwriting each when its day comes around again. Rewritable discs cost only a little more than recordable discs.

NOTE

If you're burning music files to a CD, the procedure is different. See "Burn an Audio CD" in Chapter 5.

BUY RECORDABLE CDS OR DVDS

First, you'll need suitable CDs or DVDs for your burner. There are three main considerations:

- **Recordable or rewritable** These days, most burners can handle both recordable discs (discs that can be written to only once) and rewritable discs (discs that can be erased and written to again multiple times).

- **Capacity** 650MB and 700MB are the most widely used capacities for CDs. 650MB is enough space for 74 minutes of CD-quality audio; 700MB holds 80 minutes. Standard DVDs hold 4.7GB, while dual-layer DVDs hold 9.4GB.

- **Speed** CDs and DVDs come in different maximum speed ratings. Check the speed of your burner and buy accordingly. Both CDs and DVDs use an X measurement for speed: 1X, 2X, 4X, and so on. But DVD drive speeds are approximately nine times faster than CD speeds, so a 16X DVD drive is very fast.

SEND FILES TO A CD OR DVD

Before burning a CD or DVD, you need to copy the files you want on the disc to a temporary storage area that represents the disc.

1. Open a Windows Explorer window, and browse to the folder that contains the files you want to copy to the disc. For example, click the **Start** button, and click **Documents**.

2. Select the files you want to copy.

3. Right-click the selection, click **Send To**, and click **DVD RW Drive**. (Your drive may have a different description, such as CD-RW Drive.) The files are copied to the temporary storage area, and a balloon is displayed above the notification area to alert you to their presence.

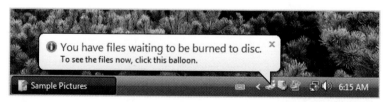

4. Click the balloon to open a Windows Explorer window showing the contents of the storage area.

WORKING WITH ZIPPED FOLDERS

Windows Vista lets you create and open folders compressed in the widely used Zip format. Zipped folders have the extension .zip and are compatible with programs like WinZip and TurboZip. You can use zipped folders to make files take less room on your hard drive and to enable you to transmit files across the Internet faster.

CREATE A ZIPPED FOLDER

To create a new zipped folder and drag files to it:

1. Open the folder in which you want to create the zipped folder. For example, click the **Start** button, and click **Documents**.

2. Right-click a blank area in the detail pane, highlight or click **New**, and then click **Compressed (Zipped) Folder**. A new zipped folder is created, and an edit box is displayed around its default name.

3. Type the name you want to give the zipped folder, and press **ENTER**.

4. Drag files and folders into the zipped folder. Windows Vista adds them to it, compressing them in the process.

SEND A FILE OR FOLDER TO A ZIPPED FOLDER

1. In Windows Explorer, right-click a file or folder you want to compress.

2. Click or highlight **Send To**, and click **Compressed (Zipped) Folder**. A zipped folder is created containing the original file or folder. The zipped folder has the name of the file or folder plus the .zip extension.

If you compress multiple files or folders using this technique, Windows names the zipped folder Archive.zip. To rename the zipped folder, click it to select it,

Continued . . .

Burn a CD or DVD

After you've copied all the files to the storage area:

1. Click the **Burn To Disc** button on the toolbar. The Burn To Disc Wizard starts and prompts you to insert a disc.

2. Insert a blank CD or DVD, and then either click **Next** or wait for the wizard to notice the disc. The wizard displays the Prepare This Disc screen (see Figure 2-18).

3. Type the name for your CD or DVD in place of the default name (the current date). You can use up to 16 letters.

4. In the **Recording Speed** drop-down list, choose the speed at which to burn the disc—for example, 4X or 8X. The wizard normally chooses the fastest speed supported by your burner and the disc you've inserted, but you may need to choose a slower speed if you find burns fail.

5. If you want the wizard to close after burning the disc, select the **Close The Wizard After The Files Have Been Written** check box.

6. Click **Next**. The wizard writes the files to the disc and then ejects it.

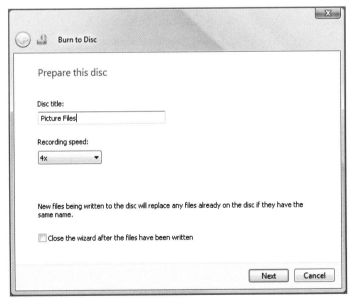

Figure 2-18: *Name your CD or DVD and choose whether to close the wizard when it has finished burning the disc.*

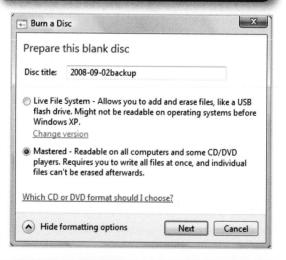

7. Click **Finish**.

8. Remove the disc from the drive and label it. Then reinsert it and ensure that the files have been burned correctly.

Erase a Rewritable Disc

Before you can use a rewritable disc again, you must erase it.

1. Insert the disc in your burner drive.

2. Click the **Start** button, and click **Computer** to open a Computer window.

3. Click the icon for the burner drive, and click the **Erase This Disc** button on the toolbar. The Burn To Disc Wizard starts.

4. Click **Next**. The wizard erases the files from the disc, and then the Completing the CD Writing Wizard dialog box appears.

5. Click **Finish**.

You can then write files to the disc as you did before.

Choose Between the Mastered and Live File System Formats

Windows Vista lets you burn data discs in either of two formats:

- **Live File System** makes the CD or DVD behave like a USB flash drive. You can write files to the disc whenever you want and delete files from the disc. This is handy, but you lose some capacity on the disc, and the disc may not work on versions of Windows before Windows XP or on other operating systems (for example, Mac OS X or Linux).

- **Mastered** lets you write files to the disc only once, so you line up the files and burn them to the disc all at once. The Mastered format is good for backing up, and you can use mastered discs in almost all CD and DVD players and with all operating systems.

To choose the format, click the **Show Formatting Options** button in the Burn A Disc dialog box, and then select the **Live File System** option button or the **Mastered** option button.

Chapter 3

Connecting to and Using the Internet

The Internet provides a major means of worldwide communications between both individuals and organizations and for locating and sharing information. For many, having access to the Internet is the primary reason for having a computer.

To use the Internet, you must have a connection to it, either through a dial-up connection or a broadband connection. You can then send and receive e-mail, access the World Wide Web, and use instant messaging.

Connect to the Internet

You can connect to the Internet using a telephone line, a TV cable, or a satellite link. With a telephone line, you can connect through either a *dial-up* connection or a DSL (digital subscriber line) connection (see comparison in Table 3-1). DSL, cable TV, and satellite connections are called *broadband* connections because of

FEATURE	DIAL-UP	DSL
Cost	From around $10/month	From around $15/month
Speed	Up to 48Kbps* download**, 33Kbps upload	Speeds vary: download 512Kbps upward, upload 128Kbps upward
Connection	Dial up each time	Always connected
Use of line	Ties up line, may want a second line	Line can be used for voice and fax while connected to the Internet

* Kbps is Kilobits (thousands of bits, 1 or 0) per second
** Download is transferring information from the Internet to your PC

Table 3-1: Comparison of Dial-Up and DSL Connections

their higher (than dial-up) speeds and common setup (see comparison in Table 3-2). You must have access to at least one of these forms of communication in order to connect to the Internet. You must also set up the Internet connection.

Set Up a Broadband Connection

A broadband connection—which typically uses a DSL phone line, a TV cable, or a satellite connection—is normally made with a device that connects to your wired or wireless local area network (LAN) and allows several computers on the network to use the connection. (See Chapter 8 for instructions on setting up a network.) With a network setup, your computer connected to the network either via a network cable or a wireless link, and a broadband service connected to the network, your computer is connected to the broadband service. There is nothing else you need to do to set up a broadband connection.

SERVICE	DOWNLOAD SPEED	UPLOAD SPEED	MONTHLY COST	RELIABILITY
Dial-Up	48Kbps	33.6Kbps	$10	Fair
DSL	768Kbps to 6Mbps or more	128Kbps to 1Mbps	$15	Good
Cable Internet	1Mbps to 6Mbps or more	500Kbps	$35	Good
Satellite Internet	1Mbps	150Kbps to 512Kbps	$50	Fair

Table 3-2: Representative Speeds, Costs, and Reliability for Internet Connections

NOTE

Sometimes a DSL or TV cable connecting device is called a "modem," but it is not an analog-to-digital converter, which is the major point of a **mo**dulator-**dem**odulator; instead, the data remains in digital form throughout. For this reason, this book doesn't describe DSL and cable connecting devices as modems.

NOTE

Because Internet Explorer is normally included with Windows Vista and is the default browser, this book assumes that you will use Internet Explorer as your browser.

NOTE

See Chapter 6 for instructions on upgrading, installing, and configuring hardware.

NOTE

The first time you open the Phone And Modem Options dialog box, the Location Information dialog box appears. Select your country, type the area code, specify any carrier code and numbers to dial for accessing an outside line, and choose between tone and pulse dialing. Then click **OK** to display the Phone And Modem Options dialog box.

To verify that the Internet connection is working, click the **Start** button, and then click **Internet**. If an Internet web page is displayed, your connection is configured and working.

Set Up a Dial-up Connection

Before you can set up a dial-up connection, you may first need to install a modem in your PC, as described next.

INSTALL A MODEM

If a modem came with your PC or if one was already installed when you upgraded to Windows Vista, your modem should already be installed and you don't need to do anything more. Skip ahead to "Create the Dial-Up Connection." Otherwise, to install the modem:

1. For an internal modem, install it in your PC. For an external modem, attach it to your PC via the serial cable or USB (universal serial bus) cable. Most USB modems draw power through the USB cable, while serial modems require their own power supply. Connect the phone line to the modem. If the modem has a power switch, turn it on.

2. Click the **Start** button, and click **Control Panel**. If Control Panel is in Control Panel Home view, click the **Classic View** link. Double-click **Phone And Modem Options**. The Phone And Modem Options dialog box appears.

3. Click the **Modems** tab. If the list shows Unknown Modem, select that and click **Remove**. If the list shows a modem by name, as shown next, Windows Vista has identified and installed your modem. Skip to "Create the Dial-Up Connection."

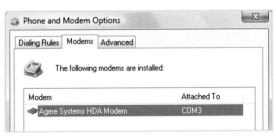

4. Click **Add** and then go through User Account Control for the Add Modems program to open the Add Hardware Wizard. Click **Next**. If the wizard finds and installs the correct modem, go to step 7. If the wizard finds several modems, select the check box for the correct modem, clear the other check boxes, and skip the next step. If the wrong modem or Unknown Modem is shown, select it and click **Change**. If no modem is found, click **Next**.

5. If you have a disk or CD containing Windows Vista drivers for your modem, click **Have Disk**, insert the disk, select the drive, click **OK**, select the manufacturer and model, and click **OK**. If you don't have a disk, select **Standard Modem Types** under Manufacturer and the speed of your modem under Model, and then click **Next**.

6. Select the COM (communications) port to which the modem is connected (see the Note), and click **Next**.

7. When the wizard tells you that your modem has been installed successfully, click **Finish** to close the wizard, and then click **OK** to close the Phone And Modem Options dialog box.

8. Click the **Close** button (the × button) to close Control Panel.

CREATE THE DIAL-UP CONNECTION

With a modem installed and working, you can set up a *dial-up connection* that uses the modem to connect via your phone line to a computer at your ISP.

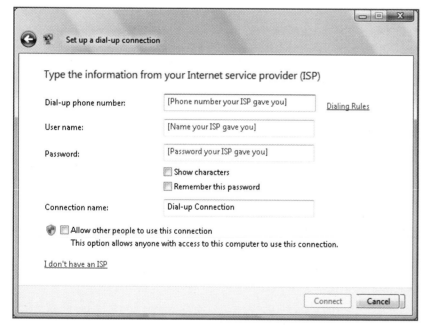

Figure 3-1: *Enter the information for your dial-up connection. Select the Allow Other People To Use This Connection check box if you want to make the connection available to other users of your PC.*

1. Click the **Start** button, and then click **Connect To**. Windows launches the Connect To A Network Wizard.

2. Click the **Set Up A Connection Or Network** link to display the Choose A Connection Option screen.

3. Click **Set Up A Dial-Up Connection**, and then click **Next**. Windows launches the Set Up A Dial-Up Connection Wizard (see Figure 3-1).

4. Type the ISP's dial-up phone number, your username, and password. Select the **Show Characters** check box if you want to verify the password as you type it rather than seeing dots. Select the **Remember This Password** check box if you don't want to type it each time you connect.

5. Type the name for your connection (this can be any name that suits you; descriptive is usually better).

6. If you want to share this dial-up connection with other users of your PC, select the **Allow Other People To Use This Connection** check box, and then go through User Account Control for the Network Connections program.

7. Click the **Connect** button to connect. You should hear your modem dialing and going through the *handshaking* (beeps and pinging sounds) with the equipment at your ISP's end.

TIP

If you think your modem has been set up properly, yet it is not connecting when you open Internet Explorer, look at the Internet Options in Internet Explorer by clicking the **Tools** menu, clicking **Internet Options**, and then clicking the **Connections** tab. See if you have a dial-up connection specified and that it dials the connection. If not, make the necessary corrections.

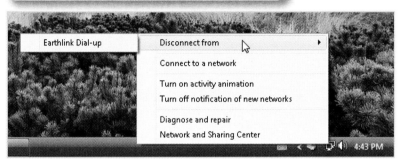

8. When the wizard displays the You Are Connected to the Internet screen, click **Close**.

9. If Windows launches the Set Network Location Wizard to let you choose the network type, click **Public Location**.

You are now connected to the Internet, and can browse the Web, send e-mail, and so on. To verify that the Internet connection is working, click the **Start** button, and then click **Internet**. If an Internet web page is displayed, your connection is configured and working.

To disconnect, right-click the connection icon in the notification area, highlight **Disconnect From**, and then click the name of the dial-up connection.

Use the Web

The *World Wide Web*, usually called simply the *Web*, is the sum of all the websites in the world. Websites range from enormous corporate sites (such as IBM's website), news sites (such as CNN), and online stores (such as Amazon.com) all the way down to minute sites promoting an individual's hobbies, opinions, or skills.

To access the Web, you use a web browser. Most copies of Windows Vista come with Microsoft's Internet Explorer web browser built-in and configured as the default browser. This section assumes you have Internet Explorer running. To start Internet Explorer:

- Click the **Start** button, and click **Internet**.

  –Or–

- If the Quick Launch toolbar (the icon area next to the Start button) is displayed, click the **Internet Explorer** icon on the Quick Launch toolbar.

Search the Internet

You can search the Internet in two ways: using the search facility built into Internet Explorer and using an independent search facility on the Web.

SEARCH FROM INTERNET EXPLORER

1. Click in the **Search** box in the upper-right corner of the Internet Explorer window.

2. In the text box, type what you want to search for, and press **ENTER**. Internet Explorer displays a list of matching websites from the search engine. Figure 3-2 shows an example.

3. Click the link of your choice to go to that site.

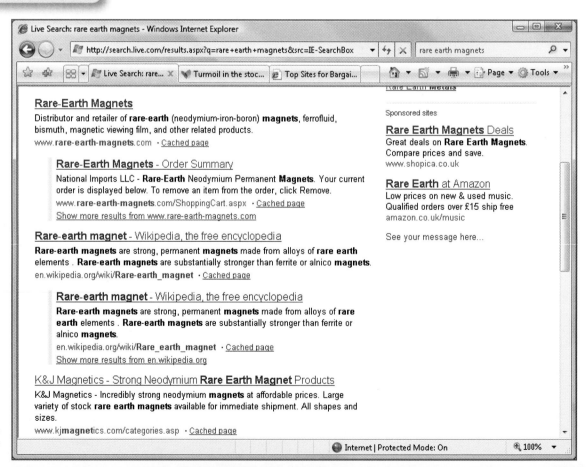

Figure 3-2: The results of a search using Internet Explorer's built-in search feature.

When you enter search criteria, place double quotation marks around them to return only results that contain the literal phrase you type. For example, searching for **lightbulb jokes** returns results that include the words "lightbulb" and "jokes," both together and separately, whereas searching for "**lightbulb jokes**" returns only results that contain that phrase.

SEARCH FROM AN INTERNET SITE

There are many independent Internet search sites. One of the most popular is Google. To access Google:

1. In Internet Explorer, click the icon to the left of the Address bar to select the current address (as shown

here), type **www.google.com**, and either click the **Go** button (the button with the blue arrow) or press **ENTER**.

2. In the text box, type what you want to search for, and click **Google Search**. The list of matching websites is shown in a full web page, as illustrated in Figure 3-3.

3. Click the link of your choice to go to that site.

Access Your Favorite Sites

When you find a website that you would like to be able to return to quickly, use Internet Explorer's Favorites feature to save it and then easily reopen it.

Figure 3-3: The results of a search using Google

BROWSING THE INTERNET

Browsing the Internet is using a web browser, such as Internet Explorer, to go from one site to another to see the sites' content. You can browse to a site by directly entering a site address, by clicking a link to a site on another site, or by using the browser controls. First, open your browser by clicking the **Start** button and clicking **Internet**.

GO TO A SITE DIRECTLY

To go directly to a site:

1. Open your browser and click the icon to the left of the Address bar to select the current address.

2. Type the address of the site you want to open, and either click the arrow button next to the Address bar or press **ENTER**.

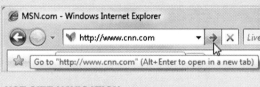

USE SITE NAVIGATION

Site navigation is using links or menus on one web page to find and open another web page, either on the same site or on another site.

- **Links** can be words, phrases, sentences, or graphics that take you to another page when clicked. Links are often underlined—if not initially, then when you hover the mouse pointer over them. When you move the mouse pointer over a link, the mouse pointer changes to a hand with the forefinger pointing upward.

North Korea - ECONOMIC SETTING
As of mid-1993, **North Korea**'s economy remained one of the world's ... Under the system, **factory** managers still are assigned **output** targets but are given more discretion

Continued . . .

SAVE A FAVORITE SITE

To add a site to your Favorites list:

1. In Internet Explorer, navigate to the site.

2. Click the **Add To Favorites** button, and then click **Add To Favorites**. The Add A Favorite dialog box appears.

3. Edit the name in the text box (or type a new name) so the name will remind you of the site.

4. Open the **Create In** drop-down list and choose the folder in which to store the Favorite.

5. Click **OK** to add the Favorite.

OPEN A FAVORITE SITE

To open a Favorite site you have saved, click the **Favorites** button to open the Favorites panel, and then click the site you want.

DISPLAY THE LINKS BAR FOR EASIER NAVIGATION

Internet Explorer versions before version 7 automatically displayed a toolbar called the Links bar that allowed you to create

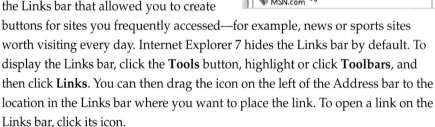

buttons for sites you frequently accessed—for example, news or sports sites worth visiting every day. Internet Explorer 7 hides the Links bar by default. To display the Links bar, click the **Tools** button, highlight or click **Toolbars**, and then click **Links**. You can then drag the icon on the left of the Address bar to the location in the Links bar where you want to place the link. To open a link on the Links bar, click its icon.

1
2
3
4
5
6
7
8
9
10

BROWSING THE INTERNET *(Continued)*

- **Menus** contain one word or a few words, in either a horizontal or vertical list, that take you to a linked page when you click them. When you move the mouse pointer over a menu, the mouse pointer changes to a hand with the forefinger pointing upward.

USE BROWSER NAVIGATION

Browser navigation is using your browser's controls to go to another web page. Internet Explorer provides several navigation tools (including the Links bar, Favorites list, and History), which are discussed in the next few pages.

You can also navigate using the **Back** and **Forward** buttons, which take you to the previous or next page in the stack of pages you have viewed most recently. Alternatively, click the **Recent Pages** button and choose the site from the Recent Pages list.

TIP

Having multiple home pages can be very helpful. However, if you have a slow Internet connection, multiple home pages may take a long time to load.

Change Your Home Page

When you first start Internet Explorer, it automatically displays a specific web page called your *home page*. (You can also display your home page at any time by clicking the **Home** icon on the toolbar.) You can have one home page or multiple home pages. When you have multiple home pages, Internet Explorer opens each page on a different tab in the same window.

To change your home page or add a new home page:

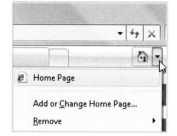

1. Navigate to the site you want to use as your home page.

2. Click the drop-down button next to the **Home** button on the toolbar, and then click **Add Or Change Home Page**.

3. In the Add Or Change Home Page dialog box, select the **Use This Webpage As Your Only Home** option button or the **Add This Webpage To Your Home Page Tabs** option button, as appropriate.

4. Click **Yes** to close the Add Or Change Home Page dialog box.

Access Your Web History

Internet Explorer keeps a history of the web pages you visit so that you can easily return to a site you've visited in the past. You can set the length of time to

QUICKSTEPS

ORGANIZING FAVORITE SITES

If you add many Favorite sites, it can become hard to easily find the one you want. Internet Explorer provides three ways to organize your Favorite sites.

REARRANGE FAVORITES ON THE LIST

The items in the Favorites Center appear in the order you added them unless you drag them to a new location or sort the list.

- In the Favorites Center, drag a site to where you want it to appear on the list.

  –Or–

- Right-click an item in the Favorites Center, and choose **Sort By Name** to sort the list alphabetically.

PUT FAVORITES IN FOLDERS

The Favorites list comes with several default folders installed by Windows Vista and by your PC's manufacturer. You can also add further folders for categorizing your Favorites, and you can put sites in folders.

1. Navigate to the site you want to add to your Favorites list.
2. Click the **Add To Favorites** button, and then click **Add To Favorites** on the menu.
3. Edit the name in the text box as needed, click **Create In**, select the folder to use, and click **OK**.

CREATE NEW FOLDERS

To create your own folders within the Favorites list:

1. Click the **Add To Favorites** menu, and then click **Organize Favorites**.
2. Click **New Folder**, type a name for the folder, and press **ENTER**.
3. Drag the desired Favorites to the new folder, and then click **Close**.

keep sites in that history; Internet Explorer clears the sites after the period you specify. You can also clear your history manually.

USE THE HISTORY FEATURE TO REVISIT A PAGE

To use the History feature to return to a page you've visited recently:

1. Click the **Favorites Center** button on the toolbar to open the Favorites Center.
2. Click the **History** button in the Favorites Center to display your browsing history.
3. To change the view, click the drop-down button next to **History** and choose the view you want: **By Order Visited Today, My Most Visited, By Site**, or **By Date**. Alternatively, click **Search History** to search your history for a particular site.

4. Click the site you want to open. Internet Explorer automatically closes the Favorites Center.

CHOOSE HOW MUCH HISTORY TO KEEP

You can set the length of time to keep your web history, and you can clear your history manually.

1. Click the **Tools** menu, and then click **Internet Options** to open to the Internet Options dialog box.
2. On the General tab, go to the Browsing History area, and then click the **Settings** button to open the Temporary Internet Files And History Settings dialog box (see Figure 3-4).
3. Use the **Days To Keep Pages In History** spinner to set the number of days.
4. Click the **OK** button to close the Temporary Internet Files And History Settings dialog box.
5. If you want to clear your browsing history immediately, click the **Delete** button on the General tab of the Internet Options dialog box. In the Delete Browsing History dialog box, click the **Delete History** button. You may also want to click the **Delete Files** button to delete temporary Internet files. However, deleting these files will make

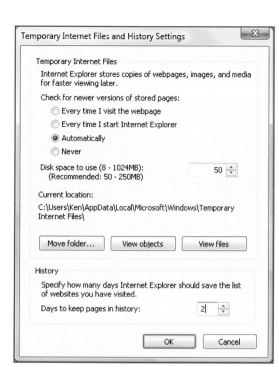

Figure 3-4: Use the Temporary Internet Files And History Settings dialog box to tell Internet Explorer how many days worth of browsing history to keep.

TIP

You can sort your history by clicking the **History** drop-down list button in the Favorites Center and choosing **By Date**, **By Site**, **By Most Visited**, or **By Order Visited Today**. You can delete a site or a page by right-clicking its entry, clicking **Delete**, and then clicking **Yes** in the Warning dialog box.

your next visit to web pages you've visited before take longer, as your browser must download all the data on each page rather than retrieving some information from temporary Internet files. Click the **Close** button to close the Delete Browsing History dialog box.

6. Click **OK** to close the Internet Options dialog box.

Use Tabs and Windows

If you want to open two or more web pages at the same time, you have a choice. You can:

- Open the web pages in separate tabs in the same window. This is useful when you need to see only one web page at once.
- Open the web pages in separate windows. This is useful when you want to compare the web pages (you can arrange the windows next to each other so you can see both).

OPEN EXTRA TABS

You can open a new tab in several ways:

- Right-click a link and choose **Open In New Tab**.
- Click the **New Tab** button on the tab bar.

- Right-click an existing tab and then click **New Tab**.
- Press **CTRL+T**.

WORK WITH TABS

Tabs are easy to work with:

- Click a tab to display its contents.
- Click the **Close Tab** button on the active tab to close that tab.

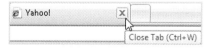

- Right-click a tab and click **Close Other Tabs** to close all other tabs but this one.
- Drag a tab along the row of tabs to move it to a different position.
- To see miniature versions of each tab so you can pick the one you want visually, click the **Quick Tabs** button. Click the picture of the tab you want to view.

QUICKSTEPS

CONTROLLING INTERNET SECURITY

Internet Explorer allows you to control several aspects of Internet security to help keep your browsing sessions safe. To configure security settings, open the Internet Options dialog box by clicking the **Tools** button and then clicking **Internet Options**.

CATEGORIZE WEBSITES

Internet Explorer allows you to categorize websites into four zones: Internet (sites that are not classified in one of the other ways), Local Intranet, Trusted Sites, and Restricted Sites. To work with these zones, you use the Security tab of the Internet Options dialog box (see Figure 3-5).

From the Internet Options dialog box:

1. Click the **Security** tab. Click the **Internet** zone. Note its definition.

2. Make sure the **Enable Protected** Mode check box is selected.

3. Optionally, drag the **Security Level For This Zone** slider to change the security level—for example, from **Medium High** to **High**.

4. Click each of the other zones where you can identify either groups or individual sites to place in a particular zone.

HANDLE COOKIES

Cookies are small files containing text data that websites store on your computer so that they can identify your PC when you return to the website. Cookies have a positive side: they can save you from having to enter your name and ID frequently. Many e-commerce websites (sites where you can execute a payment transaction over

Continued . . .

WORK WITH WINDOWS

You can open a new window in any of these ways:

- Right-click a link, and then click **Open In New Window**.
- Click the **Page** button, and then click **New Window**.
- Press CTRL+N.

You can then open extra tabs within the new window if you want.

Copy Internet Information

You'll sometimes find information on the Internet that you want to copy—a picture, some text, or a web page.

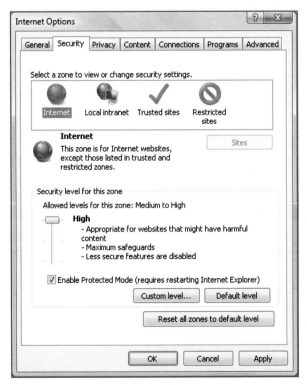

Figure 3-5: You can increase your security by using the controls on the Security tab of the Internet Options dialog box to categorize web content into security zones.

QUICKSTEPS

CONTROLLING INTERNET SECURITY *(Continued)*

the Web) require cookies for their shopping carts and payment mechanisms to work at all.

Cookies can also be dangerous, enabling websites to identify you when you do not want them to be able to do so and potentially letting outsiders access sensitive information on your PC. The Privacy tab of the Internet Options dialog box lets you determine the types and sources of cookies you will allow and what those cookies can do on your PC (see Figure 3-6).

From the Internet Options dialog box:

1. Click the **Privacy** tab. Select a privacy setting by dragging the slider up or down: Block All Cookies, High, Medium High, Medium, Low, or Accept All Cookies. Medium High or a higher setting is advisable.

2. If you want to set custom settings, click **Advanced** to open the Advanced Privacy Settings dialog box. Select the **Override Automatic Cookie Handling** check box, and choose the settings you want to use. For example, you can accept first-party cookies (those from the sites you navigate to) but block third-party cookies (from associated sites). Click **OK** to return to the Internet Options dialog box.

CONTROL CONTENT

You can control the amount of bad language, nudity, sex, and violence that Internet Explorer displays. These content controls work only for sites that have ratings; be aware that many sites do not have ratings, no matter how offensive their content.

Continued . . .

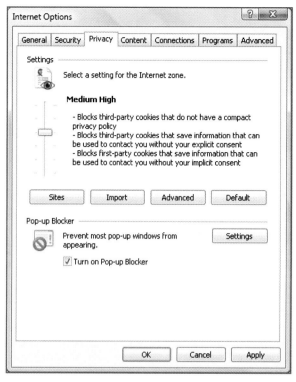

*Figure 3-6: **Determine how you want to handle cookies that websites ask to store on your PC.***

COPY A PICTURE FROM A WEB PAGE

To copy a picture from the open web page to your hard drive:

1. Right-click the picture you want to copy, and click **Save Picture As**. The Save Picture dialog box appears.

2. Locate the folder in which you want to save the picture.

3. Click **Save**.

COPY TEXT FROM A WEB PAGE

To copy some text from the open web page to a text editor or word processor:

1. Drag across the text to select it.

QUICKSTEPS

CONTROLLING INTERNET SECURITY *(Continued)*

From the Internet Options dialog box:

1. Click the **Content** tab. Click **Enable** and go through User Account Control for the Content Advisor program to open the Content Advisor dialog box (see Figure 3-7).

2. Select the category you want to affect, and drag the slider to the level you want to allow. Repeat for the other categories.

3. Click **OK** to close the Content Advisor dialog box.

USE PARENTAL CONTROLS

To control which websites a user can visit, you can use Windows Vista's Parental Controls. See "Use Parental Controls" in Chapter 7 for details.

BLOCK POP-UP WINDOWS

Web scripting (programming) languages enable web developers to automatically open extra windows, called *pop-up windows*, when you display a page or take actions on it (such as following a link or attempting to leave the page). Pop-up windows occasionally display helpful content, but they're usually used to display ads or show you content that you probably wouldn't have chosen to see.

To block pop-ups, from the Internet Options dialog box:

1. From the Privacy tab, select the **Turn On Pop-Up Blocker** check box.

2. Click **Settings** to display the Pop-Up Blocker Settings dialog box.

Continued . . .

2. Right-click the selection, and click **Copy**.

3. Open or switch to the text-editing application (for example, Notepad) or the word processor (for example, Microsoft Word). Open the document in which you want to paste the text.

4. Right-click where you want the text, and click **Paste**.

Material you copy from the Internet is normally protected by copyright laws, so what you can do with it legally is limited. Basically, you can store it on your hard drive and refer to it. You cannot put it on your website, sell it, copy it for distribution, or use it for a commercial purpose without the permission of the owner.

COPY A WEB PAGE FROM THE INTERNET

To store a copy of the open web page on your hard drive:

1. Click the **Page** button, and click **Save As**. The Save Webpage dialog box appears.

2. Select the folder in which to save the page, enter the filename you want to use, and click **Save**.

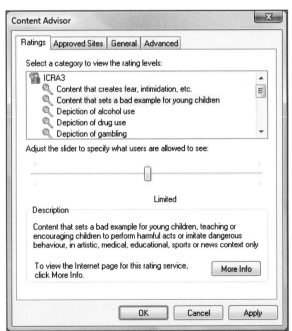

*Figure 3-7: **The Content Advisor dialog box lets you set the level of offensive content allowed in four categories.***

CONTROLLING INTERNET SECURITY *(Continued)*

3. To allow a particular site to display pop-ups, type its name in the **Address Of Web Site To Allow** text box, and click **Add**.

4. Under Settings, choose whether Internet Explorer should play a sound or display the Information bar across the top of the web page on blocking a pop-up, and whether to block pop-ups opened from links you click.

5. To control how aggressively the blocker works, open the **Filter Level** drop-down list and choose **High**, **Medium**, or **Low**, as appropriate.

6. Click **Close** to close the Pop-Up Blocker Settings dialog box.

If you choose High blocking, you can override blocking by pressing **CTRL+ALT** while clicking a link that displays a pop-up window you want to see.

When you have finished choosing security options, click **OK** to close the Internet Options dialog box.

NOTE

To play audio and video files from the Internet without interruptions, you should have a broadband Internet connection.

Play Internet Audio and Video

You can play audio and video files from the Internet directly from a link on a web page or by using the separate Windows Media Player program.

Many web pages have links to audio and video files, such as those shown in the Yahoo! Movies page in Figure 3-8. To play such a file, simply click its link. If you have more than one audio or video player installed, Internet Explorer asks you which player you want to use. Make that choice, and the player opens and plays the requested file.

For instructions on playing Internet radio and other audio with Windows Media Player, see Chapter 5.

*Figure 3-8: **Click an audio or video link on a web page to play the audio or video file.***

Use E-mail

E-mail has been described as the "killer application" for the Internet—the feature for which users feel they simply must have Internet access. Windows Vista includes Windows Mail, a powerful e-mail application.

Establish an E-mail Account

To send and receive e-mail, you must set up an e-mail account with an ISP and configure Windows Mail to use that account. The section, "Connect to the Internet," earlier in this chapter, discussed how to set up an account with an ISP and listed the information you need, including:

- Your e-mail address
- The type of mail server the ISP uses (POP3, IMAP, or HTTP)
- The addresses of the incoming and outgoing mail servers
- The username and password for your Internet account or e-mail account

After obtaining this information and establishing your Internet connection, set up your e-mail account in Windows Mail.

1. Click the **Start** button, and click **E-Mail**. (If **Windows Mail** is not your default e-mail program, click the **Start** button, click **All Programs**, and click **Windows Mail**.) Windows Mail launches the Setup Wizard so that you can enter your details.

2. On the Your Name screen, type the name you want people to see in your messages, and then click **Next**.

3. On the Internet E-mail Address screen, type your e-mail address, and click **Next**.

4. On the Setup E-mail Servers screen, select the type of mail server used by your ISP, and type the addresses of your ISP's incoming and outgoing mail servers. Select the **Outgoing Server Requires Authentication** check box if the outgoing server requires you to log on to it. Click **Next**.

5. On the Internet Mail Logon screen, type your account name and password. Select the **Remember Password** check box if you want Windows Mail to remember your password so that you don't have to type it each time you sign on to the mail server. Click **Next**.

6. On the Congratulations screen, click **Finish**. Windows Mail downloads any mail folders from the mail server.

Use the next three sections—"Create and Send E-mail," "Receive E-mail," and "Respond to E-mail"—to test your setup.

Create and Send E-mail

To create and send an e-mail message:

1. Open **Windows Mail** and click **Create Mail** on the toolbar. The New Message window opens, similar to the one in Figure 3-9.

2. Start typing a name in the **To** text box. If your Contacts list contains a match for the name (see the QuickSteps "Using the Contacts List" in this chapter), Windows Mail will suggest the match, and you can accept the suggestion by pressing **ENTER**. If Windows Mail doesn't suggest a match or if the suggested match is wrong, type the rest of the e-mail address.

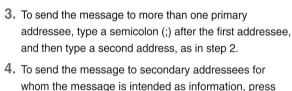

3. To send the message to more than one primary addressee, type a semicolon (;) after the first addressee, and then type a second address, as in step 2.

4. To send the message to secondary addressees for whom the message is intended as information, press **TAB** or click in the **Cc** text box. Type the secondary addressee (and, if necessary, subsequent addressees) using the same techniques.

5. Press **TAB** to move the insertion point to the Subject text box (or click in the **Subject** text box). Type the subject, press **TAB** to move the insertion point to the message box, and type your message.

6. When you have completed your message, click **Send**. Leave the Windows Mail program running if you want to continue working with e-mail.

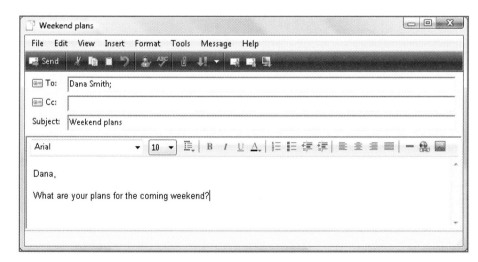

*Figure 3-9: **Sending an e-mail message is a swift and easy way to communicate with people who may not be online at the same time as you.***

Receive E-mail

Depending on how Windows Mail is set up, it may automatically download any e-mail that has been sent to you when you establish a connection to your ISP. If not, or if you need to establish a dial-up connection to your ISP manually, do so

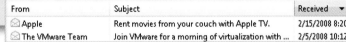

and then click **Send/Receive** or press CTRL+M to send and receive all messages.

If you have set up multiple e-mail accounts, you can check for messages separately by clicking the **Send/Receive** drop-down button and choosing the account from the list.

In any case, Windows Mail will place the e-mail you receive in your Inbox. To open and read your e-mail:

1. Open **Windows Mail** and click **Inbox** in the Folders list to open your Inbox, which contains all of the messages that you have received and haven't yet moved to another folder or deleted. (Depending on your configuration, Windows Mail may display the Inbox by default when it opens.)

2. Click a message in the Inbox to read it in the Preview pane at the bottom of the window, or double-click a message to open the message in its own window, as shown in Figure 3-10.

3. Print or delete a message in either the Inbox or its own window by clicking the appropriate button on the toolbar.

4. Click the Close button (the × button) to close the message window.

Respond to E-mail

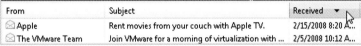

You can respond to messages you receive in three ways by first clicking the message in your Inbox and then:

● Clicking **Reply** to send a response to just the person who sent the original message

QUICKSTEPS

USING THE CONTACTS LIST

The Contacts list allows you to collect addresses and other information about your contacts, the people with whom you correspond or otherwise interact. To open the Contacts list, click **Contacts** on the Windows Mail toolbar or click the **Start** button, click **All Programs**, and then click **Windows Contacts**.

ADD A NEW ADDRESS

To add a new address to the Contacts list:

1. Click **New Contact** on the toolbar. The Properties dialog box for the contact appears.

2. Enter as much of the information that you have that you want to store. For e-mail, you must enter a name and an e-mail address. You can have several e-mail addresses for each contact. Type each e-mail address in the E-Mail text box, and then click **Add**.

3. After entering the information, click **OK** to close the Properties dialog box for the contact.

   –Or–

   Right-click a message in your Inbox, and then click **Add Sender To Contacts**.

   –Or–

   Right-click an e-mail address in an e-mail message, and click **Add To Contacts**.

Either of the latter two methods creates a new contact and opens the Properties dialog box so that you can add such further information as you have about the contact.

Continued . . .

Print   **Delete**   **Previous**   **Next**   **Contacts**   **Windows Calendar**

Figure 3-10: *You can read messages in the Preview pane in the Inbox, but you can see more of a message by opening it in its own window.*

- Clicking **Reply All** to send a response to all the addressees (both To and Cc) in the original message

- Clicking **Forward** to relay a message to people not shown as addressees of the original message

When you take any of these actions, Windows Mail displays a window similar to the New Message window, in which you can add or change addressees and the subject and add a message. Click **Send** when you have completed the reply or forwarded message and are ready to send it.

USING THE CONTACTS LIST *(Continued)*

ADD A GROUP OF ADDRESSES

To add a group of addresses that you want to be able to send a single message to:

1. Click the **New Contact Group** button on the toolbar. The Properties dialog box for the group appears.

2. Type the group name, and click **Add To Contact Group**. The Add Members To Contact Group dialog box appears. Use the controls in the dialog box to select contacts and add them to the group.

3. After adding contacts to the group, click **OK** to close the Add Members To Contact Group dialog box, and click **OK** again.

CAUTION

Not all e-mail programs can successfully receive HTML messages, so some recipients may receive versions of your messages that are hard to read. Most e-mail programs released since 2000 can send and receive HTML without problems.

Apply Formatting to Messages

The simplest e-mail messages are sent in plain text—text without any formatting. These messages are compact, so they take minimal bandwidth, can be received quickly, and can be received and read by e-mail programs that don't support formatting.

If you want, you can send messages that are formatted using HTML (Hypertext Markup Language), the formatting language used to create most websites. You can use formatting either for a single message or for all the messages you send.

APPLY FORMATTING TO AN INDIVIDUAL MESSAGE

To apply formatting to an individual message you're creating in Windows Mail, click the **Format** menu, and click **Rich Text (HTML)**.

APPLY FORMATTING TO ALL MESSAGES

To apply formatting to all messages you create in Windows Mail:

1. Click the **Tools** menu, and click **Options**. The Options dialog box appears.
2. Click the **Send** tab.
3. In the Mail Sending Format area, select the **HTML** option button.
4. Click **OK**.

CONVERT A FORMATTED MESSAGE TO PLAIN TEXT

After starting a formatted message, to convert it to plain text:

1. In the New Message window, click the **Format** menu, and click **Plain Text**.
2. In the dialog box warning you that you will lose any current formatting, click **OK**.

SELECT A FONT AND A COLOR FOR ALL MESSAGES

To use a particular font and font color on all HTML messages you send:

1. Click the **Tools** menu, and click **Options**.
2. Click the **Compose** tab. In the Compose Font area, click **Font Settings** opposite Mail. The Font dialog box opens.
3. Select the font, style, size, effects, and color that you want to use for all your messages, and then click **OK**.
4. Click **OK** to close the Options dialog box.

ADD A SIGNATURE

To add a *signature*, or canned closing, to all of the e-mail messages you send:

1. Click the **Tools** menu, and click **Options**.
2. Click the **Signatures** tab (see Figure 3-11), and click **New**. Under Edit Signature, type the signature text you want to use; or click **File**, browse to the file that contains the text for the signature, click the file, and click **Open**.
3. Select the **Add Signatures To All Outgoing Messages** check box. Ensure that the **Don't Add Signatures To Replies And Forwards** check box is selected so that replies and forwarded messages you send do not receive a signature.
4. Click **OK**.

Attach Files to Messages

You can attach and send files, such as documents or pictures, with e-mail messages.

1. Click **Create Mail** on the toolbar to open a new message.
2. Click **Attach** to display the Insert Attachment dialog box. Select the file you want to send, and click **Attach**.
3. Address, type, and send the message as you normally would.

Receive Attached Files

When someone sends you a file attached to a message, you can save the file:

1. In your **Inbox**, click the message in the message list so that it appears in the preview pane.
2. Click the **paper clip** icon at the right end of the bar above the preview pane, and click **Save Attachments** to display the Save Attachments dialog box.

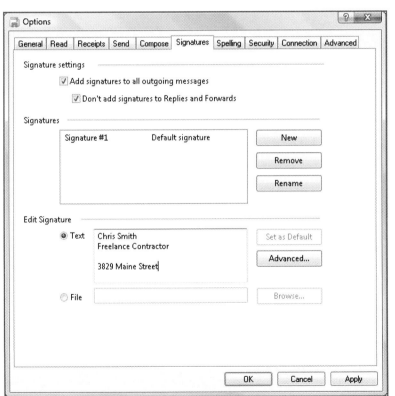

Figure 3-11: An e-mail "signature" is a standard closing for your messages. You can use one signature for all messages, create multiple signatures and choose among them, or use different signatures for different e-mail accounts.

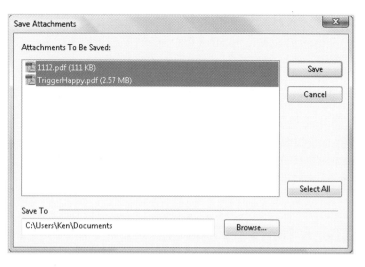

3. Verify that the folder in the Save To box is the location where you want to save the file. If necessary, change it by clicking **Browse**, selecting the folder you want, and clicking **OK**.

4. Click the file in the Attachments To Be Saved list, and then click **Save**.

Use Instant Messaging

Windows Live Messenger is an application for *instant messaging*, or *IM*—instantly sending and receiving messages with one or more people who are online at the same time as you. Instant messaging is often referred to as "chat" or "online chat," and the people with whom you chat are called your "contacts."

Beyond text messages, Windows Live Messenger also lets you have audio-only or audio-and-video conversations with one contact at a time, providing an inexpensive form of telephony and videoconferencing.

Download and Install Windows Live Messenger

Depending on who set up Windows Vista on your PC, you may or may not have Windows Live Messenger installed. To download Windows Live Messenger:

1. Click the **Start** button, click **All Programs**, and then click **Windows Live Messenger Download**. An Internet Explorer window opens to the Windows Live Services website.

2. Click the link to reach the Windows Live Messenger page.

3. In the Set Up Your Messenger area, clear the check box for any setting you do not want to implement or any additional program you do not want to install. For example, clear the **Set My Browser Home Page To MSN.com** check box if you don't want to change your home page, and clear the **Toolbar** check box if you don't want to install the Windows Live toolbar.

4. Click the **Install** button. The File Download – Security Warning dialog box appears.

5. Click the **Run** button. (Alternatively, you can click the **Save** button, save the file to disk, and then double-click the file in a Windows Explorer window to run it.)

Figure 3-12: Windows Live Messenger requires you to have a Windows Live ID, such as a Hotmail e-mail address. If you don't have one, click the Sign Up For A Windows Live ID link.

6. In the Internet Explorer – Security Warning dialog box, click the **Run** button and then go though User Account Control for the Windows Live Installer program.

7. The Windows Live Installer window shows the progress of the installation process and lets you add further components if you think this wise. When the installation has finished, click Close. Windows Live Messenger opens automatically (see Figure 3-12).

ESTABLISH A PASSPORT

To use Windows Live Messenger, you must have an online account called a Windows Live ID, which is the latest version of an identifier that used to be called Microsoft Passport and was then Microsoft .NET Passport. You create a Windows Live ID automatically when you set up a Hotmail account or an MSN account, so if you have one of these accounts, you already have a Windows Live ID. If you don't have a Windows Live ID, Windows Live Messenger walks you through the process of acquiring one.

1. If you don't have a Windows Live Messenger window open already (after installing the program), click the **Start** button, click **All Programs**, click **Windows Live**, and then click **Windows Live Messenger**.

2. Click the **Sign Up For A Windows Live ID** link to open an Internet Explorer window to the Get Windows Live website.

3. Click the **Sign Up** button, and then follow through the process of creating the Windows Live ID. You can create an address at hotmail.com or at live.com, the umbrella site for Windows Live.

SIGN IN TO WINDOWS LIVE MESSENGER

Once you have a Windows Live ID, you can sign in to Windows Live Messenger:

1. In the Windows Live Messenger window, type your Windows Live ID in the E-mail Address text box and your password in the Password text box.

2. Select the **Remember Me** check box if you want Windows Live Messenger to store your Windows Live ID. This is usually helpful.

3. Select the **Remember My Password** check box if you want Windows Live Messenger to store your password. This too is helpful but may allow other people to sign on to Windows Live Messenger using your Windows Live ID if you leave your PC running and unlocked.

Add a Contact

Help

General	Instant Messaging Address:
Contact	randall_poe@live.com
Personal	Example: example@live.com, example@yahoo.com
Work	Personal invitation:
Notes	Randall: Please add me to your contacts list! Best, Liss Johns

☐ Also send an e-mail invitation to this contact

Mobile device: (Used for text messages)

Choose a country or region ▾

Nickname: Group:
RP   Friends ▾

☑ Subscribe to updates for this contact

Learn about Windows Live Contacts

[Add contact] [Cancel]

Figure 3-13: **The five categories on the left of the Add A Contact window let you add all sorts of details about a contact. To start with, type the contact's instant messaging address, a personal invitation, and a nickname, and choose the group to which you want to assign the contact.**

4. Select the **Sign Me In Automatically** check box if you want Windows Live Messenger to sign you in the moment you log on to Windows. This is handy only if you use Windows Live Messenger heavily.

5. Click the **Sign In** button.

ADD CONTACTS TO WINDOWS LIVE MESSENGER

The first time you sign in to Windows Live Messenger, your Contacts list will be empty. You must add contacts in order to communicate with them.

1. Click the **Add A Contact** button, as shown here, to open the Add A Contact window (see Figure 3-13).

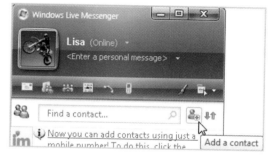

2. Type the contact's e-mail address in the Instant Messaging Address text box.

3. Type a message in the Personal Invitation text box. The message should make clear who you are (it may not be obvious from your e-mail address) and say something about your relationship with the contact (so that they can be sure it's you rather than someone impersonating you).

4. Select the **Also Send An E-mail Invitation To This Contact** check box if you want to send an e-mail invitation as well as an instant message.

5. Type the name you'll use for the contact in the Nickname text box.

6. Open the **Group** drop-down list and choose the appropriate group—for example, **Friends** or **Family**.

7. Fill in other information as needed, and then click the **Add Contact** button. Windows Live Messenger sends the invitation.

QUICKSTEPS

PERSONALIZING WINDOWS LIVE MESSENGER

Windows Live Messenger offers many configuration options. To display the Options dialog box (see Figure 3-14), click the **Show Menu** button, click or highlight **Tools**, and then click **Options**.

PERSONAL TAB OPTIONS

Type your name as you want it to appear, and choose the picture used for your instant messages. You can also add a personal message or display the name of the song you're playing in Windows Media Player.

GENERAL TAB OPTIONS

This tab contains the most important settings:

- Whether Windows Vista starts Windows Live Messenger automatically when you log on

- Whether Windows Live Messenger runs in the background when you close its window or whether it signs you out and stops running

- Whether Windows Live Messenger displays your contacts' pictures (which is usually helpful).

- Whether Windows Live Messenger displays the Video Carousel of advertisements (which is usually not helpful).

MESSAGES TAB OPTIONS

The Messages tab lets you choose the font used for your messages and decide whether to use emoticons (smileys and the like), nudges, winks, and voice clips.

You can also decide whether to keep a history of your conversations, which can be helpful. If you keep history, you can choose to load your last conversation with a

Continued . . .

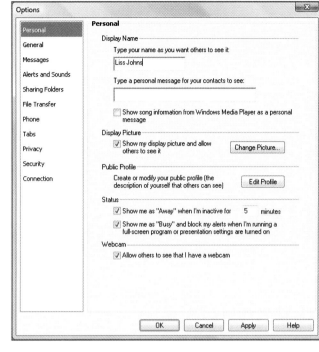

Figure 3-14: The Windows Live Messenger Options dialog box includes options for controlling when and how Windows Live Messenger runs, who can contact you and who is blocked, and which of your phone numbers you share with your contacts.

When you add a contact, the contact receives a message. Similarly, when someone else adds you to his or her contact list, Windows Live Messenger lets you choose whether to allow the person to contact you or block the person from contacting you, as shown here. You can also choose whether to add the person to your contact list.

PERSONALIZING WINDOWS LIVE MESSENGER *(Continued)*

particular contact in a new conversation window that you open with that contact, so you can resume the conversation.

ALERTS AND SOUNDS TAB OPTIONS

The Alerts And Sounds tab lets you choose when to display alerts—for example, when you receive an e-mail or instant message, or when a contact comes online. You can also control events (such as nudges or voice calls) and cause a sound to be played.

SHARING FOLDERS TAB OPTIONS

The Sharing Folders tab lets you choose whether to use the Sharing Folders feature for sharing files with contacts. Sharing Folders usually simplifies the process of sharing files, so you will probably want to set up Sharing Folders for your main contacts.

FILE TRANSFER TAB OPTIONS

The File Transfer tab lets you choose where to save files you receive, whether to scan them, and whether to reject transfers of unsafe types of files.

PHONE TAB OPTIONS

Use the Mobile Settings button to add any phone numbers—home, work, or cellular—that you want your contacts to be able to view.

TABS TAB OPTIONS

The Tabs tab lets you change the order of the tabs that appear in the Windows Live Messenger window—for example, the eBay tab and the MSN Radio tab. You can also hide the tabs by selecting the **Hide Tabs** check box.

Continued . . .

Send and Receive Instant Messages

You can send and receive text messages and files with several contacts at a time, either in the same conversation or in separate conversations. You can have only one audio or audio-and-video chat at a time and only with one contact.

SEND A MESSAGE TO A CONTACT

To send a message to a contact who is online:

1. Double-click the contact to open a Conversation window.

2. Type a message in the text box. To add an emoticon, or "smiley," click **Emoticons** and then click the emoticon in the drop-down list.

3. Press **ENTER** or click **Send**.

4. If your contact replies, the Conversation window shows who said what (see Figure 3-15).

RECEIVE A MESSAGE

When a contact tries to start a conversation with you, Windows Live Messenger displays a pop-up window above the notification area. Click this pop-up window to open the Conversation window with the contact so that you can reply.

SEND A FILE

To send a file to a contact you're chatting with:

- Drag the file from a Windows Explorer window (or the desktop) to the Conversation window.

QUICKSTEPS

PERSONALIZING WINDOWS LIVE MESSENGER (Continued)

PRIVACY TAB OPTIONS

The Privacy tab enables you to control who can contact you and what actions Windows Live Messenger can take on your behalf:

- Use the **Allow List** and **Block List** to control which contacts can see your online status and send you messages.

- Select the **Only People On My Allow List Can See My Status And Send Me Messages** check box if you want to protect yourself from unwanted attentions.

- Choose whether to be alerted when other people add you to their contact list.

SECURITY TAB OPTIONS

The Security tab lets you choose settings including:

- Whether to enter your password manually when a website requests your Microsoft Passport or allow Windows Live Messenger and Windows Vista to supply it automatically (the default).

- Whether to block Windows Live Messenger from displaying links in the conversation window.

- Whether to encrypt your stored contact information (usually a good idea).

CONNECTION TAB OPTIONS

Windows Live Messenger automatically detects your Internet connection, so you shouldn't need to change the options on this tab unless Windows Live Messenger doesn't work.

Figure 3-15: *When a conversation is in progress, you can see who said what in the Conversation window.*

–Or–

- Click the **Share Files** button in the Conversation window, and then click **Send A File Or Photo**. Select the file in the resulting Send A File dialog box, and click **Open**.

Whichever method you use, your contact receives a message that you want to send the file. Your contact can choose whether to accept the file or reject it.

RECEIVE A FILE

When a contact sends you a file, Windows Live Messenger prompts you to accept it or decline it. Click the appropriate link. If you choose to receive it,

Windows Live Messenger receives the file and displays a link that you can click to access it directly.

HAVE AN AUDIO CONVERSATION

If your PC includes a sound card, speakers, and a microphone, you can have an audio conversation over the Internet with one of your contacts.

- From an existing Conversation window with that contact, click **Call A Contact**, and then click **Call Computer**.

–Or–

- To start a new conversation, click the **Show Menu** button in the main Windows Live Messenger window, click or highlight **Actions**, click or highlight **Call**, and then click **Call A Contact's Computer**. Select the contact, and click **OK**.

HAVE AN AUDIO-AND-VIDEO CONVERSATION

If your PC has a video camera or webcam as well as a sound card, speakers, and a microphone, you can have an audio-and-video conversation over the Internet with one of your contacts.

- From an existing Conversation window with that contact, click **Start Or Stop A Video Call**.

–Or–

- To start a new conversation, click the **Show Menu** button in the main Windows Live Messenger window, click or highlight **Actions**, click or highlight **Video**, and then click **Start A Video Call**. Select the contact, and click **OK**.

Chapter 4
Installing and Using Programs

Once you've got your PC set up and configured the way you want, you're likely to spend most of your time using programs to accomplish tasks. As discussed in the previous chapter, Windows Vista comes with programs for accessing the Internet, sending e-mail, and other functions. For other tasks, you can use the programs that come with Windows Vista or install other software.

This chapter introduces you to some of the capabilities that you'll find built into Windows Vista and the programs that come with it. The chapter also describes the ways in which you're most likely to want to go beyond these capabilities and suggests how to find software that will help you to do so.

Run and Stop Programs

The standard way of running a program is to open the Start menu by clicking the **Start** button, locate the item for the program you want to run, and then click the item. You can also start a program in several other ways.

Run a Program Using the Run Dialog Box

Windows Vista includes various system tools that don't have Start menu items because you're meant to run them only in special circumstances. For example, the program Msconfig controls what happens during the Windows startup process (see Chapter 10). To run such programs, use the Run dialog box.

1. Press **WINDOWS KEY–R**. The Run dialog box appears.

2. Type the name of the program, and press **ENTER** or click **OK**.

Run a Program from the Command Prompt

Some of Windows Vista's system programs, and some older programs, need to be run from the Command Prompt window. For example, Ipconfig lets you examine the details of your network connection (see Chapter 8). To run such a program:

1. Click the **Start** button, click **All Programs**, click **Accessories**, and then click **Command Prompt**. The Command Prompt window opens (see Figure 4-1).

2. Type the program name, and press **ENTER**. The program runs or opens.

3. When you have finished using the Command Prompt window, click its **Close** button to close it.

QUICKSTEPS

SWITCHING AMONG PROGRAMS

You can switch among your open (started) programs by clicking a window, using the taskbar, or using one of the Windows Flip features.

SWITCH PROGRAMS BY CLICKING A WINDOW

If you can see the program to which you want to switch, click its window to make it active.

SWITCH PROGRAMS USING THE TASKBAR

Click the taskbar button for the window you want to make active. Use the pop-up windows and ScreenTips to help identify the correct window.

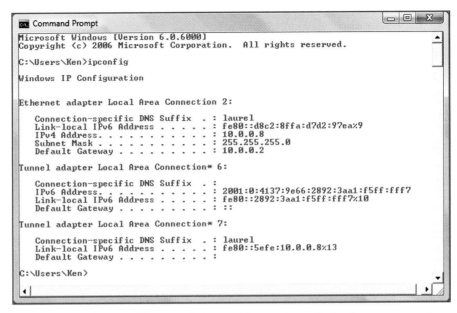

Figure 4-1: The Command Prompt window enables you to run text-only programs and older programs. You can also execute commands that you type.

If the window's button has been collapsed into a group of similar buttons to enable the buttons to fit on the taskbar at a readable size, click the group button, and then click the window you want.

Continued . . .

Stop a Program

To stop a program:

- Click the **Close** button in the upper-right corner of the window.

  –Or–

- Click the **File** menu, and then click **Exit**. For a Microsoft Office 2007 program such as Word 2007, click the **Microsoft Office** button, and then click **Exit**.

  –Or–

- Press **ALT-F4**.

SWITCH PROGRAMS USING THE KEYBOARD

To switch programs using the keyboard, use Windows Flip 3D or regular Windows Flip.

To use Windows Flip 3D (only with the Vista Aero user interface):

1. Hold down **WINDOWS KEY** and press **TAB** to display your open windows in a rotating stack.

2. Still holding down **WINDOWS KEY**, press **TAB** to bring the window you want to the front.

3. Release **WINDOWS KEY** to display the window.

To use regular Windows Flip:

1. Hold down **ALT** and press **TAB**. The task list is displayed.

2. Still holding down **ALT**, keep pressing **TAB** until you select the program you want.

3. Release **ALT**. Windows Vista makes the selected program active.

Continued . . .

Meet Windows Vista's Included Programs

Windows Vista comes with a set of programs that can take care of basic computing needs. Because these programs are supplied with most copies of Windows Vista, it can be hard to distinguish which are features of Windows Vista and which are separate programs. For example, while Windows Explorer (discussed in Chapter 2) is considered a built-in and irremovable component of Windows Vista, and Internet Explorer (discussed in Chapter 3) is considered a built-in but substitutable component, programs such as Windows Mail (discussed in Chapter 3) are considered separate programs. The main difference is that it's possible for your PC manufacturer to have substituted different programs for Internet Explorer, Windows Mail, and Windows Media Player.

Table 4-1 lists the programs you're likely to find included on a PC running Windows Vista.

Create Text Documents

Whether you use your PC for work or play, you're likely to want to create text documents: business proposals, memos, letters, schedules, recipes—anything from a few words up to many hundred pages.

Choose a Word Processor

Windows Vista includes two tools for creating text documents:

- Notepad (shown on the left in Figure 4-2) is a *text editor*—a program for creating and editing files that contain only unformatted text. Notepad is good for writing quick notes but not for creating documents that require formatting.

QUICKSTEPS

SWITCHING AMONG PROGRAMS

(Continued)

On either type of Windows Flip, you can add the **CTRL** key to the initial keypress to display the Flip stack or panel without your needing to keep holding down **WINDOWS KEY** or **ALT**:

- **Windows Flip 3D:** Hold down **WINDOWS KEY-CTRL** and press **TAB**.

- **Windows Flip:** Hold down **ALT-CTRL** and press **TAB**.

NOTE

Different versions of Windows Vista contain different programs. The difference you're most likely to notice is that Windows Vista Home Premium Edition and Windows Vista Ultimate Edition contain Windows Media Center (which includes TV-watching and recording features) and Windows DVD Maker.

NAME	USE	DISCUSSED IN
Windows Contacts	Store addresses and other contact details	Chapter 3
Windows Calendar	Store details of appointments	Not discussed
Windows Mail	Send and receive e-mail and attachments	Chapter 3
Calculator	Perform basic or scientific calculations	Chapter 4
Command Prompt	Issue advanced commands	Chapter 4
Notepad	Create and edit text documents without formatting	Chapter 4
Paint	Create and edit pictures	Chapter 5
Windows Movie Maker	Import video from a DV camcorder, edit it, and create your own movies	Chapter 5
WordPad	Create and edit text documents with simple formatting and objects (such as pictures)	Chapter 4
Windows Media Player	Play CDs, digital audio, video, and DVDs; listen to Internet radio; burn CDs	Chapter 5
Windows Photo Gallery	Send and receive instant messages and files; hold video and audio chats; share applications	Chapter 3
Backup	Back up data for safekeeping and restore it after disaster strikes	Chapter 7
Character Map	Insert special characters in documents you create using other programs	Chapter 4

Table 4-1: Programs Normally Included with Windows Vista

- WordPad (shown on the right in Figure 4-2) is a simple *word processor*—a program for creating documents that include limited formatting. WordPad documents can contain *objects*, or items created in other programs, such as pictures, charts, sounds, or video clips.

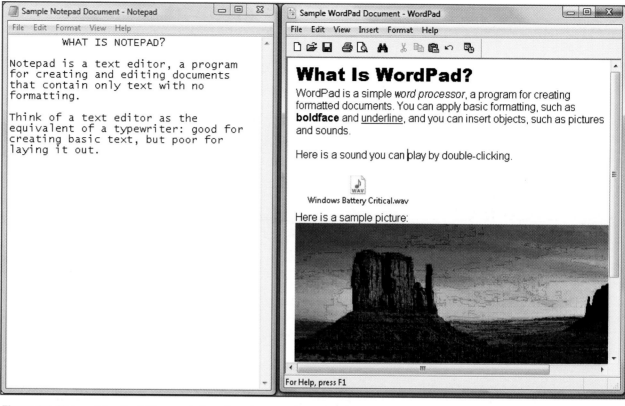

Figure 4-2: Notepad (on the left) can create only unformatted-text documents, while WordPad (on the right) can create documents that contain formatting, pictures, and inserted objects (such as sounds).

TIP

To make a program easier to access on the Start menu, add it to the "pinned" section—the list of items that doesn't change. To pin a program, click the **Start** button, locate the program item (for example, open the All Programs menu), right-click the item, and click **Pin To Start Menu**.

If you create more than even a few documents, you'll probably need a more advanced word processor than WordPad. The following are the main word processors to consider:

- **Microsoft Word** is the industry-standard word processor for Windows. Word (see Figure 4-3) offers a full set of features and is widely used. You can buy Word on its own, but it's prohibitively expensive. Instead, look for Word bundled with Microsoft Works, a basic suite of programs suitable for home or light office use, or buy Word as part of Microsoft Office, Microsoft's industry-leading productivity suite. Several

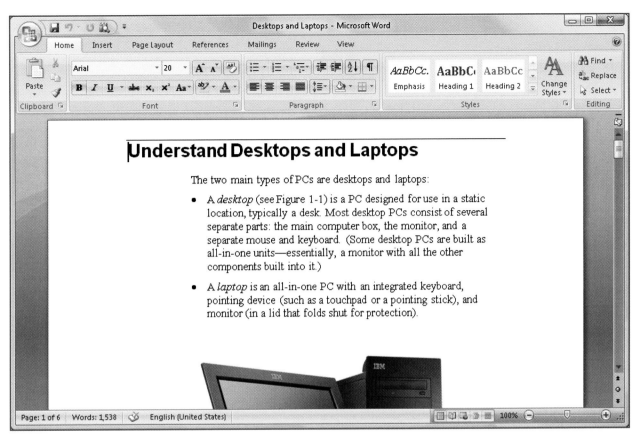

Figure 4-3: A full-featured word processor, such as Microsoft Word 2007, enables you to create a wide variety of text-based documents.

TIP

In many cases, the best time to buy a suite of productivity software is when you buy your PC. So if you're thinking about buying a new PC, explore your options for buying a productivity suite with it and compare the cost to that of buying the suite separately.

versions of Microsoft Office are available with different sets of programs—for instance, Microsoft Office Professional Edition includes the Access database program, which is typically used only in business settings. If you are a student or teacher, you may qualify for an academic edition of Office at a considerable discount.

- **Corel WordPerfect** is the latest version of WordPerfect, the leading word processor of the late 1980s. WordPerfect is the linchpin product in Corel WordPerfect Office, another productivity suite that competes with Microsoft Office. WordPerfect is a powerful word processor, and WordPerfect Office is usually around half the price of Microsoft Office. Some PC manufacturers bundle WordPerfect Office with their PCs.

UNDERSTANDING FREEWARE AND SHAREWARE

Commercial software is relatively straightforward: you pay for either a shrink-wrapped box or a file that you download. You then have certain limited rights to install the software on one or more computers (depending on what you bought). A typical commercial software package offers a limited amount of support but no compensation for any loss of data incurred if the software doesn't work the way it's supposed to.

Some software authors choose to share the fruits of their labors with other people for free. The programs they create are called *freeware*, and you can use them freely without paying. Some authors ask you to make a donation toward their costs if you like the program; such software is sometimes called *donationware*.

Other software authors provide full or lightly restricted versions of their software for download and evaluation. If you like the software enough to keep using it, you're supposed to pay the author for it (and you may have to pay in order for it to keep working). Such software is called *shareware* and is a popular way for software authors to distribute their work without incurring the large costs associated with commercial production.

TIP

In Microsoft Office 2007, the Microsoft Office button (the round button in the upper-left corner of the window) replaces the File menu. Commands such as Save, Print, and Exit appear on this menu. For example, to create a new document in Word 2007, click the **Microsoft Office** button, and then click **New**.

- **OpenOffice.org** is a freeware productivity suite that includes a word processor (called Writer), a spreadsheet (called Calc), a presentation program (called Impress), a drawing program (called Draw), and database connectivity tools. OpenOffice.org Writer has fewer features and less polish than Word, but it offers enough features to meet most home and many business needs. You can download OpenOffice.org from the OpenOffice.org website, www.openoffice.org.

- **Sun StarOffice** is a productivity suite based on OpenOffice.org but sold and supported as both commercial software and as a part of the free Google Pack (www.google.com). Like OpenOffice.org, StarOffice has fewer features and less polish than Word (and the other Microsoft Office applications), but it offers enough features to meet most home and many business needs. Even the paid version of StarOffice is much less expensive than Microsoft Office and comes bundled with some inexpensive PCs.

Create a Text Document

Whichever word processor you use, the process of creating a text document is the same. This example uses WordPad.

1. Start the word processor. To open WordPad, click the **Start** button, click **All Programs**, click **Accessories**, and then click **WordPad**.

2. Most word processors automatically open a new blank document when you start them. If necessary, click the **File** menu, and click **New** to create a new document. Often, you can also create a new document by pressing **CTRL-N**.

3. Enter the text of your document by typing it or copying it from another source and pasting it into your document.

4. Insert any other objects your document needs. For example, in WordPad, you might insert pictures or sounds.

5. Format the document using the available formatting options. For example, in WordPad, you can select the font and the font size; make text bold, italic, underlined, or a particular color; and apply left, center, or right alignment to any paragraph.

6. When you want to save the document, click the **File** menu, and click **Save**. The Save As dialog box appears. Choose the location, type the name for the file, and click **Save**.

TIP

WordPad doesn't offer the Close command, but you can close the open document without closing WordPad by starting a new document: click the **File** menu, click **New**, choose the document type in the **New** dialog box, and click **OK**. If the open document contains unsaved changes, WordPad prompts you to save them.

UICKSTEPS

INSERTING SPECIAL CHARACTERS

Many word processors include custom commands for inserting symbols and special characters. For example:

- In Word 2007, you click the **Insert** tab of the Ribbon, go to the **Symbols** group, and click the **Symbol** button.
- In Word 2003, you click the **Insert** menu, click **Symbol**, and then work in the Symbol dialog box.

To insert special characters in programs that don't have custom commands for symbols, use Character Map:

1. Click the **Start** button, click **All Programs**, click **Accessories**, click **System Tools**, and then click **Character Map**. Character Map opens (see Figure 4-4).

2. Select the font for the special character in the **Font** drop-down list.

3. Double-click the character to copy it to the Clipboard.

4. Click the **Close** button to close Character Map.

5. Activate the program in which you want to insert the character, right-click at the appropriate location, and click **Paste**.

7. You can view how the document will look when it is printed. Click the **File** menu, and click **Print Preview** to preview the document for gross layout errors. Press **ESC** to cancel the preview.

8. Print the document by clicking the **File** menu and clicking **Print**. The Print dialog box appears. Choose your printing options, and then click **Print**.

9. In WordPad, or in another word processor that doesn't have a Close command, click the **File** menu, and click **Exit** to close the document and the word processor. In most word processors, you can click the **File** menu, and click **Close** to close the document but leave the word processor open for creating other documents.

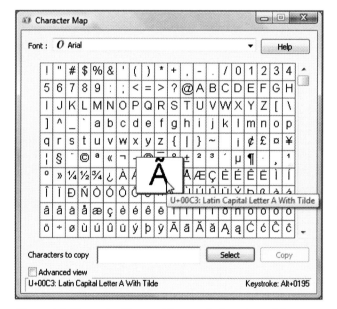

Figure 4-4: Character Map enables you to insert special characters in a document in any Windows program.

Create Other Office Documents

To create office documents other than text documents, you must install additional programs on Windows Vista. The three types of programs you're most likely to need for standard office work are

- **Spreadsheet programs**, such as Microsoft Excel, Corel Quattro Pro, OpenOffice.org Calc, and the Calc module in StarOffice (shown in Figure 4-5), enable you to organize, calculate, summarize, and present data. Typical uses of spreadsheets include planning and tracking budgets, analyzing sales, and charting results.

- **Presentation programs**, such as Microsoft PowerPoint, Corel Presentations (see Figure 4-6), OpenOffice.org Impress, and the Presentation module in StarOffice, let you quickly create visually impressive presentations for business or social purposes. You can show your presentations using a PC or a slide projector.

- **Database programs**, such as Microsoft Access and Corel Paradox, enable you to store large amounts of data in databases that you can search and query for particular data. Databases tend to be used in business settings; few homes and home offices require full-scale databases. You can create small databases in spreadsheet programs or store your data in an address book program (such as Windows Contacts, discussed in Chapter 3) or a personal information manager (PIM) program.

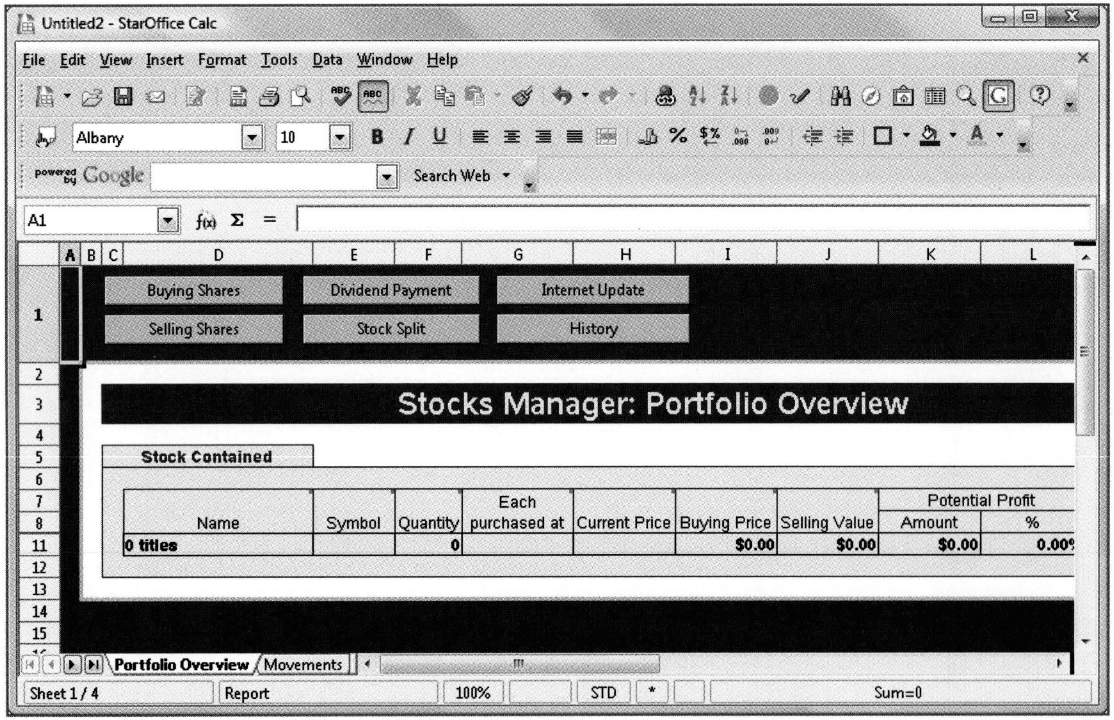

Figure 4-5: Spreadsheet programs are for analyzing data and presenting it effectively.

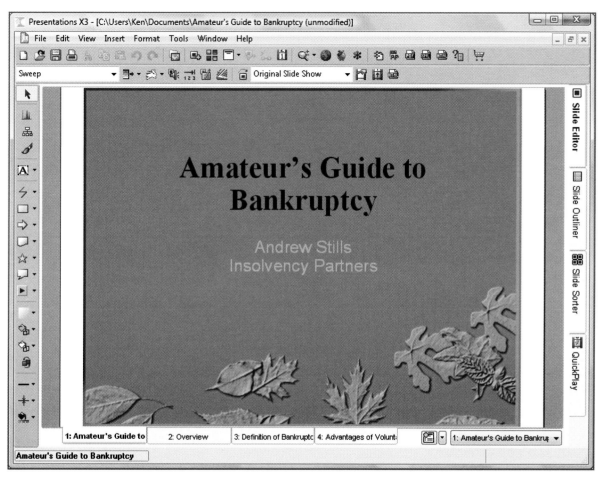

Figure 4-6: Presentation programs enable you to put together simple or complex presentations on any subject.

Beyond these office-standard programs, you can find other programs for just about any computer-based task you need to perform, be it creating illustrations, laying out publications, designing websites, or managing a company's relationships with its customers.

QUICKSTEPS

PERFORMING CALCULATIONS

Windows Vista's Calculator hides a powerful scientific calculator behind its default appearance as a basic calculator.

1. Click the **Start** button, click **All Programs**, click **Accessories**, and then click **Calculator**. Calculator opens.

2. To switch to Scientific mode (see Figure 4-7), click the **View** menu, and then click **Scientific**. (To switch back, click the **View** menu, and then click **Standard**.)

3. Type the numbers and mathematical signs, or click the buttons to enter them and perform calculations.

4. To copy a calculation to another program, click the **Edit** menu, and then click **Copy**. Activate the other application, right-click at the appropriate location, and then click **Paste**.

5. Click the **Close** button to close Calculator.

TIP

Before installing any program, it's a good idea to close all the programs you're running. Windows Vista reduces the likelihood of the installation conflicting with programs you're running, but conflicts can still occur. You may also need to restart Windows Vista after installing the new program.

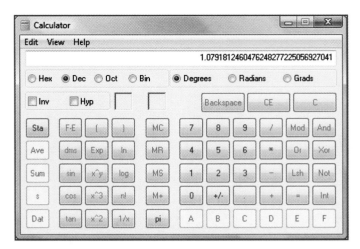

Figure 4-7: The Scientific view of the Calculator provides enough advanced functions for some mathematical and scientific usage.

Install and Remove Programs

Before you can use a new program, you must get a copy of the program and install it on your PC. These days, there are two main ways of getting programs:

- Buy a retail package from a physical or online store. Such programs come on CDs or DVDs.

  –Or–

- Download a program from the Web using a web browser (for example, Internet Explorer, discussed in Chapter 3). You can buy commercial software for download from online stores. You can also find shareware and freeware programs on software-distribution sites.

Install a Program from a CD or DVD

To install a program from a CD or DVD:

1. Insert the CD or DVD.

2. If Windows Vista doesn't automatically launch the disc's installation program, click the **Start** button, click **Computer**, right-click the optical drive in the Computer window, and click **AutoPlay** to launch the installation program.

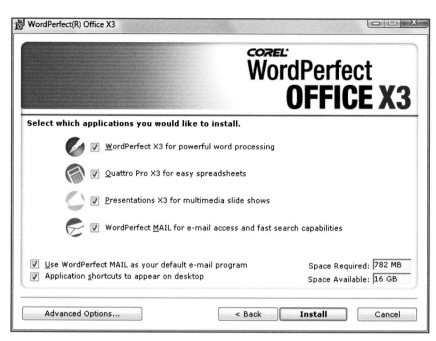

Figure 4-8: Most installation programs follow a standard series of steps that include choosing whether to install the entire program or just some of its components. For example, you may prefer to omit components you don't need in order to save space on your PC.

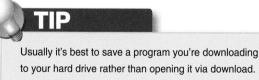

TIP

Usually it's best to save a program you're downloading to your hard drive rather than opening it via download. That way, if there is a problem when you try to install the program, you can restart the installation without having to download the program a second time.

3. Follow the instructions in the installation program for accepting the license agreement; entering any product key or security code required; and choosing options, such as the folder in which to install the program and which components to include. Figure 4-8 shows a typical installation program.

4. After the installation program finishes you'll usually need to click **Finish** or **OK** to close it. If you need to restart Windows Vista, the installation program will prompt you to do so. Save any unsaved work before letting the installation program restart Windows Vista.

Download and Install a Program

To download and install a program from the Web:

1. Click the **Start** button, and click **Internet** to open Internet Explorer.

2. Locate the website that contains the program you want to download. Purchase the program, if necessary, and click the link for the download.

3. The File Download – Security Warning dialog box appears (see Figure 4-9), asking whether you want to open the program or save it to your PC. Click **Save**. The Save As dialog box appears. Select the folder in which to store the downloaded file—your Desktop folder is usually the most convenient location—and click **Save**.

Figure 4-9: When the File Download – Security Warning dialog box asks you whether to open or save a program, it's usually best to click Save. That way, you can restart the installation easily if it fails.

NOTE

Sometimes you will download a zipped (compressed) file rather than an executable file (a file you can simply run). In this case, you will need to extract its contents. Double-click the file to display its contents in a Windows Explorer window, and then drag them to your desktop. Double-click the resulting file to start the installation. If extracting the contents of the zipped file results in a folder full of files, double-click the file named **setup.exe**.

4. When you are told the download is complete, click **Run**.

5. Follow the instructions in the installation program for accepting the license agreement; entering any product key or security code required; and choosing options, such as the folder in which to install the program and which components to include.

Download complete

Download Complete

iTunesSetup.exe from appldnld.apple.com.edgesuite.net

Downloaded: 56.4MB in 5 min 50 sec
Download to: C:\Users\Ken\Do...\iTunesSetup.exe
Transfer rate: 165KB/Sec

☐ Close this dialog box when download completes

[Run] [Open Folder] [Close]

6. After the installation program finishes installing the program, you'll usually need to click **Finish** or **OK** to close the installation program. If you need to restart Windows Vista, the installation program prompts you to do so. Save any unsaved work before letting the installation program restart Windows Vista.

Remove a Program

When you install a program, the installation program typically puts files in many folders, not just in the folder you designated. The installation program also creates entries in the Windows Vista registry, a central database of configuration settings. When you remove a program, you must do so in a way that removes all files and registry settings.

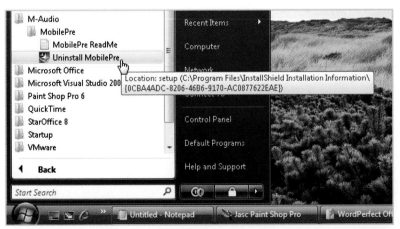

To remove a program:

1. Close all open programs.

2. Click the **Start** button, click **All Programs**, and display the program's folder on the Start menu to see if the program has a custom uninstall option. If it does (as in the example here), click the uninstall option and follow the instructions on the resulting screens.

3. If the program doesn't have an uninstall option and the All Programs menu is still open, click the **Back** button to close the All Programs menu. With the Start menu still open, click **Control Panel**. In Control Panel Home view, click the **Uninstall A Program** link. The Programs And Features window opens (see Figure 4-10).

QUICKSTEPS

STARTING A PROGRAM AT LOGON

If you always use a program when using Windows Vista, make Windows Vista start the program automatically when you log on.

1. Click the **Start** button, click **All Programs**, right-click the menu item for the program, and click **Copy**.

2. On the All Programs menu, right-click **Startup** and click **Open All Users**. A Windows Explorer window opens showing the Start Menu\Programs\Startup folder. Programs in this folder are started automatically when you log on or any other user logs on.

3. Right-click open space in the folder, and then click **Paste** to paste the copied item.

4. Click **Close** to close the Windows Explorer window.

The next time you log in, Windows Vista starts the program automatically.

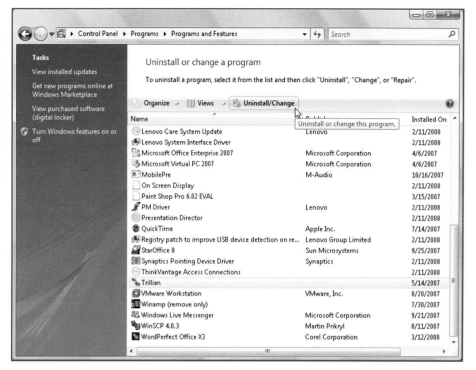

Figure 4-10: If a program doesn't have a custom uninstall option, use the Programs And Features window to remove it.

4. Click the program you want to remove, and click **Uninstall** or **Uninstall/Change** (which button is shown depends on the program), and then go through User Account Control for the Uninstall Or Change An Application program. Follow the onscreen procedure for removing the program. The details of the procedure depend on the program you're removing; you may be asked to choose between removing the entire program and removing only some parts of it.

5. When the program has been removed, click **Close** to close the Programs and Features window, and then click **Close** to close the Control Panel window.

Configure Programs

After installing most current or recent programs, you can run them simply by clicking their entries on the Start menu. You may need to configure some older programs, however, before they will run on Windows Vista. You also often need to set configurable options in your programs so that they work the way you want them to.

Use Compatibility Mode to Run Older Programs

Because Windows Vista is based on very different software than earlier versions of Windows (such as Windows 95, Windows 98, and Windows Me; and Windows 2000, Windows XP, and Windows Server 2003), some programs designed for those versions of Windows won't run properly on Windows Vista. To make them work, you must use Windows Vista's Compatibility Mode, which provides the Windows settings that the program expects to find.

To set up Compatibility Mode for a program:

1. Click the **Start** button, click **All Programs**, and locate the menu item for the program.

2. Right-click the menu item, and click **Properties** to display the Properties dialog box for the program.

3. Click the **Compatibility** tab (see Figure 4-11).

4. Select the **Run This Program In Compatibility Mode For** check box, and select the operating system in the drop-down list box: Windows 95, Windows 98/Windows Me, Windows NT 4.0 (Service Pack 5), Windows 2000, Windows XP (Service Pack 2), or Windows Server 2003 (Service Pack 1).

5. For programs that are many years old, and for some games, you may need to experiment with the Settings options to reduce color depth to 256 colors; reduce the screen resolution to 640×480 pixels; or disable Windows Vista's visual themes, desktop composition, or display scaling.

6. If the program needs to be run with the privileges of an administrator (as many programs designed for Windows 95, 98, and Me require), select the **Run This Program As An Administrator** check box.

7. Click **OK** and then try to run the program. If it fails to run and displays an error message, try different compatibility settings.

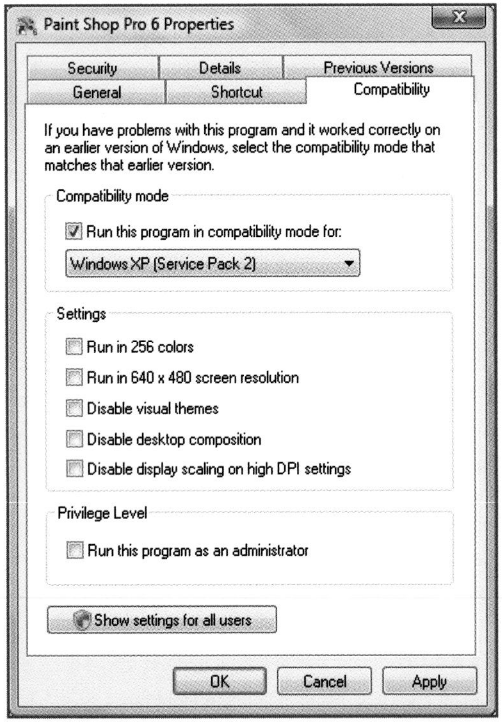

Figure 4-11: To make older programs run on Windows Vista, you may need to set Compatibility Mode for an earlier version of Windows, lower the color depth, or reduce the screen resolution.

Set Configurable Options

Most complex programs contain many configurable options that you can change to control the way the program behaves. The standard location for configurable options in Windows programs is the Options dialog box, which you typically access in one of these ways:

- Click the **Tools** menu and then **Options**.
- (Office 2007) Click the **Microsoft Office** button, and then click the **Options** button.

Figure 4-12 shows the Word Options dialog box for Microsoft Word 2007, which contains nine categories (on the left) with options for controlling everything

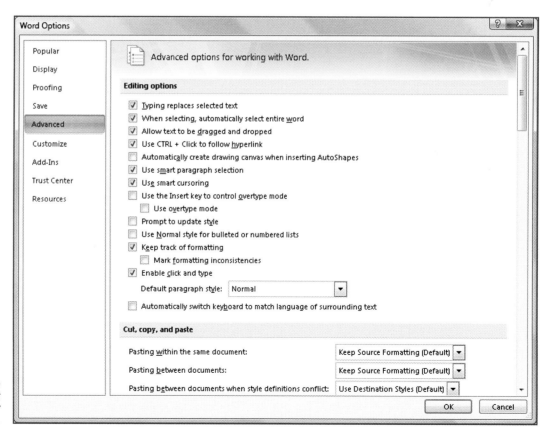

Figure 4-12: You can configure the appearance and behavior of most Windows programs by using their Options dialog boxes.

NOTE

If the Target text box on the Shortcut tab of the Properties dialog box is dimmed and unavailable, you need to create another shortcut to the program file. Open a Windows Explorer window to the Program Files folder, locate the program, right-click it, and choose Send To | Desktop (Create Shortcut). You can then customize the resulting shortcut on the Desktop.

from the screen elements that the program displays to the way it converts documents created in other word processors.

Set Program Startup Options

You may also want to configure how a program starts.

1. Click the **Start** button, click **All Programs**, and locate the menu item for the program.

2. Right-click the menu item, click **Properties** to display the Properties dialog box for the program, and then click the **Shortcut** tab. Figure 4-13 shows an example.

3. In the Target text box, you can add to the command for starting the program any specific *switches*, or command modifiers, that you want to apply. For example, you can make Microsoft Word create a new document based on a particular template by using a /t switch and the template path and filename (with no spaces between the two).

4. To create a shortcut key for running the program, click the **Shortcut Key** text box, and then press the desired key. Windows Vista creates a shortcut using **CTRL-ALT** and that key. For example, if you press **S**, Windows Vista creates the shortcut **CTRL-ALT-S**.

5. To control the initial window size for the program, choose **Normal Window**, **Maximized**, or **Minimized** in the **Run** drop-down list box.

6. Click **OK** to close the Properties dialog box.

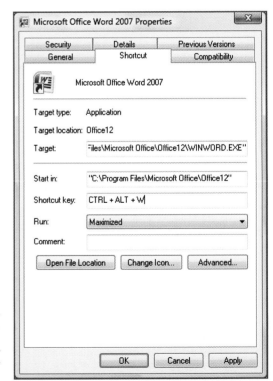

Figure 4-13: The Shortcut tab of the Properties dialog box for a program shortcut lets you choose whether to run the program maximized or set up a keyboard shortcut for launching the program.

How to...

Chapter 5

Installing and Using Audio and Video Hardware

Most PCs include powerful audio and video capabilities that Windows Vista enables you to use with minimal effort. This chapter shows you how to use those capabilities to listen to CDs and Internet radio, copy CDs to your PC, and watch videos and DVDs. The chapter also shows you how to attach a digital camera (so that you can import pictures from it), a scanner (so that you can scan physical documents into your PC), a DV camcorder (so that you can import video), and a printer (for printing any text or graphical documents).

Connect Cameras, Scanners, and Printers

Before you can work with video hardware, you must connect it to your computer. This section shows you how to connect a digital camera, a webcam, a video camera, a scanner, and a printer.

CHOOSING A DIGITAL CAMERA

There are three key factors to consider when choosing a digital camera:

- **Resolution**   Camera resolution is measured in megapixels, or millions of pixels, by multiplying the horizontal resolution of the camera's sensor by the vertical resolution. For example, 2048×1536 resolution gives approximately 3 megapixels. The important number is *effective* pixels, which is usually substantially lower than the total pixel number that is normally quoted. Higher resolutions enable you to make larger prints without graininess. You can enlarge 2-megapixel pictures to 8×6 inches, 3-megapixel pictures to 10×8 inches, 5-megapixel pictures to around 13×10 inches, and 8-megapixel pictures to around 16×12 inches.

- **Lens zoom**   Digital cameras use two types of zoom: *optical zoom* moves the lens elements and delivers full quality, while *digital zoom* enlarges the pixels to create the effect of zoom. Optical zoom is the important measurement, but you will sometimes want to use digital zoom as well to zoom in on faraway objects beyond the reach of optical zoom.

- **Memory type and capacity**   Digital cameras typically use removable memory cards, such as CompactFlash, Secure Digital, and Memory Stick. If you already have devices that use one of these types of cards, you may prefer that type; otherwise, all the types work well. Most cameras come with a small memory card; buy a larger card when you buy the camera so that you can take plenty of photos before needing to download them to your PC.

Connect Cameras and Scanners

Windows Vista makes the process of connecting cameras and scanners to your PC as straightforward as possible. The process is different for different types of cameras—digital still cameras, webcams, and video cameras—and for scanners.

CONNECT A DIGITAL CAMERA

How you connect a digital camera to your PC depends on the camera model and the medium it uses to store the pictures.

Some older digital cameras connect directly to your PC via a serial cable. Serial cables transfer data far more slowly than USB, so if you have the choice between USB and serial, choose USB. Many newer PCs do not have serial ports, so you may not even have the choice.

- If your digital camera has fixed (nonremovable) storage, you typically connect it directly to your PC via a USB (Universal Serial Bus) cable. For some (typically older) cameras, you may need to install driver software that came with the digital camera to enable the PC to identify the digital camera's storage.

  –Or–

- If your digital camera has a removable memory card, you remove the memory card and insert it in a card reader attached to your PC via a USB port. Depending on the camera, you may also be able to connect it directly to your PC via a USB cable.

When you plug in the USB cable or insert the memory card in the card reader, Windows Vista detects the camera or card as a removable disk drive and installs any driver needed, as shown here. You can then access the contents of the camera or the memory card using Windows Explorer.

CONNECT A WEBCAM

Many laptops and some desktops have webcams built in. Otherwise, you can connect an external webcam. Almost all external webcams connect to your PC via USB. Simply plug the webcam's connector into a USB port on your PC or a USB hub attached to your PC.

NOTE

Webcams (short for "web cameras") are fixed video devices that stay with your computer. They are different from digital camcorders ("camera recorders"), which are portable video devices that can operate separately from a computer. Digital camcorders are discussed later in this chapter.

CHOOSING A SCANNER

For scanning photos and documents, your best buy is typically a *flatbed scanner*—a scanner that has a flat sheet of glass on which you place the object to be scanned. The scanner's lens then moves along the area occupied by the object to capture its image. Flatbed scanners deliver good scanning for most general purposes and start at less than $50. Most modern flatbed scanners connect via USB 2.0, which is the most convenient form of connection for PCs.

The other three main types of scanners are *sheet-fed scanners* (ones that feed the document past the scanner lens), *slide scanners* (specialized scanners for scanning film and slides), and *drum scanners* (high-quality scanners in which the paper being scanned is wrapped around the inside of a drum on which the scanner's lens revolves).

You can also buy a scanner as part of a multifunction device that includes a printer, fax, copier, and sometimes other features. These devices can be handy for saving space and typically deliver good enough features for general use.

The measurement of a scanner's quality is its resolution, which is given in horizontal and vertical measurements in dots per inch (dpi). Entry-level scanners now start at 1200×2400dpi, which is more than enough for

Continued . . .

Windows Vista recognizes many USB webcams and automatically loads drivers for them. For some webcams, you may need to supply the drivers.

CONNECT A DV CAMCORDER

To connect a DV camcorder to your PC, you typically need a FireWire port on the PC. "Import Video from a Camcorder," later in this chapter, discusses how to add a FireWire port to your PC (if necessary) and how to import video from your camcorder.

CONNECT A SCANNER

To create high-quality pictures of hard-copy photographs and other documents, use a scanner. With optical character recognition (OCR) software, you can also use a scanner to enter the text from hard-copy original documents, either typed or printed, on to your PC without retyping all the text. If you don't have a scanner, see the "Choosing a Scanner" QuickFacts for advice on choosing one.

Most modern scanners are Plug and Play devices (you plug them in, Windows detects them automatically, and you can start to use them).

1. Connect the scanner to your PC via the USB port or the parallel port. (If you have a choice between the two, choose USB.) If the scanner is Plug and Play, Windows Vista attempts to find and install a driver for the scanner.

2. If Windows Vista finds and installs a driver successfully, it displays a pop-up message above the notification area to let you know, as shown here. If Windows Vista prompts you to provide a driver for the scanner or allow it to access Windows Update to search for a driver, provide the driver or give permission for the search. Follow through the installation process until the scanner is successfully installed.

Install a Printer

Sooner or later, you'll probably need to print documents from your PC. First, you must install a printer.

QUICK**FACTS**

CHOOSING A SCANNER (Continued)

scanning text documents. For scanning pictures, look for 2400×4800dpi; for professional quality, look for 4800×9600dpi. Make sure that this resolution is *optical* (produced by the scanner's hardware) rather than *interpolated*, in which the scanner's software doubles the optical resolution by adding extra rows of pixels between the real rows.

If you need to produce text versions of scanned documents, you'll need OCR software. Many scanners include "lite" versions of optical character recognition (OCR) software, but you may need to buy more powerful software if you scan many text documents. If you have Microsoft Office 2007 or 2003, you can use the OCR feature built into the Microsoft Office Document Imaging program.

QUICK**FACTS**

CHOOSING A PRINTER

Printers come in two main types:

- **Inkjet printers** spray ink from tiny nozzles onto the paper as it is fed through the printer. Most inkjet printers can print in color as well as in black and white and produce printouts of a high enough quality for most use. Inkjets start at less than $40, and most consumer printers are inkjets. Higher-quality (and more expensive) inkjets use more colors of ink and can print photos well.

- **Laser printers** use a laser to create the image. Laser printers are usually more expensive than inkjet printers and are typically used in companies, although "personal" laser printers start at relatively

Continued . . .

How you install a printer depends on whether it's a local printer (one attached directly to your PC) or a network printer and on whether the printer supports the Plug and Play specification, which enables the PC to detect the printer.

OPEN THE PRINTERS WINDOW

To work with printers and faxes, use the Printers window in the Control Panel.

1. Click the **Start** button, and then click **Control Panel**.

2. In Control Panel Home View, go to the **Hardware and Sound** category, and then click the **Printer** link. In Classic View, double-click the **Printers** icon. The Printers window opens.

For quick access to the Printers window, add a Printers link to the Start menu:

1. Right-click the **Start** button, and click **Properties**. The Taskbar And Start Menu Properties dialog box appears.

2. On the Start Menu tab, click the top **Customize** button to open the Customize Start Menu dialog box.

3. In the Start Menu Items list box, select the **Printers** check box.

4. Click **OK**, and then click **OK** again.

CONNECT THE PRINTER

Before installing the printer in Windows Vista, connect the printer to your PC or network.

1. If necessary, unpack the printer and assemble it.

2. Load the printer with ink or toner and with paper.

3. Connect the printer to your PC or to the network.

   - Most recent consumer printers connect via USB.

   - Older consumer printers connect via a parallel port (see Chapter 1).

   - Most network printers connect via Ethernet to a network switch or hub (see Chapter 8).

   - For a wireless printer, you don't need to establish a physical connection provided you have a wireless access point (see Chapter 8).

4. Plug the printer into an electrical outlet, and turn it on.

CHOOSING A PRINTER *(Continued)*

low prices. For business purposes, most companies use monochrome laser printers for black-and-white documents, reserving their color laser printers for color documents.

When buying a printer:

- If you need to print photos, buy a high-quality inkjet printer and special photo paper.

- If you need to produce many high-quality black-and-white business documents, buy a monochrome laser printer.

- Factor the cost of ink (for inkjet printers) or toner (for laser printers) refill cartridges into the cost of the printer. If you use an inkjet extensively, refills may soon cost more than the printer did.

- If you need to network the printer, buy a printer that connects via Ethernet (see Chapter 8) rather than the standard USB connection. If you're planning a wireless-only network, consider either a printer that includes a wireless connection or a wireless access point that offers a printer connection.

- If you also need to scan, photocopy, and fax items, consider a multifunction printer that includes these capabilities.

TIP

Some printers include custom software utilities for automating printer installation, calibrating the printer, and managing your printouts. If your printer includes a custom installation utility, you may not need to take the steps described here.

INSTALL A LOCAL PLUG AND PLAY PRINTER

To install a Plug and Play printer, connect it to your PC, as described in the previous section. Then:

1. Start Windows Vista if it isn't running. Windows Vista should detect the printer and automatically install a driver if it has one available. If so, Windows Vista displays a notification-area message telling you that the printer was successfully installed. Skip the rest of this list.

2. If the Found New Hardware Wizard starts and displays a dialog box such as the one shown here, click the **Locate And Install Driver Software** button, and then go through User Account Control for the Device Driver Software Installation program.

3. The wizard then searches for a suitable printer driver and, if it finds one, installs it. If not, the wizard displays a dialog box such as the one shown in Figure 5-1.

4. Choose how to proceed:

- If your printer included a disc, insert it in your PC's optical drive. The wizard detects the disc and proceeds with the installation.

- If you don't have a disc but have a driver file on your PC's hard disk, click the **I Don't Have A Disc. Show Me Other Options** button. On the next screen, click the **Browse My Computer For Driver Software** button. Click the **Browse** button, locate the folder in the Browse For Folder dialog box, click **OK**, and then click **Next** to start the installation.

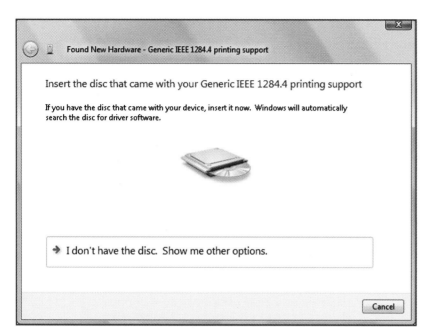

Found New Hardware - Generic IEEE 1284.4 printing support

Insert the disc that came with your Generic IEEE 1284.4 printing support

If you have the disc that came with your device, insert it now. Windows will automatically search the disc for driver software.

→ I don't have the disc. Show me other options.

Cancel

Figure 5-1: *If the wizard can't find a suitable printer driver, it prompts you to provide one.*

NOTE

If Windows Update doesn't produce a driver for your printer, download the driver from the printer manufacturer's website, and then expand the file if it is compressed. On the Install Printer Software page, click **Have Disk**. Then use the resulting dialog boxes to specify the location where you saved the driver file, and select the printer.

• If you have neither a disc nor a driver file, click the **I Don't Have A Disc. Show Me Other Options** button. On the next screen, click the **Check For A Solution** button to see if Windows Update can provide a driver.

5. Click the **Start** button, and then click **Printers**. The Printers window opens, showing the printer you installed. Hover the mouse pointer over the printer to display its status, as shown in Figure 5-2. (If your printer isn't listed in the Printers And Faxes window, Windows Vista didn't install it. Go to the next section, "Install a Local Other Printer.")

6. To check that the printer is working, right-click the printer and click **Properties**, and then click the **Print Test Page** button on the General tab of the resulting Properties dialog box. In the dialog box that tells you the page has been sent, click the **Close** button.

7. Click **OK** to close the Properties dialog box, and then click **Close** to close the Printers window.

INSTALL A LOCAL OTHER PRINTER

If your printer doesn't install automatically using the steps in the previous section, install it manually.

1. If your printer included a disc with software for Windows Vista, insert the disc in your PC's optical drive, and follow the onscreen instructions to install the printer. When the installation procedure is complete, click the **Start** button, and then click **Printers** to open the Printers window. Right-click the printer and click **Properties**, and then click **Print Test Page** on the General tab of the resulting Properties dialog box. If the test page prints satisfactorily, click **OK** and skip to step 9.

2. If your printer didn't include a disc, click the **Start** button, click **Printers**, and then click **Add A Printer** on the toolbar in the Printers window. The Add Printer Wizard starts.

3. On the Choose A Local Or Network Printer page, click the **Add A Local Printer** button. The Choose A Printer Port page is displayed.

4. Select the **Use An Existing Port** option button, and select the port in the drop-down list box. Usually, you'll need to select **LPT1** for a printer attached to a parallel port or **USB001** for a printer attached via USB.

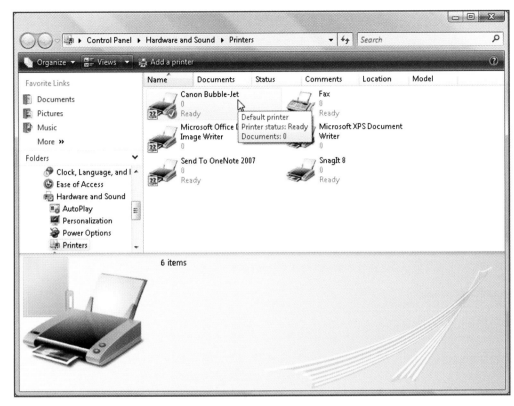

Figure 5-2: *Windows Vista should automatically detect and install a Plug and Play printer that you connect to your PC.*

NOTE

The Add Printer Wizard lets you set any printer you install as your default printer, the printer used when you don't specify another printer. You can change your default printer at any time by opening the Printers window (click the **Start** button, and then click **Printers**), right-clicking the printer, and clicking **Set As Default Printer**.

5. Click **Next**. The Install The Printer Driver page is displayed (see Figure 5-3).

6. Select the manufacturer and model of the printer you want to install. If you can't find your printer, click **Windows Update** to download the latest printer drivers, and then search for the manufacturer and model once more. After finding the correct printer, click **Next**. The Type A Printer Name page is displayed.

7. Change the default name for the printer to a more helpful name, if you want; choose whether to use this printer as your default printer; and click **Next**. The You've Successfully Added [Printer] page is displayed.

8. Click **Print A Test Page** if you want to print a test page, and then click **Finish**.

9. Click **Close** to close the Printers window.

INSTALL A NETWORK PRINTER

A network printer is a printer made available to your PC via a network in one of three ways:

● The printer is connected to someone else's PC and has been shared.

● The printer is connected to a dedicated printer server.

● The printer is directly connected to the network through its own network interface.

The first two types of network printers are installed as described in the following section. The third type of printer is installed (usually automatically) as a local printer, as described in the previous two sections.

1. Click the **Start** button, click **Printers**, and then click **Add A Printer** on the toolbar in the Printers window. The Add Printer Wizard starts and displays the Choose A Local Or Network Printer page.

2. Click the **Add A Network, Wireless Or Bluetooth Printer** button. The Searching For Available Printers page is displayed (see Figure 5-4).

Figure 5-3: *To install a printer manually, you must specify the printer manufacturer and model and select the port into which the printer is plugged.*

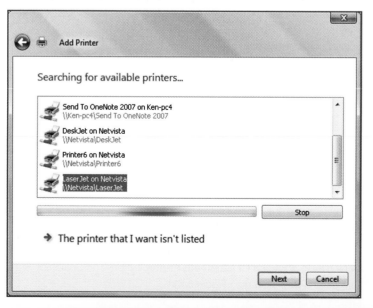

Figure 5-4: *A printer attached to another PC must be shared by that PC before you can use it from your PC.*

3. Look at the list of available printers:
   - If the printer you want appears in the list box, click it, and click the **Next** button. Then follow through the rest of the installation routine and skip the remainder of this list.
   - If the printer you want isn't listed, click **The Printer I Want Isn't Listed** to display the Find A Printer By Name Or TCP/IP Address page. Click the **Select A Shared Printer By Name** option button. If you know the names of the computer sharing the printer and the shared printer you can simply type the name in the text box using the format \\computername\printername. Otherwise, click **Browse**, double-click the sharing computer, and then double-click the shared printer. Click the **Next** button.

4. Name the printer, and choose whether to make it your default printer.

5. Click **Finish** and then click **Close** to close the Printers And Faxes window.

SHARE YOUR PC'S PRINTER

You can share the printer attached to your PC so that other people on your network can print using it.

1. Click the **Start** button, and click **Printers** to open the Printers window.

2. Right-click the printer, and then click **Sharing**. The Sharing tab of the Properties dialog box for the printer is displayed.

3. If the controls in the Share This Printer group box are grayed out and unavailable, click the **Change Sharing Options** button, and then go through User Account Control for the Change Printing Settings program. Windows enables the controls in the group box.

4. Select the **Share This Printer** check box.

5. Type a descriptive name of no more than 12 characters in the Share Name text box.

6. If you want the PC sending the print job to do the work of processing the print job (rather than having the PC sharing the printer do the processing), select the **Render Print Jobs On Client Computers** check box. This is usually a good idea unless the other PCs are severely underpowered.

7. Click the **OK** button.

8. Click **Close** to close the Printers window.

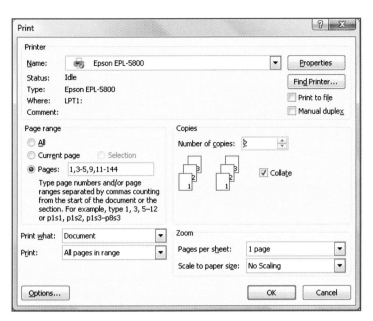

Figure 5-5: *The controls in the Print dialog box vary from program to program, but most Print dialog boxes let you choose the printer, print range, and number of copies to print.*

Print Documents and Photos

Most programs provide similar features for printing documents, although the specific options vary depending on the contents of the document the program produces. For example, Microsoft Word has different features for printing word-processing documents than Microsoft Excel has for printing spreadsheets because word-processing documents and spreadsheets have different features.

PRINT A DOCUMENT

To print a document other than a photo:

1. Open the program and open the document you want to print. Alternatively, open the **File** menu (or the **Microsoft Office button** menu in Office 2007), and click **Preview** to view the document in print preview. Check for errors and correct any that you find.

2. Open the **File** menu (or the **Microsoft Office button** menu in Office 2007), and click **Print**. The Print dialog box appears. Figure 5-5 shows an example of a Print dialog box.

3. Choose the printer in the drop-down list.

4. Choose other options for printing (depending on the program). For example, you might choose to print only some pages.

5. Click **OK**.

PRINT A PHOTO

You can print a photo directly from a graphics program, such as Paint or Photoshop Elements, but Windows Vista also provides the Print Pictures Wizard.

1. Open a Windows Explorer window and browse to the folder that contains the photos you want to print. For example, click the **Start** button, and click **Pictures** to open your Pictures folder.

2. Select the photos to print, and click Print on the toolbar. The Print Pictures Wizard starts (see Figure 5-6).

TIP

To print using the Print Pictures Wizard from any folder other than the Pictures folder, customize the folder so that Windows Vista knows that it contains photos. In the Address bar, click the folder to the left of the current folder to display the parent folder of the current folder. Right-click the folder that contains the photos, and click **Properties** to display the Properties dialog box. Click the **Customize** tab, click **Pictures And Videos** in the **Use This Folder Type As A Template** drop-down list, and then click **OK**. Double-click the folder to display its contents again.

TIP

You can choose further options for printing your pictures by clicking the Options link in the lower-right corner of the Print Pictures Wizard and then choosing settings in the Print Settings dialog box. Select the **Sharpen For Printing** check box if you want the Wizard to apply automatic sharpening to the pictures; clear this check box if the pictures look overcooked. Clear the **Only Show Options That Are Compatible With My Printer** check box if you want to see options that your printer supposedly doesn't support—but don't expect the extra options to give good results if your printer genuinely doesn't offer them. When you've finished choosing settings, click **OK** to return to the Print Pictures Wizard.

Figure 5-6: The Print Pictures Wizard enables you to print selected photos using various layouts. Click the Next arrow *button and* Previous arrow *button below the preview to move from one picture to another.*

3. In the **Printer** drop-down list, make sure the correct printer is selected. (If you have installed only one printer, it will be selected already.)

4. In the **Paper Size** drop-down list, choose the paper size—for example, **Letter** for full-size 8.5×11-inch paper.

5. In the **Quality** drop-down list, choose the quality at which you want to print—for example, 600×600 dots per inch. Which choices you have depend on the printer you're using. For best results, you'll typically want to choose the highest resolution available.

6. Set the number of copies in the **Copies Of Each Picture** box.

7. Select the **Fit Picture To Frame** check box if you want to print the picture as large as possible within the area available to it.

QUICKFACTS

CHOOSING ILLUSTRATION PROGRAMS

If Paint doesn't provide the tools you need for graphical work, get a more advanced illustration program.

- **Paint Shop Pro** from Corel Corporation (www.corel.com; around $100) provides powerful features for creating and editing graphics.

- **Photoshop Elements** from Adobe Systems, Inc. (www.adobe.com; around $120) is a stripped-down version of Photoshop, Adobe's market-leading graphics program.

- **Deneba Canvas** from ACD Systems of America, Inc. (www.acdsee.com; around $350) is a professional-quality graphics program.

- **Photoshop** from Adobe Systems, Inc. (www.adobe.com; around $650, but less if purchased as part of Adobe Creative Suite) is the tool that most professionals use for editing graphics.

You can download evaluation versions of all these programs from the URLs provided.

---

8. On the right side of the Print Pictures Wizard, select the layout you want—anything from **Full Page Photo** (one picture per sheet) to **Contact Prints** (many tiny pictures per sheet).

9. Click the **Print** button to print the pictures. The wizard closes.

Create and Import Pictures and Video

Once your video hardware is connected (as discussed earlier in this chapter), you can use Windows Vista's features and programs to work with pictures and video.

Work with Pictures Using Paint

Windows Vista's Paint accessory program is useful for creating simple illustrations, capturing still pictures from a webcam, and converting digital pictures from one format to another.

CREATE A PICTURE

To create a picture using Paint:

1. Click the **Start** button, click **All Programs**, click **Accessories**, and then click **Paint**. Paint opens.

2. Use the tools in Paint to create your picture (see Figure 5-7). Hover the mouse pointer over a tool to display a ScreenTip describing it.

3. Click the **File** menu, and click **Save As**. The Save As dialog box appears. Select the folder, enter the filename, and click **Save** to save the picture.

4. Click the **File** menu, and click **Exit** to close Paint and the picture.

If you need to capture all or part of the screen, use Windows Vista's Snipping Tool. Click the **Start** button, click **All Programs**, click **Accessories**, and then click **Snipping Tool**. Click the **New** drop-down button, and then choose the type of capture you want: **Free-Form Snip**, **Rectangular Snip**, **Window Snip**, or **Full-Screen Snip**.

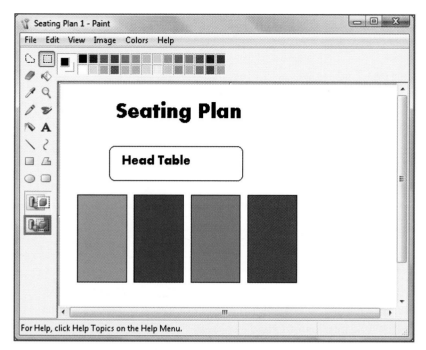

Figure 5-7: *Paint offers preset shapes and colors for creating basic diagrams. You can also create pictures.*

CAPTURE STILLS FROM A WEBCAM

To capture still pictures from a USB webcam using Paint:

1. Connect your USB webcam to your PC as discussed in "Connect a Webcam," earlier in this chapter.

2. Click the **Start** button, click **All Programs**, click **Accessories**, and then click **Paint**. Paint opens.

3. Click the **File** menu, and click **From Scanner Or Camera** to open the Capture Pictures From Video dialog box.

4. Aim the camera at your subject so that the picture in the Capture Pictures From Video dialog box shows what you want to capture.

5. Click **Capture**. Paint adds the captured picture to the list box on the right side of the dialog box. Click **Capture** again to capture further pictures as necessary.

6. In the list box, select the picture you want to keep.

7. Click **Get Picture**. Paint closes the Capture Pictures From Video dialog box and displays the picture in the Paint window.

8. Click the **File** menu, and click **Save**. The Save As dialog box appears.

9. Choose the folder, type the filename, and choose a suitable format in the **Save As Type** drop-down list (see the "Choosing the Best Picture Format" QuickFacts for advice), and then click **Save**.

10. If you've finished working with Paint, open the **File** menu, and click **Exit**.

CONVERT A PICTURE TO A DIFFERENT FORMAT

To convert a picture to a different format using Paint:

1. Click the **Start** button, click **All Programs**, click **Accessories**, and then click **Paint**. Paint opens.

2. Click the **File** menu, and click **Open**. The Open dialog box appears. Select the picture and click **Open**.

3. Click the **File** menu, and click **Save As**. The Save As dialog box appears.

4. Choose the format in the **Save As Type** drop-down list (see the "Choosing Picture Formats" QuickFacts for advice). If the new format uses the same extension as the current format (for example, when you're converting one type of bitmap to another), change the filename so that the new picture doesn't overwrite the old picture.

QUICKFACTS

CHOOSING THE BEST PICTURE FORMAT

There are many different formats for digital pictures. These formats differ in the amount of data they save for the picture and the way in which they save it. Paint can open and save files in five of the most widely used formats.

BITMAP

Bitmap is a standard format that stores the details of the data contained in each pixel of the picture. Bitmaps are

Continued . . .

CHOOSING THE BEST PICTURE FORMAT *(Continued)*

uncompressed, so they take up more disk space than most other graphics formats. Paint offers four grades of bitmap:

- Use Monochrome Bitmap when you want to convert a picture to black and white.

- Use 16 Color Bitmap when you want to strip a picture down to 16 colors. This sometimes gives desirable artistic effects, but typically wrecks any picture that contains complex colors.

- Use 256 Color Bitmap (8-bit) when you want to reduce a picture to 256 colors. The effects are better than 16 Color Bitmap, but they change most pictures considerably for the worse.

- Use 24-Bit Bitmap (more than 16 million colors) when you want to save as much data as possible about your picture; 24-bit bitmaps take up a considerable amount of space.

JPEG

JPEG (Joint Photographic Experts Group) is a graphics format widely used on the Web. JPEG uses *lossy compression*, compression that discards some of the data, to give a smaller file size. Use JPEG when you want to produce compact pictures with reasonable quality for Web use.

GIF

GIF (Graphics Interchange Format) is an older standard graphics format also widely used on the Web. GIF provides a good balance of picture quality with file size, but, unfortunately, has legal constraints on its use—in theory, you should pay a royalty each time you create a GIF picture.

Continued . . .

5. Click **Save**.

6. If you've finished working with Paint, click the **File** menu, and click **Exit**.

Work with Digital Pictures

Windows Vista makes it easy to import pictures from a digital camera and view them in the Windows Photo Gallery program.

IMPORT PICTURES FROM A DIGITAL CAMERA

To import pictures from a digital camera:

1. Connect the digital camera or its memory card to your PC, as discussed in "Connect a Digital Camera," earlier in this chapter.

2. Click the **Start** button, click **All Programs**, and then click **Windows Photo Gallery**. Windows Photo Gallery opens. (If the AutoPlay dialog box appears, you won't need to do this.)

3. Click the **File** button, and then click **Import From Camera Or Scanner** to open the Import Pictures And Videos dialog box.

4. Click the icon for the camera or memory card. If you don't see the icon, click the **Refresh** button to make Windows read the devices again.

5. Click the **Import** button. Windows Photo Gallery displays the Importing Pictures And Videos dialog box, shown here.

6. In the Tag These Pictures box, either type any tags (terms) you want to apply to the pictures, or pick a term you've used before from the drop-down list.

QUICKFACTS

CHOOSING THE BEST PICTURE FORMAT *(Continued)*

TIFF

TIFF (Tagged Image File Format) is a standard graphics format for storing full-quality pictures. There are various subtypes of TIFF file; Paint creates TIFF files compressed with LZW compression, *lossless compression* (compression that does not discard data), which reduces the file size. Use TIFF when you want to create high-quality pictures for print use that take up less space than 24-bit bitmaps.

PNG

PNG (Portable Network Graphics) is a relatively new graphics format developed for Internet usage. PNG uses lossless compression to create a high-quality picture with as small a file size as possible. Use PNG when you want to produce a full-quality picture for Web use.

TIP

If you want to change the way in which Windows Photo Gallery imports the pictures, click the **Options** link in the Importing Pictures And Videos dialog box. The Import Settings dialog box opens. In the **Settings For** drop-down list at the top, choose **Cameras**, **CDs And DVDs**, or **Scanners**, as appropriate. You can then use the other controls to specify which folder to put the files in, how to name the subfolder and the files, whether to erase the photos from the camera, and whether to open Windows Photo Gallery automatically after importing the pictures. Click **OK** when you've finished making choices.

7. Click the **Import** button. Windows Photo Gallery starts importing the pictures.

8. Select the **Erase After Importing** check box if you want Windows Photo Gallery to erase the pictures from the camera after importing them. Normally, it's safer to check the imported pictures first, and then delete them from the camera manually.

9. At the end of the import, Windows Photo Gallery opens automatically (unless you have set it not to in the Import Settings dialog box). You can then view your pictures as described in the next section.

10. Click the **Safely Remove Hardware** icon in the notification area, and then click the item for the removable disk drive on the resulting menu.

11. Detach the camera or remove the memory card from the card reader.

VIEW PICTURES IN WINDOWS PHOTO GALLERY

To view pictures in Windows Photo Gallery:

1. If Windows Photo Gallery is not already open, click the **Start** button, click **All Programs**, and then click **Windows Photo Gallery**.

2. If you have just imported pictures as described in the previous section, Windows Photo Gallery will have selected the Recently Imported category in the left pane, as in Figure 5-8. If not, click the category you want to view—for example, **Pictures**.

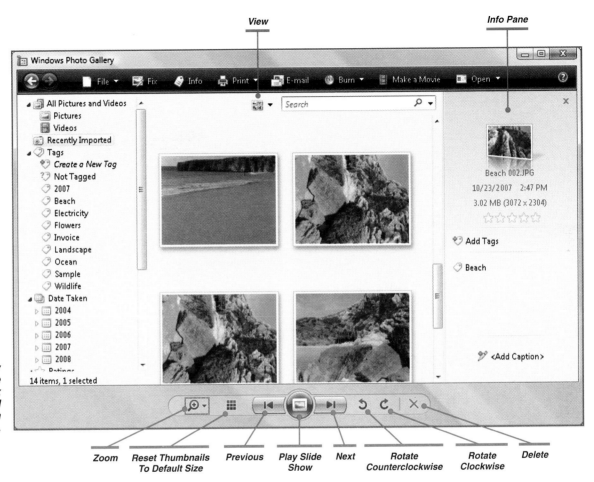

View

Info Pane

Windows Photo Gallery

File ▼ | Fix | Info | Print ▼ | E-mail | Burn ▼ | Make a Movie | Open ▼ | ?

◢ All Pictures and Videos
   Pictures
   Videos
   Recently Imported
◢ Tags
   Create a New Tag
   Not Tagged
   2007
   Beach
   Electricity
   Flowers
   Invoice
   Landscape
   Ocean
   Sample
   Wildlife
◢ Date Taken
   ▷ 2004
   ▷ 2005
   ▷ 2006
   ▷ 2007
   ▷ 2008

Search

Beach 002.JPG
10/23/2007   2:47 PM
3.02 MB (3072 x 2304)

Add Tags

Beach

<Add Caption>

14 items, 1 selected

Zoom | Reset Thumbnails To Default Size | Previous | Play Slide Show | Next | Rotate Counterclockwise | Rotate Clockwise | Delete

Figure 5-8: Windows Photo Gallery view enables you to browse quickly through your pictures, fix and rotate them as necessary, and apply tags and ratings. You can also browse through your videos.

3. To change the way in which pictures are displayed, click the View button, and then choose **Thumbnails**, **Thumbnails With Text**, or **Tiles**, as appropriate. Thumbnails shows just the picture; Thumbnails With Text shows brief information about the picture; and Tiles shows more details, including the rating.

4. To change the size at which each picture is displayed, click the Zoom button, and then drag the slider up (to enlarge the pictures) or down (to reduce them).

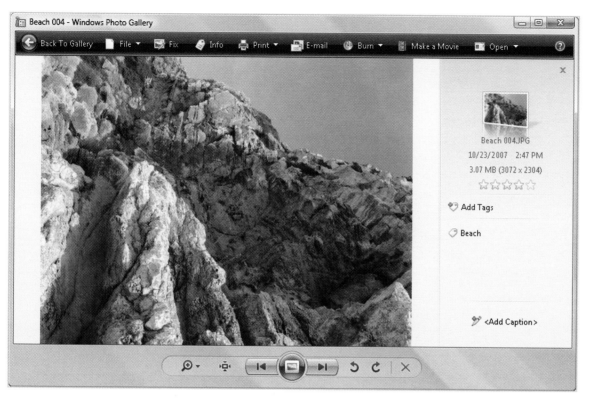

5. To view a single picture as large as it will go in the window, double-click it. Windows Photo Gallery displays the picture, as shown here. You can then manipulate the picture as described next, or click the **Back To Gallery** button to return to the gallery view.

6. Click the **Previous arrow** or the **Next arrow** to move from one picture to the next, or click the picture you want to display.

7. If a picture is on its side or upside-down, click it and click **Rotate Clockwise** or **Rotate Counterclockwise** until it is right-side up.

8. To tag the selected picture, click the **Add Tags** link in the Info pane. (If the Info pane is not displayed, click the **Info** button on the toolbar.) Type the text for the tag, and then press ENTER. Similarly, you can add a caption or a rating in the Info pane.

9. To change the coloring or cropping on a picture, click the **Fix** button. Windows Photo Gallery opens the picture in a separate window (unless it was already displayed in one) and displays the Fix pane (shown here). Use the controls to adjust the picture—for example, changing the brightness or contrast, or removing red eye. Use the **Undo** button to remove a change that didn't have the desired effect.

10. To view the pictures as a full-screen slideshow, click the **Play Slide Show** button.

- To create a slideshow of only some pictures, select them before clicking **Play Slide Show**.
- Use the control toolbar that appears near the bottom of the screen to control the slideshow.
- Click the **Themes** button to change the overall theme of the slideshow.
- Click the **Settings** button (the one with a cog wheel) to change the speed of the slideshow, shuffle the pictures, turn looping on or off, or mute the audio.
- Click the **Exit** button or press ESC to end the slideshow.

11. Click the **Close** button when you have finished viewing your pictures and want to close Windows Photo Gallery.

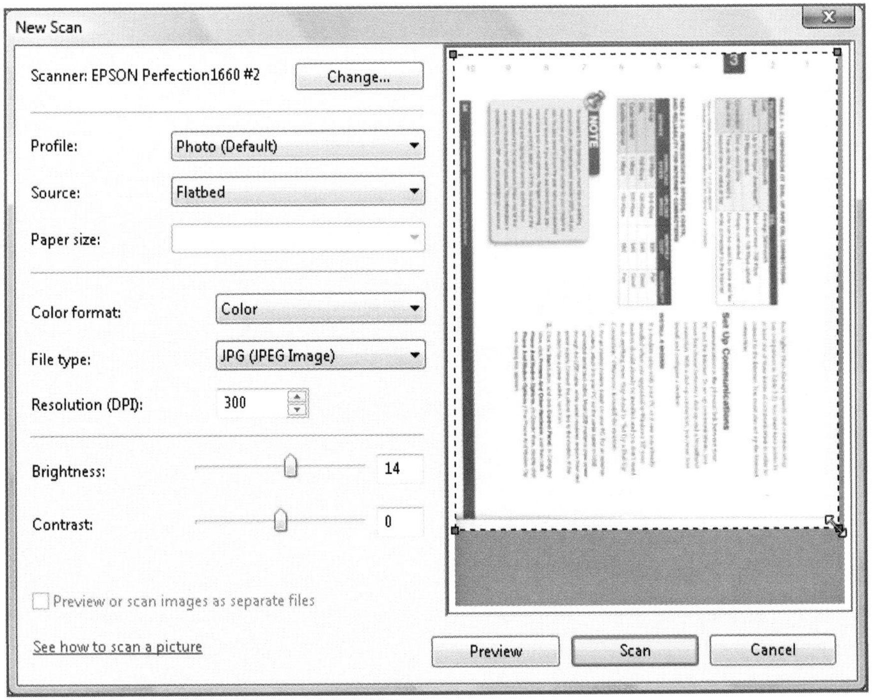

Figure 5-9: Click the Preview *button to display a preview of the picture or document you're scanning, and choose settings for the type of document and the kind of file you want to create.*

Scan a Picture or Document

With your scanner connected and installed (as discussed in "Connect a Scanner," earlier in this chapter), you can scan a picture or a document.

1. Place the picture or document on the scanner, aligning it carefully with the guides.

2. Click the **Start** button, click **All Programs**, and then click **Windows Photo Gallery** to open Windows Photo Gallery.

3. Click the **File** button, and then click **Import From Camera Or Scanner** to open the Import Pictures And Videos dialog box.

4. Click the icon for the scanner. If you don't see the icon, click the **Refresh** button to make Windows read the devices again.

5. Click the **Import** button. Windows Photo Gallery displays the New Scan dialog box (see Figure 5-9).

6. In the **Profile** drop-down list, choose **Photo** if you're scanning a picture. Choose **Documents** if you're scanning a document (for example, text).

7. In the **Color Format** drop-down list, choose the type of file you want to create: **Color**, **Grayscale**, or **Black And White**.

8. In the **File Type** drop-down list, choose the file format: **BMP (Bitmap Image)**, **JPG (JPEG Image)**, **PNG (PNG Image)**, or **TIF (TIFF Image)**. See the "Choosing the Best Picture Format" QuickSteps, earlier in this chapter, for advice on picture file formats.

9. In the **Resolution** box, set the resolution you want to use for the picture. Try 300dpi (dots per inch) for general purpose scans and 600dpi when you need higher quality.

10. Click the **Preview** button to display a preview on the right side of the New Scan dialog box. Drag the corner handles to select the portion of the image that you want to keep.

11. If necessary, drag the **Brightness** slider or **Contrast** slider to adjust the image.

12. Click the **Scan** button. Windows Photo Gallery scans the document and then displays the Importing Pictures And Videos dialog box.

13. In the Tag These Pictures box, either type any tags (terms) you want to apply to the scan, or pick a term you've used before from the drop-down list.

14. Click the **Import** button. Windows Photo Gallery imports the picture to the Recently Imported category and selects it.

15. View the picture and make sure the scan was successful before you close Windows Photo Gallery. Remove the document from the scanner.

Import Video from a DV Camcorder

If your PC has one or more FireWire ports, you can import video directly from a DV camcorder using Windows Movie Maker (which is usually included with Windows Vista) or another video program. A DV camcorder stores its data in a digital format that you can easily transfer to your PC. By contrast, an analog camcorder stores its data in an *analog format*—as a continuous but varying signal. To transfer analog footage from a camcorder to your PC, you need a video capture card that can create digital data from the analog signal.

FireWire is a standard technology for data transfer (it competes with USB), but most PCs use USB rather than FireWire. Some high-end PCs include FireWire, and if you're buying a PC with the intention of capturing video, you should ensure that FireWire is built into your PC. Otherwise, you'll need to add FireWire in one of these ways:

- Install a FireWire PCI card in a desktop PC.
- Insert a FireWire PC Card in a laptop PC.

NOTE

Windows Movie Maker is a relatively limited program and isn't always effective in capturing video from an analog signal fed into a video capture card. If you can't get Windows Movie Maker to capture the video satisfactorily, use the software that came with the video capture card to capture the video to a file. Then, import that file into Windows Movie Maker so that you can work with it.

NOTE

If your DV camcorder supports streaming video over USB, you can connect it via USB rather than FireWire.

See Chapter 6 for instructions on installing cards in your PC.

With a FireWire port available, you can capture video as follows:

1. With your PC turned on and Windows Vista running, plug your DV camcorder into one of the FireWire ports on your PC, and turn on the camcorder. The AutoPlay dialog box appears.

2. Click **Import Video**. Windows Vista launches Windows Movie Maker and opens the Video Capture Wizard, which walks you through the process of capturing the video.

Listen To and Record Audio

Windows Media Player, a multimedia player that comes built into most copies of Windows Vista, enables you to play audio, video, and (with a hardware or software decoder) DVDs. Sound Recorder, a program included with Windows Vista, enables you to record audio from a microphone or another audio source.

Configure Your Audio Setup

When you set up your PC (see Chapter 1), you connected your external speakers (or a receiver or amplifier) to the line output of your sound card. To get good sound, you may need to configure your audio setup.

1. Right-click the Volume icon in the notification area, and then click **Playback Devices** in the context menu to open the Sound dialog box with the Playback tab at the front (see Figure 5-10).

2. Click the playback device in the list box (you may have only one device, as in the example), and then click the **Configure** button to launch the Speaker Setup Wizard.

3. On the Choose Your Configuration screen (see Figure 5-11), choose the speaker setup, and then click the **Next** button.

4. On the Select Full-Range Speakers screen, identify your full-range speakers—those that play the full range of sound rather than only part of it. Click the **Next** button.

5. On the Configuration Complete screen, click the **Finish** button to apply your choices to your speaker setup.

6. Click **OK** to close the Sound dialog box.

Figure 5-10: The Sound dialog box lets you configure your playback devices, recording devices, and system sounds.

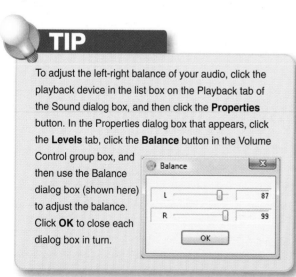

Figure 5-11: *Make sure Windows Vista knows which speaker setup you're using so that your audio sounds right. You can click the* Test *button to test all speakers at once, or click the icon for a speaker to test only that speaker.*

TIP

To adjust the left-right balance of your audio, click the playback device in the list box on the Playback tab of the Sound dialog box, and then click the **Properties** button. In the Properties dialog box that appears, click the **Levels** tab, click the **Balance** button in the Volume Control group box, and then use the Balance dialog box (shown here) to adjust the balance. Click **OK** to close each dialog box in turn.

SET THE VOLUME

You can control the volume at which audio plays in three ways:

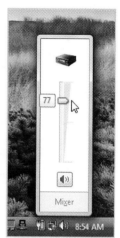

- Use the volume control in the program that's playing sound.

- Use the volume control in the notification area or the master volume control to set the overall output volume for your PC.

- Use the physical volume control on your speakers or your receiver or amplifier to set the volume they produce.

Listen to CDs and Digital Audio

To listen to an audio CD:

1. Insert the CD in your PC's optical drive.

2. If the AutoPlay window doesn't appear, click the **Start** button, click **Computer**, right-click the optical drive, and click **Open AutoPlay**. Depending on the software installed on your PC, the choices in the AutoPlay dialog box may be different from the example shown here.

3. Click the **Play Audio CD Using Windows Media Player** link. Windows Media Player opens (see Figure 5-12) and starts playing the CD.

4. Use the playback controls to control the playback of the CD.

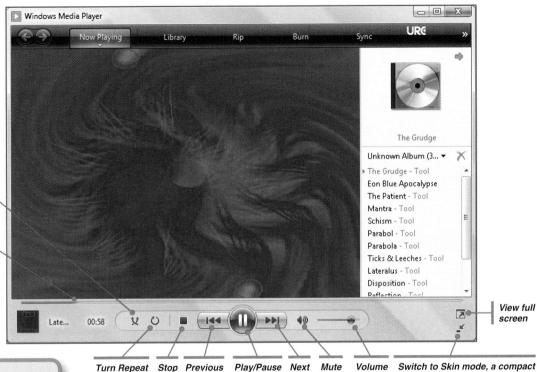

Figure 5-12: *If you have an Internet connection, Windows Media Player automatically downloads information about the CD you've inserted.*

Turn Shuffle on or off

Seek; drag to move forward or back through the current song

View full screen

Turn Repeat on or off | Stop | Previous | Play/Pause | Next | Mute | Volume | Switch to Skin mode, a compact mode in which you can apply different "skins" (looks) to Windows Media Player

QUICKFACTS

UNDERSTANDING COPY PROTECTION

The material on most CDs and DVDs is owned and copyrighted by some combination of the composer, the artist, the producer, and the publisher. Copyright law prohibits using copyrighted material in ways that are not beneficial to the copyright holders, including giving or selling the content without giving or selling the original CD or DVD.

To prevent people from violating copyright law, some audio discs are protected to make copying difficult. Such audio discs (which are technically *not* CDs because they don't comply with CD standards) typically carry a warning, such as "Copy Protected," or a notice, such as "Will *not* play on PC or Mac." Some of these copy-protection technologies

Continued . . .

Copy Audio CDs to Your PC

Windows Media Player enables you to copy tracks from audio CDs to compressed audio files on your hard disk, to create and organize a library of your music, and to create recordable CDs containing selections of this music. To copy from a CD:

1. Insert the CD.

2. If the AutoPlay window doesn't appear, click the **Start** button, click **Computer**, right-click the optical drive, and click **Open AutoPlay**.

3. Click **Rip From CD Using Windows Media Player**, and then click **OK**. Windows Media Player starts copying the music from the CD to your hard disk.

Listen to Internet Radio

Windows Media Player's Radio Tuner feature lets you listen to radio stations around the world that broadcast their programs across the Internet, either in addition to conventional broadcasting or instead of it. Internet radio works best over a broadband connection that delivers at least 128Kbps (see Chapter 3 for details on Internet connections), but you can also listen to lower-quality radio broadcasts over a dial-up connection.

To start listening to Internet radio:

1. Click the **Start** button, click **All Programs**, and then click **Windows Media Player**.
2. Click the **Media Guide** button on the toolbar to display the WindowsMedia.com site.
3. Click the **Internet Radio** link.
4. Find a radio station in one of three ways:
   - Click a link in the Featured Stations list.
   - Click a link in the Find More Stations list, and use the resulting screen to browse by genre, search by keyword, or search by ZIP code.
   - In the Search text box, drag over **Search Keyword**, type the call letters of a radio station, and either press ENTER or click the **Search** arrow. The Search Results page is displayed.
5. After selecting a station, click the **Play** link.

Here are three quick hints for working with Internet radio:

- To find radio stations that broadcast in a given language, at a specific speed, or on a particular band, click the **Use Advanced Search** link.
- Some radio stations don't have a Play link. Instead, you must click the **Visit Website To Play** link to open a web page showing the station, and then start it playing from there. Often, you must register with the station first.
- You can also click the **Add To My Stations** link to add a radio station to your station list. You can then listen to it easily next time by opening **Media Guide**, clicking **Internet Radio**, clicking **My Stations**, and then clicking the station.

Figure 5-13: *Before you can record audio, you must tell Windows Vista which sound source to monitor.*

Burn an Audio CD

Windows Media Player makes it easy to burn an audio CD that will play on almost any CD player:

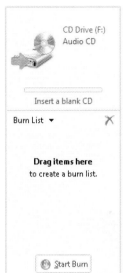

1. In Windows Media Player, click the **Burn** tab in the toolbar. Windows Media Player displays the Burn pane on the right and prompts you to insert a blank CD, as shown here.

2. Insert the CD in your PC's optical drive, and wait for Windows Media Player to take control of it.

3. Drag songs from your music library to the Burn List area in the Burn pane.

4. Drag the songs into the order in which you want them to play.

5. Click the **Start Burn** button to start burning the CD.

6. When the burn is complete, remove the CD from the drive, and label it. Then put it back in the drive, and make sure it works.

Record Audio

Sound Recorder, a small program included with Windows Vista, can record audio input through the line input or microphone input on your sound card. You must connect the audio source and tell Windows Vista which input to monitor.

CONNECT THE AUDIO SOURCE

Connect the audio source to your sound card by using a cable with suitable connectors. For example, to connect a receiver output to a standard line input, you'll need a cable with two RCA plugs for the receiver end and a male-end stereo miniplug at the sound card end.

SPECIFY THE AUDIO SOURCE

Specify the audio source that Sound Recorder will record from.

1. Right-click the **Volume** icon in the notification area, and then choose **Recording Devices** from the context menu to display the Recording tab of the Sound dialog box (see Figure 5-13).

2. In the **Select A Recording Device Below To Modify Its Settings** list box, click the audio source—for example, **Line In**. If the device does not have a white check mark in a green circle to indicate that it is the default device, click the **Set Default** button to make it the default.

3. With the device still selected, click the **Properties** button to display the Properties dialog box for the device. Click the **Levels** tab, start playing audio on the audio source at the volume you expect to use, and then drag the slider to set the input volume. Click **OK**.

4. Click **OK** again.

START SOUND RECORDER

Start Sound Recorder by clicking the **Start** button, clicking **All Programs**, clicking **Accessories**, and then clicking **Sound Recorder**.

RECORD USING SOUND RECORDER

To record using Sound Recorder:

1. Open Sound Recorder if it is not already open.

2. Click the **Start Recording** button to start recording.

3. Start the audio playing.

4. Click the **Stop Recording** button to stop recording. Sound Recorder displays the Save As dialog box.

5. Specify a filename, choose the folder in which to store the file, and then click the **Save** button. Sound Recorder automatically closes the file you saved and creates a new blank file for you.

6. If you want to record another sound file, repeat steps 2 through 6. Otherwise, click the **Close** button to close Sound Recorder.

Watch Video Files and DVDs

You can also watch video files, video CDs, or DVDs using Windows Media Player.

CAUTION

Microphone inputs are much more sensitive than line inputs because microphones produce low levels of signal. Never plug a line-level source into a microphone input because the strong signal may damage the input. Similarly, don't plug a microphone into a line input because the microphone signal will be too weak for the line input to record it satisfactorily.

NOTE

If you have Windows Vista Home Premium Edition or Windows Vista Ultimate Edition, you can also use the Windows Media Center program to watch videos or DVDs.

5

Watch Video Files

The easiest way to play a video file using Windows Media Player is to double-click the file in a Windows Explorer window (if the file is stored on a local drive) or click a link to the file in an Internet Explorer window (if the file is stored on the Internet). Windows Media Player starts automatically and begins playing the file. Use the playback controls to control playback in much the same way as to play a music file.

Watch DVDs

To watch a DVD using Windows Media Player:

1. Press the **Eject** button on your PC to open the tray on your optical drive. Insert the DVD and press the **Eject** button to close the tray.

2. If Windows Vista does not recognize the DVD and displays the AutoPlay dialog box, click the **Start** button, click **Computer**, right-click the optical drive, and click **Open AutoPlay**.

3. Click the **Play DVD Video Using Windows Media Player** link.

4. To control the DVD playback, use the onscreen controls.

NOTE

If your version of Windows Vista includes the Windows Media Center program, you can watch DVDs in Windows Media Center instead of Windows Media Player. Windows Media Center has a more TV-like interface than Windows Media Player and is better suited to navigation with a remote control.

Understand and Change DVD Regions

DVDs are encoded for eight different regions (geographical or notional areas) to enable the movie industry to control the release dates, pricing, and content of movies in different areas of the world.

- Most movies and DVDs are released in the U.S., Canada, and Japan first. Regional encoding helps prevent DVDs sold in these countries from spoiling movie ticket sales in countries with later release dates.

- People in Region 1 (the U.S., Canada, and U.S. Territories) typically pay less for DVDs than people in Region 2 (Europe, Japan, the Middle East, and South Africa) but more than people in Region 3 (Southeast and East Asia) and Region 6 (China).

- People temporarily in Region 8 (on international flights and cruises) get versions of movies with plane crashes and maritime disasters tactfully omitted.

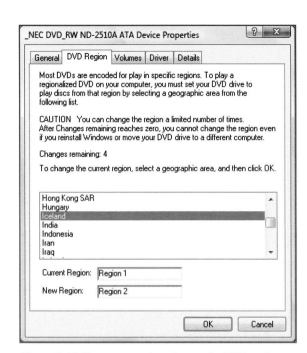

_NEC DVD_RW ND-2510A ATA Device Properties

General | DVD Region | Volumes | Driver | Details

Most DVDs are encoded for play in specific regions. To play a
regionalized DVD on your computer, you must set your DVD drive to
play discs from that region by selecting a geographic area from the
following list.

CAUTION   You can change the region a limited number of times.
After Changes remaining reaches zero, you cannot change the region even
if you reinstall Windows or move your DVD drive to a different computer.

Changes remaining: 4

To change the current region, select a geographic area, and then click OK.

Hong Kong SAR
Hungary
Iceland
India
Indonesia
Iran
Iraq

Current Region: Region 1

New Region: Region 2

OK   Cancel

Figure 5-14: *You may need to change the DVD region
before you can play a regionally-encoded DVD.*

To play a DVD, your DVD drive or player must be set for the right region. To
Hollywood's dismay, you can get some multiregion DVD players, but almost
all computer DVD drives are restricted to playing one region at a time. You can
usually switch a drive from region to region, but only a limited number of times
(five changes is typical) before it becomes locked with the last region setting.

If your DVD drive is set for the wrong region for a DVD you've inserted,
Windows Media Player displays a message. Note the region you need, and
click the **OK** button. The Properties dialog box for the DVD drive appears (see
Figure 5-14). Click the **DVD Region** tab, click the country in the list box, check
that the readout in the New Region text box matches the required region, and
then click **OK** to make the change.

Some DVDs are encoded without region restrictions. These *all-region DVDs*
work on any DVD player or drive.

Chapter 6
Upgrading, Installing, and Configuring Hardware

No matter how well equipped your PC is when you buy it, you'll probably need to add hardware to it sooner or later to extend or improve its capabilities. This chapter explains how to establish which upgrades are possible for your PC, how to choose hardware, how to install or connect it physically to your PC, and how to get it working. This chapter also shows you how to perform the three hardware upgrades you're most likely to want to perform yourself: increasing your PC's memory, adding another hard drive, and adding an optical drive. It then explains how to add a PCI card to a desktop PC and how to install drivers for the hardware you install.

Beyond the hardware upgrades discussed in this chapter, Chapter 3 covers installing a modem; Chapter 5 covers connecting cameras, scanners, and printers; and Chapter 8 covers installing network adapters.

UPGRADING THE MOTHERBOARD

Upgrading the motherboard is usually possible only for desktop PCs and not for laptop PCs. The motherboard must be the correct size for the PC case and must contain the appropriate number of expansion slots (such as PCI Express and PCI slots) for the expansion cards you need to install. Depending on your needs, the motherboard may also have other features integrated into it, such as a graphics processor, a sound chip, and a network card. Having such features integrated reduces the number of expansion slots you need, but it also makes upgrading individual components of your PC more difficult.

A motherboard upgrade affects the whole PC and requires disconnecting most cables, removing almost all components, and reinstalling the components and reconnecting the cables. Consult a PC technician unless you are highly knowledgeable in this area.

Prepare to Install Hardware

Before you buy any hardware, you must make sure that it will work with your PC and that you can attach it to your PC.

- In most desktop PCs, you can upgrade almost any component from the *motherboard*, or *system board* (the main circuit board into which the processor, memory, and add-in cards are plugged) to the memory, hard drive, internal optical drives, sound card, graphics adapter, network adapter, and more.

- In most laptops, you can add memory but cannot change any other internal components without considerable expertise, expense, or trouble.

- You can add many external devices (such as hard drives, optical drives, and network adapters) to both desktop PCs and laptop PCs via USB, FireWire, and ExpressCard or PC Card connections.

Connect Hot-Pluggable Hardware

Hot-pluggable devices are those you can plug in or unplug while Windows Vista is running and have Windows Vista automatically load or unload the appropriate driver. USB, ExpressCard or PC Card, and FireWire devices are almost always hot-pluggable. Windows Vista can sometimes detect serial devices (such as serial modems) and automatically load drivers for them, but such devices aren't normally considered hot-pluggable because some of them won't work unless they're plugged in when Windows Vista starts up.

All hot-pluggable devices connect to your PC from the outside, typically via USB ports, FireWire ports, or PC Card slots.

The first time you add a hot-pluggable device to your PC, the notification area displays an Installing Device Driver Software pop-up message, as shown here. The Found New Hardware Wizard automatically starts searching for a suitable driver that will enable your PC to use the device.

If the wizard finds a suitable driver for the device, it installs the driver without further comment and then displays a Your Devices Are Ready To Use pop-up

message, as shown here. You can then start using the device. Alternatively, you can click the pop-up message to see the details of what the wizard has installed.

If the wizard doesn't find a suitable driver for the device, it displays the Found New Hardware dialog box to let you decide how to deal with the device. Figure 6-1 shows an example. "Supply a Device Driver Using the Found New Hardware Wizard," later in this chapter, discusses this process,

Figure 6-1: **If Windows Vista can't find a driver for a hot-pluggable device, you can provide the driver yourself.**

Open a Desktop PC Case

To install hardware that's not hot-pluggable in a desktop PC, you must open the case and prepare to work inside it.

1. If Windows Vista is running, shut it down and turn off your PC.

2. Unplug the PC's power cord and any other cables (such as the keyboard and mouse cables) that could get in the way.

3. Unscrew the case or the relevant panel using a screwdriver for conventional case screws or your fingers for thumbscrews (screws with knurled, graspable sides—not instruments of torture).

4. Slide the case or panel off.

5. Before you touch anything inside the case, touch a metal object, such as your desktop PC case, to discharge any static you've built up.

6. Perform the desired operations inside the case. For example, install a drive or an adapter.

7. Replace the case or the panel.

8. Connect the cables you disconnected, and then restart the PC.

Install Memory

To add memory to a PC, follow these general steps, consulting your PC manufacturer's instructions for details:

1. If Windows Vista is running, shut it down and then turn off your PC.

2. Unplug the power cord. For a laptop PC, remove the battery.

3. For a desktop PC, open the case. For a laptop PC, open the memory compartment. Depending on the laptop PC, this usually means either lifting up the keyboard or unscrewing a memory hatch on the bottom of the laptop PC. Consult the documentation to find out how to access the memory.

4. Before you touch anything inside the case, touch a metal object, such as your desktop PC case, to discharge any static you've built up. For a laptop PC, touch a metal object other than your laptop.

5. If you need to remove one of the installed memory modules to make space for a new one (as in the PC shown in Figure 6-2, where three memory modules fill all three available slots), use the PC manufacturer's instructions to identify which module is which. For most designs, you open the spring-loaded clips (the white tabs on either end of the modules in the figure) so that the module pops up at an angle, and then work it out of the slot with your fingers.

Figure 6-2: *If all the memory slots on your PC are full, you will need to sacrifice one or more of your existing memory modules to make space for higher-capacity ones.*

Figure 6-3: ***When installing memory in a laptop, you typically open the memory compartment, slide in the memory module at a shallow angle, and then push it down gently until the slot's latches click into place.***

TIP

To transfer files and settings from your old hard drive to your new hard drive, you can use Windows Vista's Windows Easy Transfer Wizard (click the **Start** button, click **All Programs**, click **Accessories**, click **System Tools**, and then click **Windows Easy Transfer**). The Files and Settings Transfer Wizard can transfer Windows settings, programs and their information, and specific files and folders. If you want to transfer all the data from your old hard disk to your new hard disk easily, consider a tool such as Symantec's Drive Image or Norton Ghost (both products are found at www.symantec.com).

6. Slide the new module in at an angle so that it is firmly in the slot, and then push it gently until the spring-loaded clips click into place. Figure 6-3 illustrates installing a memory module in a laptop PC's memory compartment.

7. For a desktop PC, replace the case. For a laptop PC, close the memory compartment, and reinsert the battery.

8. Connect the power cord, and then start your PC. Your PC typically will notice the memory automatically; however, on some PCs, you may need to access the BIOS settings (usually by pressing **DELETE** or **F2** during startup) and configure the PC to recognize the memory. Consult your PC manufacturer's documentation for instructions.

9. To check how much memory your PC has, press **WINDOWS KEY–BREAK**, and then look at the Memory (RAM) readout in the System area, as shown here. Click the Close button (the × button) to close the System window.

System	
Rating:	**3.0** Windows Experience Index : Unrated
Processor:	AMD Athlon(tm) 64 Processor 3200+ 2.20 GHz
Memory (RAM):	2.00 GB
System type:	32-bit Operating System

Add a Hard Drive

If you need more hard drive space than you currently have, you can often add a hard disk to your PC.

- On either a desktop PC or a laptop PC, you can replace your existing hard drive with a higher-capacity model. This option involves reinstalling Windows Vista and all your programs and transferring all the data and settings you want to keep, so it is best avoided unless you have no alternative.

- On most desktop PCs, you can install a second, third, or fourth internal hard drive to work alongside your existing drive or drives. The installation process involves mounting the drive in an empty drive bay in your PC, connecting an existing drive cable or installing a new one to the motherboard, and connecting an existing power cable to the power supply unit (see Figure 6-4). This process is relatively easy, but you may prefer to have a PC technician perform it for you to avoid any confusion.

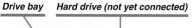

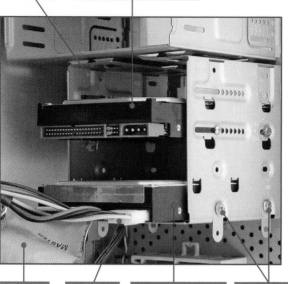

Figure 6-4: *Secure the hard drive in the drive bay with screws, and connect the drive cable and the power cable (from the bundle of cables attached to the power supply) to the rear of the drive.*

TIP

USB 2.0 is part of the standard specification for Windows PCs, so almost all PCs include USB 2.0. As a result, you can find a wide selection of USB 2.0 external hard drives at good prices. Fewer PCs have FireWire, and most that do have FireWire 400 rather than FireWire 800 (which is twice as fast). If your PC does have FireWire 800, a FireWire 800 external hard drive will give you the best performance. Otherwise, USB 2.0 is your best bet.

TIP

If Disk Management doesn't notice the new disk and display the Initialize Disk dialog box, open the **Action** menu and click **Scan Disks**.

- On either a desktop or a laptop PC, you can add an external USB 2.0 or FireWire hard drive. Provided that your PC has a USB 2.0 port or a FireWire port, this is usually the most convenient option for both desktop PCs and laptop PCs.

Set Up a New Hard Drive

After installing a new hard drive, you will normally need to initialize, partition, and format it.

INITIALIZE A NEW HARD DRIVE

1. Press **WINDOWS KEY–R**. The Run dialog box appears.

2. Type **diskmgmt.msc**, press **ENTER** or click **OK**, and then go through User Account Control for the Microsoft Management Console feature. The Disk Management window opens. When Disk Management notices the new hard disk, it displays the Initialize Disk dialog box (see Figure 6-5).

3. Click **OK**. Windows Vista initializes the drive and closes the Initialize Disk dialog box.

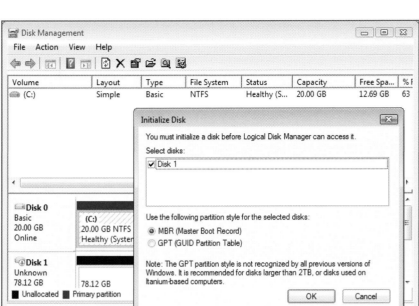

Figure 6-5: *Disk Management automatically displays the Initialize Disk dialog box when it notices the new disk you've installed.*

PARTITION A NEW HARD DRIVE

1. While still in the Disk Management window, for a drive that has been newly initialized, right-click the white box next to the drive, and click **New Simple Volume**. The New Simple Volume Wizard starts. Click **Next**. The Specify Volume Size page appears (see Figure 6-6).

2. Usually, it is most convenient to create one volume using all the space on the new drive. To do so, leave the default settings, and then click **Next**. If you want to create a smaller partition, change the **Simple Volume Size In MB** value, and then click **Next**. The Assign Drive Letter Or Path page appears.

3. Verify that the **Assign The Following Drive Letter** option button is selected, and change the drive in the drop-down list if necessary. Continue to the next section.

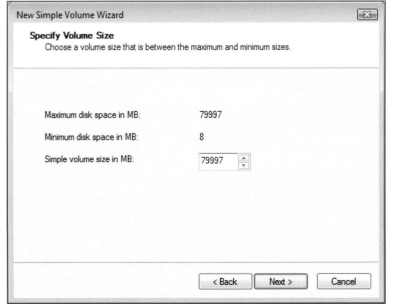

Figure 6-6: *It's usually most efficient to create a single volume that takes up all the space on the new drive.*

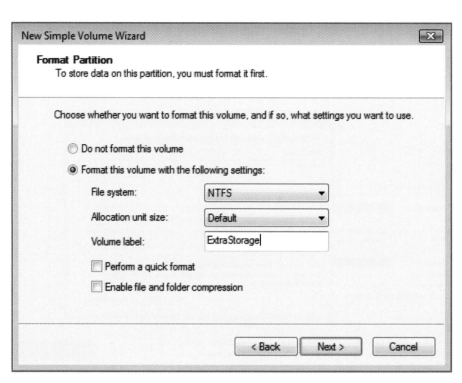

New Simple Volume Wizard

Format Partition
To store data on this partition, you must format it first.

Choose whether you want to format this volume, and if so, what settings you want to use.

◯ Do not format this volume

◉ Format this volume with the following settings:

File system: NTFS ▾

Allocation unit size: Default ▾

Volume label: ExtraStorage

☐ Perform a quick format

☐ Enable file and folder compression

< Back   Next >   Cancel

Figure 6-7: **For most hard drives, you'll get optimum results using the NTFS file system and the default allocation size.**

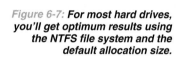

CAUTION

Compression enables you to store more files on the drive, but it reduces drive performance slightly. If you have Windows Vista Business Edition or Windows Vista Ultimate Edition, compression also prevents you from applying encryption to your files, because you cannot use both compression and encryption on the same files and folders.

FORMAT A NEW HARD DRIVE

1. Click **Next**. The Format Partition page appears (see Figure 6-7).

2. Verify that the **Format This Partition With The Following Settings** option button is selected, choose **NTFS** in the **File System** drop-down list box, and leave the **Allocation Size Unit** drop-down list set to Default.

3. Type a short name for the drive in the Volume Label box, for example, **ExtraStorage**. Verify that the **Perform A Quick Format** check box is cleared (it's best to perform a full format of your new disk), and select the **Enable File And Folder Compression** check box if you want to use compression on the drive.

4. Click **OK**. On the Completing The New Simple Volume Wizard page, verify your choices. If they're wrong, go back and fix them. Otherwise, click **Finish**. The wizard closes and begins formatting the drive.

```
Disk 1
Basic
78.12 GB      78.12 GB
Online        Formatting : (18%)
```

5. When the format is complete, open the **File** menu, and then click **Exit** to close the Disk Management window. You can then use your new drive to store files.

Add a DVD Drive

You can add a DVD drive to your PC in the following three ways:

- Replace the existing optical drive on a desktop PC.
- Add a second internal drive to a desktop PC. If you have a free drive bay for a second optical drive and your existing drive is still functional, you may prefer to add the second drive instead so that you can work with two optical discs at once when necessary.
- Attach an external optical drive to either a desktop PC or a laptop PC via USB 2.0 or FireWire. In most cases, this is the easiest solution and the most flexible: you can disconnect the drive when you don't need it, and, if you have another PC, you can connect the drive to it when needed. Many modern PCs let you boot from an external optical drive, which is useful for troubleshooting (and for installing operating systems on a PC that lacks a built-in optical drive, such as a subnotebook).

To install an internal optical drive, use these steps in conjunction with the manufacturer's specific instructions:

1. Turn off your PC, unplug the power cord, and remove the case or panel.

2. Before you touch anything inside the case, touch the case to discharge any static electricity.

3. Remove the cover from an unused drive bay at the front of the PC.

4. Slide the drive into the bay from the front, as shown here. You may want to slide it in beyond its final position so that the connectors on the back are easily accessible from the inside of the PC.

5. Connect a drive cable from the back of the optical drive to an existing drive cable or, if it's a new cable, plug it into a connector on your motherboard.

Audio cables (some drives use only one cable)

Drive cable

Power cable

6. Connect one or more audio cables (depending on the drive) from the audio outputs on the drive to your sound card.

7. Connect a power cable to the drive.

8. Slide the drive so that it is positioned flush with the front of the PC, and then screw it into place.

9. Close your PC, reattach the cables, and then restart it.

Install a PCI Card or PCI Express Card

Many add-on components for desktop PCs —sound cards, wired and wireless network adapters, and graphics adapters—are built as PCI cards. Some high-performance cards (such as graphics adapters, which need to be able to transfer a large amount of data quickly) are built as PCI Express cards, which provide faster data transfer than regular PCI. You install such cards in PCI slots or PCI Express slots on your PC's motherboard.

To install a PCI card or PCI Express card:

1. Turn off your PC, unplug the power cord, and remove the case or panel.

2. Touch the case to discharge any static electricity.

3. If the opening at the back of the case next to the PCI slot or PCI Express slot is covered, unscrew and remove the metal tab (if it's screwed on) or break off the metal tab (if it's molded).

NOTE

You also can get external optical drives that connect via SCSI or via a parallel port. These days, however, USB 2.0 or FireWire are far preferable means of connection for external drives because they're much faster than a parallel port, hot-pluggable, and easier than both SCSI and parallel-port connections.

FINDING DEVICE DRIVERS

Getting new hardware to work usually involves finding the correct device driver. The following are the best sources for device drivers.

- The **manufacturer** of the device is generally the best source, but as hardware goes out of date and becomes unprofitable to support, manufacturers stop writing new drivers. If the manufacturer provided a driver on a CD or floppy disk with the hardware, try that driver; if not, go to the manufacturer's website (search for it if necessary). Most manufacturers put a link with a name such as Downloads, Drivers, Software, or Support in a prominent position on their home page to guide you to the drivers.

- **Microsoft** has the latest drivers for the most widely used devices and, as a part of Windows Update, the ability to scan your PC and see if Windows Update has any drivers to help you. Unless you have turned off Automatic Updates, Windows Update will check periodically for new drivers. To check immediately, click the **Start** button, click **All Programs**, and then click **Windows Update**. Your browser opens and displays the Windows Update website. Click **Scan For Updates**, and see if a driver for your device is found.

- **Third-party** sources can be found using search engines, such as Google (www.google.com) or Yahoo! (www.yahoo.com), and searching for **device drivers**. Finding sites usually isn't a problem; what is a problem is determining which sites are reputable (or at least safe) and which aren't. Some of these sources charge you for drivers; others (such as the widely useful DriverGuide site: www .driverguide.com) make you either pay or watch a series of advertisements; others yet are free. Make sure that the driver will work with Windows Vista.

4. Remove the expansion card from its packaging, align it with the correct type of slot, and press it into place.

5. Attach the expansion card's metal bracket to the case with a screw.

6. Close the case.

Install a Device Driver

Windows Vista must have the correct driver for each piece of hardware on your PC before it can communicate with that hardware and use it successfully.

As mentioned earlier in this chapter, the Found New Hardware Wizard automatically searches for a suitable driver for each new hardware item it detects. If the Found New Hardware Wizard finds a suitable driver, it simply installs the driver without consulting you—so normally you will need to use the Found New Hardware Wizard only when it cannot find a driver for a piece of hardware that it has detected.

SUPPLY A DEVICE DRIVER USING THE FOUND NEW HARDWARE WIZARD

When the Found New Hardware Wizard tells you that it needs to install driver software for your hardware, you have four choices:

- **Provide a driver**   Click the **Locate And Install Driver Software** button, and then follow through the procedure described in detail in the following list.

- **Cancel the installation**   Click the **Cancel** button to stop the installation for now.

- **Stall for time**   If you don't have a suitable driver, or if your PC isn't connected to the Internet, click the **Ask Me Again Later** button. You can then try to finish installing the hardware when you have the driver or an Internet connection.

- **Give up for now**   If you want neither to install the hardware now nor cancel, click the **Don't Show This Message Again For This Device** button. This option may sound useless, but you may run into multifunction devices for which Windows Vista can install a driver that provides partial functionality but not full functionality. In this case, you may want to give up on the components that you can't get working right now.

To supply a device driver using the Found New Hardware Wizard:

1. On the Windows Needs To Install Driver Software page, click the **Locate And Install Driver Software** button, and then go through User Account Control for the Device Driver Software Installation program.

2. When the wizard displays the Insert The Disc That Came With Your Hardware page (which shows the name of the hardware, as in Figure 6-8), insert the CD or DVD in your PC's optical drive and wait for the wizard to recognize it.

3. If the wizard prompts you to select the correct driver for your device from a selection of drivers that might match, click the correct driver, and then click **Next**.

4. When the wizard finishes, click **Finish** to close it. Your new hardware should now be ready for use.

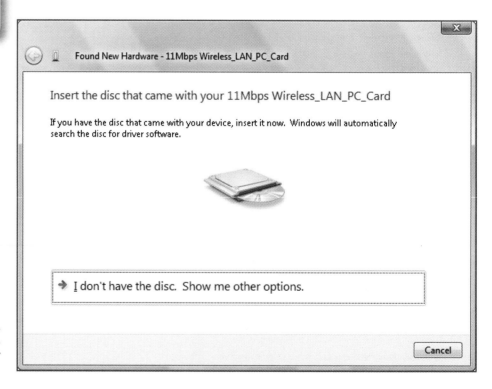

Figure 6-8: **If you have a CD or DVD containing the driver software for the hardware device you're installing, insert it when the Found New Hardware Wizard displays this screen.**

The Found New Hardware Wizard runs only if Windows Vista detects the hardware you've added. If Windows Vista doesn't detect the hardware, you can use the Add Hardware Wizard to specify the driver the hardware needs.

1. Click the **Start** button, and then click **Control Panel** to open a Control Panel window.

2. If a dot appears next to Control Panel Home in the left pane, click the **Classic View** link below it to switch to Classic view.

3. Double-click the **Add Hardware** icon to start the Add Hardware Wizard, which displays its opening page. Click **Next** to display the Wizard Can Help You Install Other Hardware page.

4. Select the **Search For And Install The Hardware Automatically** option button, and then click **Next**. The wizard then searches for new hardware that Windows Vista isn't yet using and installs any it finds, prompting you for drivers as necessary.

5. If the wizard finds no new hardware, it displays a page telling you so. Click **Next** to display the From The List Below, Select The Type Of Hardware You Are Installing page (see Figure 6-9).

6. If the type of device appears in the Common Hardware Types list box, click it. Otherwise, click **Show All Devices**, and click **Next**. The wizard displays the Select The Device Driver You Want To Install For This Hardware page (see Figure 6-10).

7. In the Manufacturer list box, click the manufacturer of the device you're installing (if the manufacturer is listed). In the Model list box, select the model (if it is listed). Click **Next**. On the The Wizard Is Ready To Install Your Hardware page, click **Next**. Skip to step 10.

8. If the manufacturer or model isn't listed, click **Have Disk**. The Install From Disk dialog box appears. Use the options in the Install From Disk dialog box to select the disk that contains the driver. If the driver is in a folder, browse to the folder, and then click **Open**. Click **OK**. The Select The Device Driver You Want To Install For This Hardware page appears.

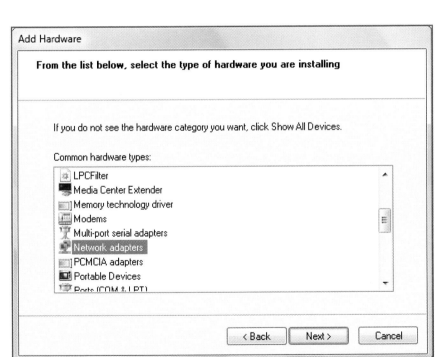

Figure 6-9: **IIf the Found New Hardware Wizard and Add Hardware Wizard are unable to find your new hardware, you may need to identify it manually.**

QUICKFACTS

UPGRADING THE GRAPHICS ADAPTER

If your desktop PC doesn't deliver adequate graphics performance, you can upgrade your graphics adapter. (On most laptop PCs, you cannot change the graphics adapter because it is integrated into the motherboard.)

Most desktop PCs use one AGP (Aperture Graphics Port) graphics card but also can use one or more PCI or PCI Express graphics cards to drive additional monitors. If you need to use multiple monitors, consider getting an AGP graphics adapter or a PCI Express adapter designed to drive two or more monitors. Multiple monitor–capable graphics adapters are more expensive than single-monitor versions, but they are easier to manage than multiple separate graphics adapters, which sometimes do not work in combination.

If your PC has an AGP graphics adapter installed in an AGP slot (rather than built into the motherboard), you should be able to upgrade easily. Check which variety of AGP your slot supports (AGP 2X, AGP 4X, or AGP 8X), buy a replacement graphics adapter that offers the features you need and that is compatible with Windows Vista, shut down your PC and disconnect the power, remove the case, and replace the graphics adapter.

If your PC has a graphics chip built into the motherboard, you will need to disable that graphics chip in order to use a different graphics adapter. Consult your PC's documentation or manufacturer on how to do this.

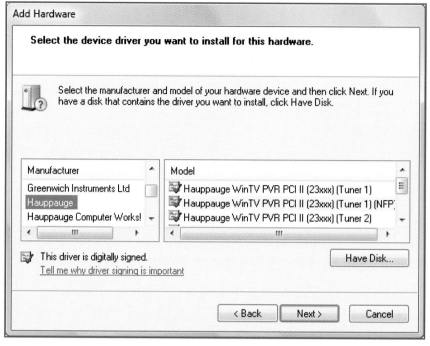

Figure 6-10: **Some devices may require you to identify the manufacturer and model. For other devices, you can use the Have Disk button to provide a driver that identifies the device.**

9. Click the driver and then click **Next**. If the Update Driver Warning dialog box appears, and you're sure you want to proceed, click **Yes**. If the Hardware Installation dialog box appears, warning you that the driver has not passed Windows Logo testing to verify its compatibility with Windows Vista, click **Continue Anyway** if you want to proceed.

10. On the Completing The Add Hardware Wizard page, click **Finish** to close the wizard. Your new hardware should now be ready for use.

Chapter 7
Securing Your PC

As you'll know if you've read a newspaper in the last few years, your PC faces a wide variety of threats. In this chapter you'll learn how to enhance your PC's physical security, prevent your PC from being used if it is stolen, install an antivirus program to defend your PC against viruses and other *malware* (malicious software), secure your PC on its local network, and secure it against attacks across the Internet. You'll also learn how to back up your data and restore it after disaster strikes.

Secure Your PC

The first (and arguably most obvious) aspect of security is securing your PC. This entails ensuring the physical security of the actual PC, setting a boot password, keeping Windows Vista updated, installing and using antivirus software, avoiding potentially dangerous programs and drivers, and using an uninterruptible power supply (UPS) if you have a desktop PC.

NOTE

This chapter assumes that your PC is running Windows Vista with Service Pack 1 (SP1). SP1 includes fixes for bugs included in the original version of Windows Vista, together with improvements to make Vista run faster and better. See the "Updating to Service Pack 1" QuickSteps, later in this chapter, if your PC doesn't have SP1 installed.

TIP

If you only need to secure your laptop against abuse from your children or your animals, buy a lockable laptop desk.

CAUTION

If you keep your desktop in a locked cabinet, safe, or room, ensure that there is adequate ventilation so that your PC doesn't overheat.

CAUTION

Most boot passwords provide effective security against any but the most expert attackers. This means that if you forget your boot password, you will be unable to start up your PC and access your data.

Implement Physical Security

First, ensure your PC's physical security as much as possible. What this entails depends on your PC (a desktop or a laptop) and your circumstances.

- Most laptops have a connector for using a cable lock to connect the laptop to a less movable object. Such cable locks deter casual theft rather than determined thieves armed with bolt-cutters but are often valuable in low- to moderate-risk situations.

- Most desktops are harder to steal discreetly than laptops because they're substantially larger and heavier and are not usually carried from place to place or used in public locations. If your desktop needs more security than your home or office provides, however, consider locking your desktop in a cabinet or custom computer safe. You'll need to deal with the awkwardness of routing all the cables into the cabinet or safe, but this is manageable.

No matter what protective measures you take, your PC's physical security may be compromised by human attack, by acts of nature, or simply by gravity. Your data will almost always be more valuable than your PC itself, so you must protect your data by backing it up regularly and frequently and by storing the backup at a different location than your PC. See "Back Up Your Data," later in this chapter.

Set a Boot Password

If your PC contains valuable data, secure it with a boot password. This is a password that you must enter when starting the PC in order to load the operating system. Consult your PC's documentation for instructions on setting a boot password.

Choose Vital Security Settings

Windows Vista includes several tools for keeping your PC secure:

- **Windows Firewall** protects your PC from attack across network connections (including the Internet).

- **Windows Defender** tries to detect malware (malevolent software) that sneaks onto your PC.

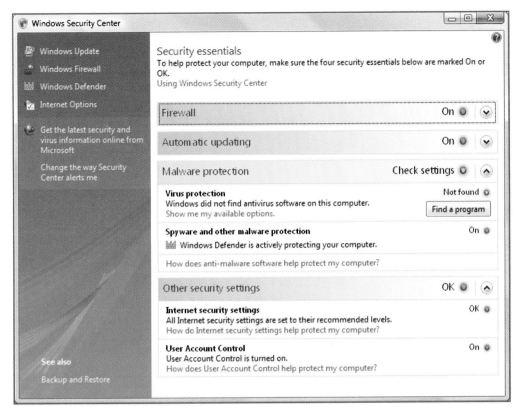

*Figure 7-1: **Windows Vista's Security Center lets you check for holes in your PC's security and configure settings to solve security problems. If all is well, each of the four categories—Firewall, Automatic Updating, Malware Protection, and Other Security Settings—has a green bar.***

- **Automatic Updating** checks automatically for Windows fixes and updates and installs them on your PC to keep Windows up to date.

- **Internet Explorer** offers many security options for protecting your PC against harmful websites.

- **User Account Control** attempts to ensure that you are the one installing any software or changing any sensitive settings (rather than a program or an attacker making such changes).

To keep your PC protected, make sure that all these tools are running. Windows Vista's Security Center gives you an overview of their status.

To open Windows Security Center:

1. Click **Start**, and then click **Control Panel** to open a Control Panel window.

2. If a dot appears next to Control Panel Home in the left pane, click the **Classic View** link to switch to classic view.

3. Double-click the **Security Center** icon to open Windows Security Center (see Figure 7-1).

4. If the Firewall line says Off rather than On, click anywhere in the red bar to display the options. Then click the **Turn On Now** button and go through User Account Control for the Security Center program to turn Windows Firewall on.

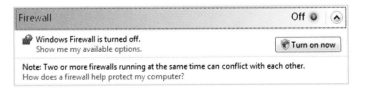

TIP

Windows Vista's default setting is to download and install updates at 3 A.M. each day. If you turn your PC off at night, use the Change Settings window to choose a more suitable time. If you put your PC to sleep at night, you needn't change the setting—Windows Vista will wake it to check for updates, and then put it back to sleep.

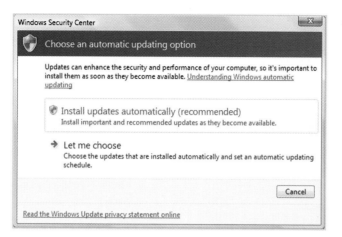

5. If the Automatic Updating line says Not Automatic or Off, click anywhere in the bar to display the options. Then click the **Change Settings** button to display the Windows Security Center dialog box shown here. The easiest option is to apply automatic updating by clicking the **Install Updates Automatically** button and then going through User Account Control for the Security Center program. If you prefer to control automatic updating, click the **Let Me Choose** button to display the Change Settings window (see Figure 7-2). Choose settings, click **OK**, and then go through User Account Control for the Windows Update program to apply the settings.

Windows Vista does not include an antivirus program. Many PC manufacturers install an antivirus program—but in many cases, it is only a trial version that expires after a short time.

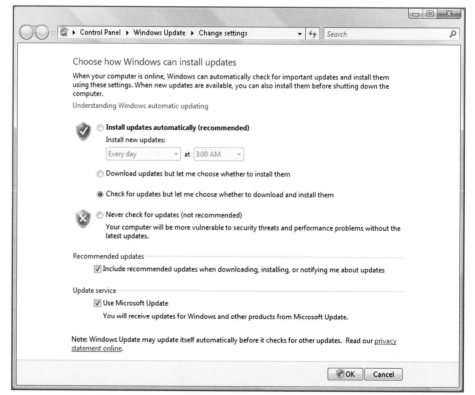

*Figure 7-2: **The Change Settings window lets you choose among automatic updating, downloading updates but installing them manually, both downloading and installing updates manually, and never checking for updates. Unless you have a slow Internet connection, Install Updates Automatically is normally the best choice.***

6. If the Malware Protection line says Check Settings, click anywhere in the red or yellow bar to display the options. Malware Protection covers two different items: Virus Protection (which Windows Vista does not provide out of the box) and Spyware And Other Malware Protection (for which Windows Vista provides Windows Defender).

> **Malware protection** Check settings ⊙ ⌃
>
> **Virus protection** Not found ⊙
> Windows did not find antivirus software on this computer.
> Show me my available options. [Find a program]
>
> **Spyware and other malware protection** On ⊙
> Windows Defender is actively protecting your computer.
>
> How does anti-malware software help protect my computer?

7. If the Virus Protection line shows Not Found, click the **Find A Program** button to open an Internet Explorer window to the Windows Vista Security Software Providers web page on Microsoft's website. Browse the available software (see the "Choosing Antivirus Software" QuickFacts for suggestions), choose antivirus software, and then install it.

8. If the Spyware And Other Malware Protection line shows Off, click the **Turn On Now** button and then go through User Account Control for the Security Center feature to turn Windows Defender on. Normally, you should run Windows Defender, even though it may slow your PC down a bit.

9. If the Other Security Settings line says Check Settings, click anywhere in the red or yellow bar to display the options. If the Internet Security Settings line shows a problem, click the **Restore Settings** button. In the dialog box that appears, click the **Restore My Internet Security Settings Now** button, and then go through User Account Control for the Security Center program.

10. If the User Account Control line says Off, click the **Turn On Now** button, and then go through User Account Control for the Security Center program.

11. When you have made sure all four bars are green, click the **Close** button (the × button) to close the Windows Security Center window.

Keep Windows Vista Updated

Once you've made sure Automatic Updating is turned on in Security Center, Windows automatically checks for updates each day, downloads any it finds, and installs them. Many updates require Windows to restart itself, so it's a good

NOTE

Instead of installing all updates, you can click the **View Available Updates** link to display the View Available Updates window, which lists the updates. You can then clear the check box for any update that you don't want to install. When you're ready, click the **Install** button and go through User Account Control for the Windows Update program to install the updates.

idea to save all your documents before leaving your PC for the night, in case an update requires a restart.

After an update that requires a restart, Windows displays a message balloon above the notification area to let you know what has happened, as shown here. You can click the message to open the View Update History window, which lists the updates that have been applied to Windows.

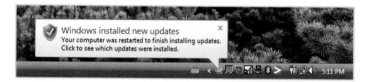

Whether you use Automatic Updating or not, you can also check for updates manually at any time:

1. Click **Start**, click **All Programs**, and then click **Windows Update** to open the Windows Update window.

2. Click the **Check For Updates** button. Windows connects to the Windows Update site and downloads details of any updates.

3. If the Windows Update window shows that updates are available, as in Figure 7-3, click the **Install Updates** button and go through User Account Control for the Windows Update program to install all the updates.

4. If Windows prompts you to restart your PC after installing the updates, close any programs you're running, and then click the **Restart Now** button.

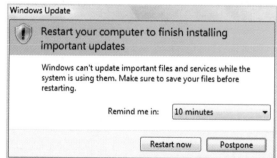

Avoid Unsigned Programs and Drivers

To help ensure that you can ascertain who created the programs and drivers you install, Windows Vista checks programs and drivers for *digital signatures*, encrypted identification information. When you try to install an unsigned

UPDATING TO SERVICE PACK 1

Windows Vista Service Pack 1 (SP1), released in March 2008, is a major update to Windows Vista. SP1 fixes many bugs that were present in the original version of Windows Vista, improves security, and may even make Windows Vista run faster and more stably.

Even if you have chosen not to use Automatic Updating, you should apply SP1 to Windows Vista:

1. Save any open documents and close all your programs.
2. Click **Start**, click **All Programs**, and then click **Windows Update** to open the Windows Update window.
3. Click the **Check For Updates** button.
4. Click the **View Available Updates** link to view all available updates.
5. Select the check box for Windows Vista Service Pack 1.
6. Follow through the installation process. This typically involves restarting your PC several times.

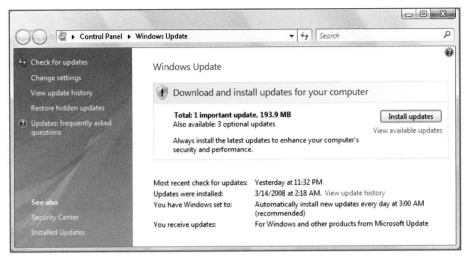

Figure 7-3: *You can use the Windows Update window to check for updates at any point.*

program or driver, or a program designed for another version of Windows, a warning dialog box appears. Figure 7-4 shows three examples of warning dialog boxes:

● The Security Warning dialog box for a program whose publisher could not be verified (click **Run** if you're sure you want to proceed).

● The Program Compatibility Assistant warning that a program has known compatibility issues (click **Run Program** if you want to try running the program anyway).

● The Security dialog box for a driver whose publisher could not be verified (click **Install This Driver Software Anyway** if you're certain you want to take the risk of trying to use the driver).

Use an Uninterruptible Power Supply

The battery in a laptop enables it to ride out power outages for up to several hours, depending on how fully the battery is charged and how much power the laptop consumes. With a desktop PC, you can use an uninterruptible power supply, or UPS, to prevent your PC from crashing when the power goes out. Your PC's power cord plugs into the UPS, which in turn plugs into a wall outlet.

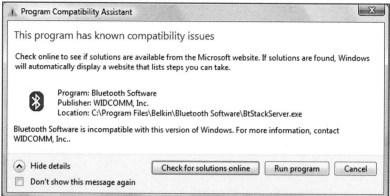

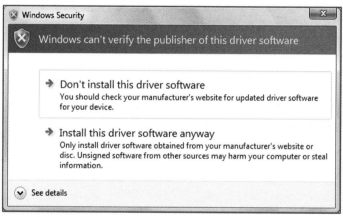

Figure 7-4: *When Windows Vista warns you that it can't verify the source or Windows Vista compatibility of a program or driver, it's best not to install that program or driver. However, you will not be able to use the program or the hardware device that needs the driver.*

The UPS contains batteries that will supply power to your PC for a short time (from 5 to 30 minutes), enough to get you through brief power interruptions or allow you to shut down your PC "gracefully" (under control) on longer outages.

A UPS helps protect your PC from electric spikes that come through the electric wires, but it's a good idea to unplug both the PC and the phone line during electrical storms in case lightning strikes nearby and sends a huge spike through the wires.

NOTE

This book talks about setting up local user accounts, which are set up on your PC. If your PC is part of a server-based network that uses domains (administrative units), your network administrator will set up user accounts through the domain.

The procedure for installing a UPS depends on the model of UPS, but in general it involves these steps:

1. Plug the UPS into an electrical outlet, and charge it for the time specified in the instructions.

2. If your PC is running, shut down Windows Vista and turn off the computer.

3. Plug your CPU, monitor, and any external hard drives into the UPS.

4. Connect the UPS to your PC via a serial cable or a USB cable (the cable may be included with the UPS). A USB cable must connect directly to a port on the PC, not through a USB hub.

5. Switch on the UPS, switch on your PC, and log on to Windows Vista.

6. If the UPS came with an installation program (or if you can download an installation program from the manufacturer's website), run the installation program. This will install the power-management software and configure Windows Vista's power options to use the UPS.

7. Most UPSes that connect via USB are configured automatically, but if the UPS includes configuration software, use that software to configure the UPS.

8. Close any open programs, and simulate a power outage by unplugging the UPS from the electric socket. Check that any actions you configured the UPS to take do actually occur—for example, that the UPS sounds the alarm, shuts down your PC, and then shuts itself down.

9. Plug the UPS back into the electric socket, switch it back on, and then restart your PC.

Implement User Security

After ensuring your PC's basic security by using locks, a boot password, a UPS, and an antivirus program, minimize threats to the PC from the people who use it. This means setting up a user account for each user of your PC, making him or her use a password, ensuring that your PC requires a password after being roused from a screen saver or sleep, and securing each user's files from all other users (except for files he or she wants to share).

Control Users and Passwords

After the boot password, your PC's first line of security is Windows Vista's login screen. To prevent an unauthorized person from logging on to Windows Vista, you must create a user account for each person who uses your PC and assign a password to each user account. You must also turn off the Guest account.

Create a User Account and Apply a Password

To create a user account:

1. Click **Start**, and then click your picture at the top of the Start menu to open the User Accounts window.

2. Click the **Manage Another Account** link, and then go through User Account Control for the User Accounts Control Panel program. The Manage Accounts window appears (see Figure 7-5).

3. Click **Create A New Account** to display the Name The Account And Choose An Account Type page.

4. Type a name of up to 20 characters in the text box.

5. Select the **Standard User** option button unless the user will need to administer the PC (in which case, select the **Administrator** option button).

6. Click **Create Account**. You are returned to the Manage Accounts window.

7. Click the account you just created to open the Change An Account window for the account.

8. Click **Create A Password**. The Create Password window opens.

9. Type the password twice, type a password hint if you think the user will need it (a password hint is always bad for security), and click **Create Password**. You are returned to the Change An Account page.

10. Click the **Manage Another Account** link to return to the Manage Accounts window so that you can work further with user accounts, or click **Close** to close the window.

11. After creating the user account and password, tell the person the username and password, and instruct him or her on how to change the password the first time he or she logs on to Windows Vista.

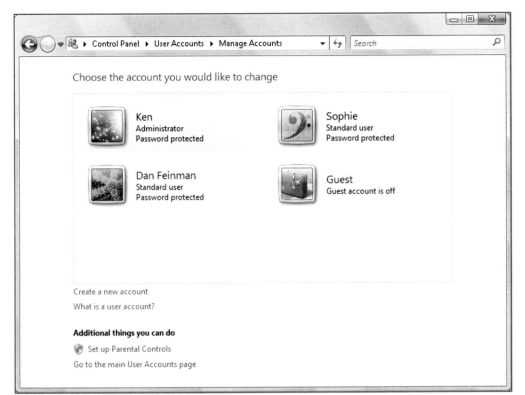

Choose the account you would like to change

Ken
Administrator
Password protected

Sophie
Standard user
Password protected

Dan Feinman
Standard user
Password protected

Guest
Guest account is off

Create a new account
What is a user account?

Additional things you can do

Set up Parental Controls
Go to the main User Accounts page

*Figure 7-5: **To help secure your PC, set up a separate user account for each user, require a password for each account, and make sure the Guest account is turned off.***

CAUTION

Never remove the password from a user account. Removing the password gives malefactors an easy route into your PC.

Set Passwords for Other Users

Every user of your PC must have a password for the PC to be even moderately secure. You can use steps 7 through 9 of the previous section to set passwords for existing users, but doing so causes them to lose access to key information, including any passwords they've stored for network resources or websites. For this reason, it's better to persuade users to change their passwords themselves by using the steps in the next section.

Change Your Own Password

You must also set a password for your own account to ensure that nobody else can log on to it.

1. Click **Start**, and then click your picture at the top of the Start menu to open the User Accounts window.

2. Click **Create Your Password** to display the Change Your Password page.

3. Type your current password in the Current Password text box (to prove that you know your password).

4. Type the new password twice in the New Password text box and the Confirm New Password text box.

5. Type a password hint if you absolutely must (it's always a bad idea).

6. Click the **Change Password** button. Windows changes the password and returns you to the User Accounts window.

7. From this window, you can also change the picture associated with your user account, change your account name or type (from Administrator to Standard), or remove your password.

Turn Off the Guest Account

The Guest account is an unprotected account intended for use by people who need to use the PC only temporarily and take only limited actions with it. You should ensure that the Guest account is turned off except when someone needs to use it. To turn off the Guest account:

1. Click **Start**, and then click your picture at the top of the Start menu to open the User Accounts window.

2. Click the **Manage Another Account** link, and then go through User Account Control for the User Accounts Control Panel program. Windows displays the Manage Accounts window.

3. Click the **Guest** icon. Windows displays the Change Guest Options window.

4. Click the Turn Off The Guest Account link. Windows turns off the Guest account, and then displays the Manage Accounts window again.

5. Click the **Close** button (the × button) to close the Manage Accounts window.

Password-Protect Your PC After Screen Saver or Standby

Usually, your screen saver kicks in when you leave your PC unattended (or when the phone or a colleague has claimed your attention). For security, make sure that whoever interrupts your screen saver has the authority to use your PC. If you use standby, ensure that waking your PC requires a password.

1. Right-click blank space on the desktop, and then click **Personalize** to open the Personalization window.

2. Click the **Screen Saver** link to open the Screen Saver Settings dialog box.

3. Make sure that a screen saver is selected in the **Screen Saver** drop-down list. If the (None) item is selected, the other controls are not available.

4. Select the **On Resume**, **Display Logon Screen** check box.

5. Click **OK** to close the Screen Saver Settings dialog box.

> **NOTE**
>
> If the person to whom you want to apply Parental Controls does not have a separate user account already, create a new user account for them now.

Apply Parental Controls

Windows Vista's Parental Controls let you restrict what a user can do on the computer to limit the damage they can do and help keep them out of harm's way. Parental Controls let you restrict:

- Website access, instant messaging, e-mail, and downloads
- The times the user can log on to Windows
- The games the user can play
- The programs the user can run

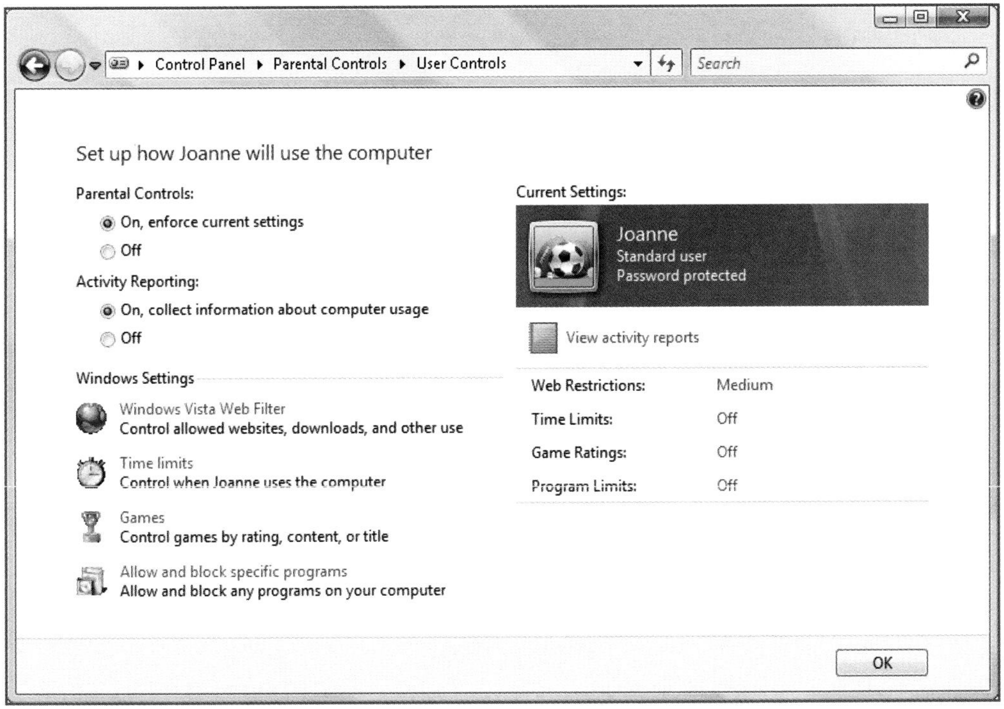

Figure 7-6: ***The User Controls window is where you set up Parental Controls that limit which actions the user can take in Windows. You can also turn Activity Reporting on or off here.***

To apply Parental Controls, log on using an administrator account, and then:

1. Click **Start**, and then click your picture at the top of the Start menu to open the User Accounts window.
2. Click **Manage Another Account**, and then go through User Account Control for the User Accounts Control Panel program to open the Manage Accounts window.
3. In the Additional Things You Can Do list, click **Set Up Parental Controls**, and then go though User Account Control for the Parental Control program to open the Parental Controls window.
4. Click the user to whom you want to apply Parental Controls. Windows opens the User Controls window (see Figure 7-6).
5. In the upper-left corner, under the Parental Controls heading, select the **On, Enforce Current Settings** option button instead of the Off option button. This is the master control for turning Parental Controls on.
6. Below that, under the Activity Reporting heading, select the **On, Collect Information About Computer Usage** option button if you want to monitor the user's activity. Normally, you will want to do this so that you can tell whether the Parental Controls are effective or need adjustment. If you don't want to monitor the user's activity, select the **Off** option button.

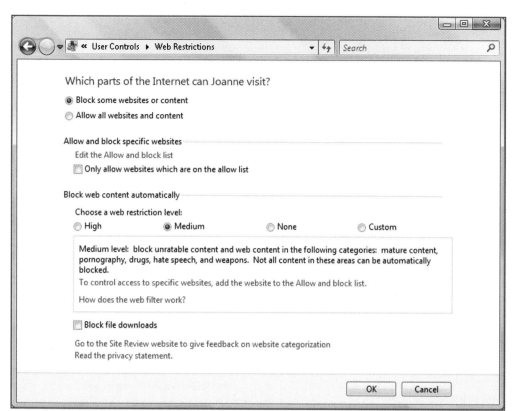

Figure 7-7: *Web Restrictions enable you to prevent the user from accessing certain websites and control whether the user can download files to the PC.*

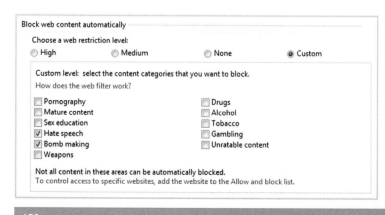

7. Under the Windows Settings heading, click **Windows Vista Web Filter** to display the Web Restrictions window (see Figure 7-7).

8. To implement Web Restrictions, as you'll often want to do to keep users safe, select the **Block Some Websites Or Content** option button. The alternative is to select the **Allow All Websites And Content** option button; if you do this, click **OK** and go to step 13.

9. Click **Edit The Allow And Block List** to open the Allow Block Webpages window:

   ● In the Website Address text box, type or paste the name of a website you want to allow or block, and then click the **Allow** button or the **Block** button, as needed, to add the site to the Allowed Websites list or the Blocked Websites list.

   ● If you want to restrict the user to only the specific websites you've permitted, select the **Only Allow Websites Which Are On The Allow List** check box. (This check box also appears in the Web Restrictions window.)

   ● When you've finished setting up the lists, click **OK** to return to the Web Restrictions window.

10. If you have not selected the **Only Allow Websites Which Are On The Allow List** check box, select the appropriate option button in the Choose A Web Restriction Level: **High**, **Medium**, **None**, or **Custom**. The **Custom** option displays check boxes that you can select to specify each category of item to block—for example, Mature Content, Hate Speech, or Bomb Making.

11. If you want to prevent the user from downloading any files, select the **Block File Downloads** check box.

12. Click **OK** to close the Web Restrictions window and return to the User Controls window.

TIP

You can transfer a list of allowed and blocked websites from one PC to another. On the PC that has the list, use the **Export** button in the Allow Block Webpages window to export the list to a file. Transfer the file to the second PC, and then use the **Import** button to import the list from the file.

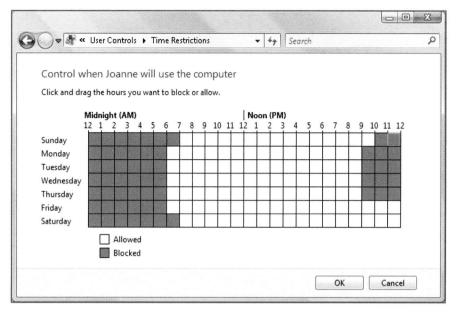

Figure 7-8: *The Time Restrictions window lets you quickly set times when the user may not use the PC.*

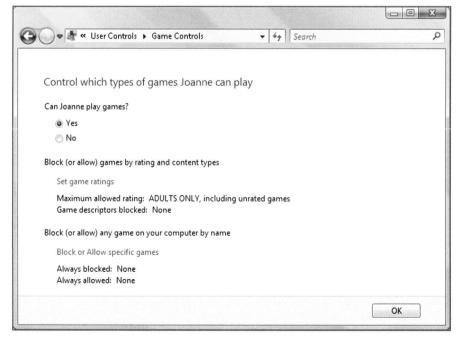

13. Click **Time Limits** to open the Time Restrictions window (see Figure 7-8).

14. Drag in the grid through the hours you want to block; click an individual box to change its color from white to blue or vice versa. When you've finished, click **OK** to return to the User Controls window.

15. Click **Games** to open the Game Controls window (see Figure 7-9).

16. If you want to prevent the user from playing games at all, select the **No** option button at the top. Otherwise, select the **Yes** option button.

Figure 7-9: *The Game Controls window lets you turn off games altogether or put together a custom list of permitted games.*

NOTE

The Game Overrides window shows only the games installed in Windows Vista's Games folder. If a game is installed in another folder, you will need to block it using the Allow And Block Specific Programs feature.

17. To block games by their ratings and content types, click **Set Game Ratings**. The Game Restrictions window opens:

- Select the **Allow Games With No Rating** option button or the **Block Games With No Rating** option button, as appropriate.

- In the Which Ratings Are OK To Play? list, select the option button for the highest Entertainment Software Rating Board level of games you want to permit: **Early Childhood**, **Everyone**, **Everyone 10+**, **Teen**, **Mature**, or **Adults Only**.

- In the Block These Types Of Content area, select the check box for each type of content you want to block—for example, **Drug Reference** or **Partial Nudity**.

- Click **OK** to return to the Game Controls window.

18. If you want to block or allow specific games, click **Block Or Allow Specific Games**. In the Game Overrides window, select the **Always Allow** option button or the **Always Block** option button for each game, and then click **OK** to return to the Game Controls window.

19. Click **OK** to return to the User Controls window.

20. If you want to block some programs, click **Allow And Block Specific Programs** to open the Application Restrictions window (see Figure 7-10).

21. Select the **User Can Only Use The Programs I Allow** option button, and then select the check box for each permitted program. Click **OK** to return to the User Controls window.

22. Click **OK** to close the User Controls window and apply the restrictions.

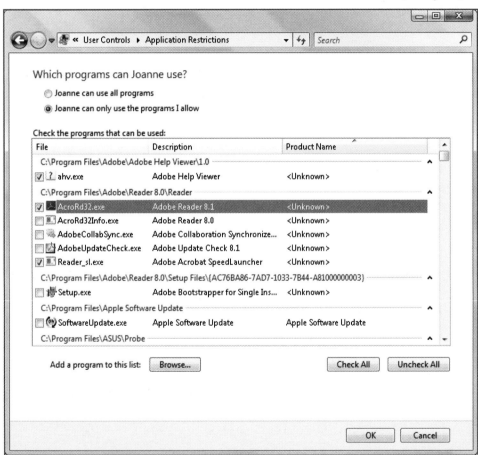

Figure 7-10: **The Application Restrictions window lets you prevent the user from running certain programs—or limit them to a short list of permitted programs. If a program doesn't appear in the list, click the Browse button and use the Open dialog box to find it.**

VIEWING ACTIVITY REPORTS FOR A USER

After applying Parental Controls to a user, it's a good idea to view activity reports to see what the user has been doing—and learn whether you need to relax the restrictions, tighten them, or simply leave them as they are.

1. Open the Parental Controls window for the user by following steps 1–4 in "Apply Parental Controls."

2. Click **View Activity Reports** to open the Activity Viewer window, which shows the actions that have been logged for the user.

3. In the left pane, click the **+** sign to expand the item for the user. Click the **+** sign to expand the category you want to view, and then click the item under it. For example, expand the **Web Browsing** category and then click the **File Downloads** item to see which files the user has downloaded.

4. When you have finished viewing activities, click the **Close** button (the **X** button) to close the Activity Viewer window.

CAUTION

Don't configure Windows Firewall manually unless you're sure of what you're doing. Otherwise, you may inadvertently open your PC, your network, or both to attack.

Implement Network and Internet Security

If your PC is part of a network or if it is connected to the Internet, you must implement adequate security to make sure that no malefactor can connect to it or otherwise harm it from a remote PC. That means turning on and configuring Windows Vista's built-in firewall, sharing folders safely, turning off any unnecessary network services, and securing your web browser as much as possible.

A *firewall* is a protective barrier between your computer and other computers to which it is connected. When turned on and configured correctly, the firewall permits only approved data to pass and blocks the passage of any data that is not approved.

Configure Windows Firewall

If your PC connects to a network or the Internet, you must turn on Windows Firewall as described in "Choose Vital Security Settings," earlier in this chapter.

Normally, Windows Vista configures Windows Firewall automatically. In order to allow some programs to communicate across your network and the Internet, however, you may need to configure Windows Firewall manually.

To configure Windows Firewall manually:

1. Click **Start**, and then click **Control Panel** to open a Control Panel window.

2. If a dot appears next to Control Panel Home in the left pane, click **Classic View** to switch to Classic view.

3. Double-click the **Windows Firewall** icon to open the Windows Firewall window.

QUICKSTEPS

RESETTING A PASSWORD

To avoid losing data if you forget your password, create a password-reset disk. This can be either a USB key or a floppy disk (if your PC has a floppy drive).

CREATE A PASSWORD-RESET DISK

1. Connect a USB key to a USB port, or insert a formatted floppy disk in your PC's floppy drive.

2. Click **Start** and then click your picture at the top of the Start menu to open a User Accounts window.

3. In the Tasks pane, click **Create A Password Reset Disk** to launch the Forgotten Password Wizard.

4. Click **Next**. The wizard displays the Create A Password Reset Disk page.

5. Select the USB key or floppy disk in the I Want To Create A Password Key Disk In The Following Drive.

6. Click **Next** to display the Current User Account Password page.

7. Type your current password, and click **Next**. After the wizard creates the disk, click **Next** and then click **Finish**.

8. Remove the disk, label it, and store it securely where nobody else can use it to access your account.

RESET YOUR PASSWORD

You'll typically need to use your password-reset disk when you find that Windows Vista's Welcome screen won't accept what you thought was your password.

1. When Windows tells you that your username or password is incorrect, click **OK**.

Continued . . .

4. Click **Change Settings**, and then go through User Account Control for the Windows Firewall Settings program, to open the Windows Firewall Settings dialog box (see Figure 7-11).

5. On the General tab, verify that the **On** option button is selected.

6. Click the **Exceptions** tab (see Figure 7-12).

7. Examine the list of exceptions. A typical Windows setup may need the following:

- Core Networking
- File And Printer Sharing (if you're sharing files or printers on your network)
- Microsoft Office Outlook (if you use Outlook)
- Network Discovery
- Remote Assistance

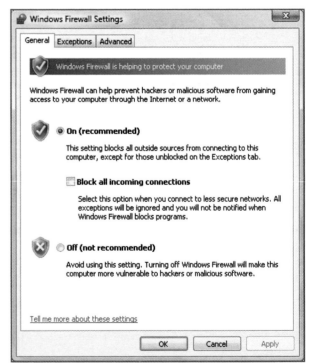

Figure 7-11: When you connect to less secure networks, you may need to select the Block All Incoming Connections check box on the General tab of the Windows Firewall Settings dialog box. For normal use, leave this check box cleared.

QUICKSTEPS

RESETTING A PASSWORD *(Continued)*

2. Click **Reset Password** under the password box (and password hint, if you have one) to launch the Password Reset Wizard.

3. Click **Next**. The wizard displays the Insert The Password Reset Disk page.

4. Connect the USB key or insert the floppy disk.

5. Open the **Password Key Disk Is In The Following Drive** drop-down list, and then select the correct drive.

6. Click **Next** to display the Reset The User Account Password page.

7. Type a new password twice, type a password hint if you think you're likely to forget your new password, click **Next**, and then click **Finish**.

8. At the Welcome screen, type your new password and press **ENTER** to log on.

From now on, use the new password. Your password-reset disk remains valid, so you don't need to create a new reset disk.

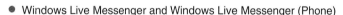

NOTE

The controls on the Advanced tab of the Windows Firewall Settings dialog box enable you to switch Windows Firewall off for any of your network connections. For example, you could turn Windows Firewall off for your local area network connection while leaving it on for your Internet connection. But for security, you must keep Windows Firewall turned on for each network connection, as an attack can come from your local network just as easily as from the Internet.

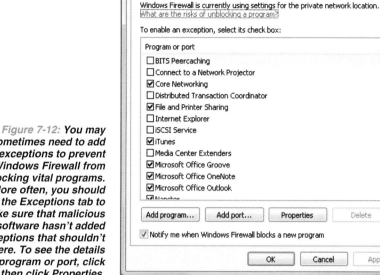

Figure 7-12: **You may sometimes need to add exceptions to prevent Windows Firewall from blocking vital programs. More often, you should scan the Exceptions tab to make sure that malicious software hasn't added exceptions that shouldn't be there. To see the details of a program or port, click it, and then click Properties.**

- Windows Live Messenger and Windows Live Messenger (Phone)
- Windows Media Player and Windows Media Player Network Sharing Service

8. If you need to make a change to allow a particular program to run, use the **Add Program** button or the **Add Port** button to add the program or configure the port.

9. Click **OK** to close the Windows Firewall settings dialog box, and then click **Close** to close first the Windows Firewall window and then the Control Panel window.

Secure Your Internet Browsing

At this writing, Internet Explorer is the most widely used web browser in the short history of the Web. Unfortunately, many security loopholes have been discovered in Internet Explorer; and these loopholes have been used by malicious hackers trying to promote products, extract sensitive information from others' PCs, or simply inflict damage. While Internet Explorer 7 is much more secure than Internet Explorer 6, it remains vital that you choose tight security settings to protect your PC from Internet attack.

SECURE INTERNET EXPLORER

If you use Internet Explorer to browse the Internet, you must secure it as much as possible by using the features in Internet Explorer's Internet Options dialog box (see Chapter 3).

- Make sure that Protected Mode is on for the Internet zone, Local Intranet zone, and Restricted Sites zone on the Security tab. (If Protected Mode is off, Internet Explorer tries to alert you to the problem.)

- Set a Medium-High or (preferably) High security level for the Internet zone on the Security tab. The disadvantage to the High security level is that it may prevent you from downloading files you need.

- Block as many cookies as you can without disabling the website functionality you need by using the controls on the Privacy tab.

- Block pop-up ads from the Privacy tab.

- Use the Restricted Sites feature (on the Security tab) and the Content Advisor (on the Content tab) to keep yourself or other users from accessing sites that are known or likely to harbor malicious or undesirable content.

- Use Parental Controls (discussed earlier in this chapter) to prevent young or otherwise susceptible users from accessing unsuitable sites or from downloading files.

USE ANOTHER BROWSER

Given that Internet Explorer is the favorite target of malicious hackers, one straightforward security strategy is to use a different browser instead of Internet Explorer. Several other browsers are available, including Mozilla Firefox (www.mozilla.org; free, Opera (www.opera.com; free) or Safari (www.apple .com; free). In time, these browsers, too, may be targeted by malefactors and security holes may be exposed, but at this writing, these browsers offer an easy way to sidestep attacks aimed at Internet Explorer.

TIP

To reduce the chance of Internet Explorer downloading malicious ActiveX controls, in Internet Explorer, choose the **High** level of security for the Internet zone and the Restricted Sites zone on the Security tab of the Internet Options dialog box. (To open the Internet Options dialog box, open Internet Explorer, click **Tools**, and then click **Internet Options**.)

AVOID OR REMOVE SPYWARE

Spyware is the term for software that is installed without your permission on your PC and that executes a function that you don't want. Examples include:

- Changing your home page to a different page (such as a pornography site) and restoring the home page to that page if you change it back manually
- Adding bookmarks to Internet Explorer, to the Quick Launch toolbar, and to your desktop
- Running a program that monitors your PC usage or attempts to show you advertisements or learn your passwords or other sensitive data

The best way to avoid spyware is to prevent it from being installed.

- If a pop-up window (see the example here) prompts you to take an action, don't take it unless you trust the site you're visiting.
- If you're prompted to install an ActiveX control (a unit of program code), as in the example here (which appears across the top of the details area in the Internet Explorer window), don't install it unless you're sure the site is trustworthy.

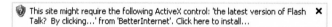

Even if you're careful in your browsing and refuse all suspicious pop-ups and ActiveX controls, spyware may still infiltrate your PC through a security loophole. To get rid of it, or simply to ensure that your PC is clean, try Spybot Search & Destroy (www.safer-networking.org [note the hyphen]; freeware) or LavaSoft Ad-aware (www.lavasoft.de; freeware). Figure 7-13 shows Spybot Search & Destroy in action.

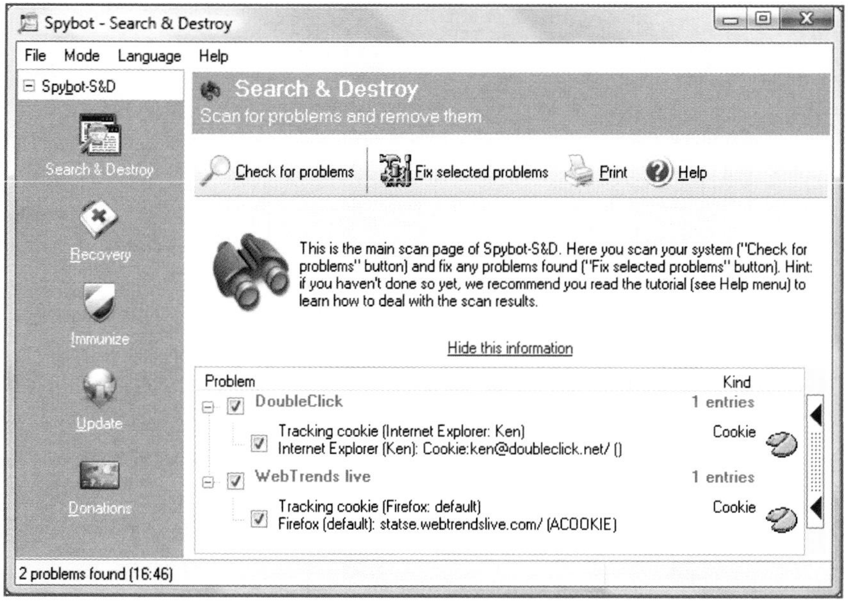

NOTE

If tools such as Spybot Search & Destroy and Ad-aware are unable to remove the spyware, consult a computer professional as soon as possible.

Figure 7-13: *Use a tool such as Spybot Search & Destroy to remove any spyware that has been installed on your PC.*

Back Up and Recover Your Data

To ensure that you don't lose your valuable data if your PC fails or is stolen, you must secure your data by backing it up to a safe location. After disaster strikes, you can then recover your data.

Back Up Your Data

Backing up your data means storing a copy of it in a safe location. Windows Vista includes a utility named Backup for backing up data.

1. Click **Start**, click **All Programs**, click **Maintenance**, and then click **Backup And Restore Center** to open the Backup And Restore Center window (see Figure 7-14).

2. Click the **Back Up Files** button, and then go through User Account Control for the Microsoft Windows Backup program. The Back Up Files Wizard starts and displays the Where Do You Want To Save Your Backup? page.

3. Choose where to store your backup:

   - Select the **On A Hard Disk, CD, Or DVD** option button if you want to use one of those media, and then choose the drive in the drop-down list. This example uses a DVD. Although this option doesn't mention USB flash drives, you can also use them.

   - To use a network drive, select the **On A Network** option button. Click **Browse**, use the Browse For Folder dialog box to select the network folder, and then click **OK**.

4. Click **Next**. If your PC has two or more hard disk partitions, the wizard displays the Which Disks Do You Want To Include In The Backup? page. Select the check box for each disk you want to include, and then click **Next** to display the Which File Types Do You Want To Back Up? page (see Figure 7-15).

5. Select the check box for each category of files you want to back up, and then click **Next** to display the How Often Do You Want To Create A Backup? page.

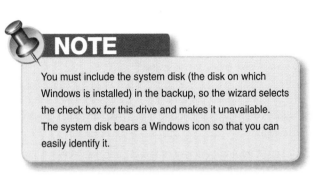
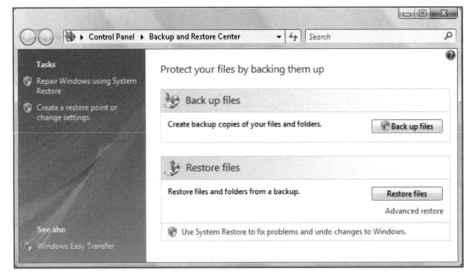

Figure 7-14: *From the Backup And Restore Center window, you can begin the process of backing up your files or restoring them from backup.*

NOTE

You should back up any data that is valuable and that you cannot easily create again. For example, back up your word-processing documents, spreadsheets, presentations, digital photos, and videos you've made, because even if you could create them again, doing so would take great effort. By contrast, if you've copied your CD collection to your PC, backing it up is probably a waste of time because you could copy your CDs to your PC again with relatively little effort. That said, if your backup medium has enough space to back up all your data, you may choose to do so.

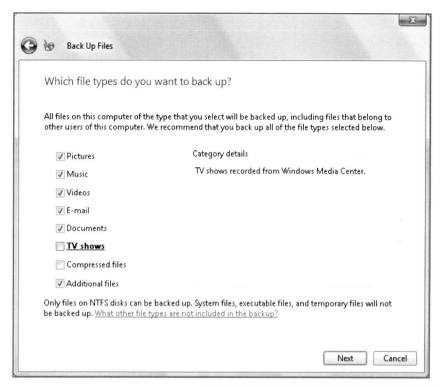

Figure 7-15: On the Which File Types Do You Want To Back Up? page of the Back Up Files Wizard, select the check box for each file type you want to include. TV Shows and Compressed Files tend to be large, so if you don't consider such files valuable, you can save space by excluding them from the backup.

NOTE

If you have Windows Vista Business Edition or Windows Vista Ultimate Edition, you can click the Back Up Computer button in the Backup And Restore Center window to back up all the files on one or more drives of your PC. If you use this option, you will need a high-capacity backup medium such as an external hard drive.

6. Use the **How Often** drop-down list, **What Day** drop-down list, and **What Time** drop-down list to set up a backup schedule.

7. Click the **Save Settings And Start Backup** button to start the backup. If you're using CDs or DVDs as the backup medium, insert the first disc when prompted, and then click **OK**. Insert further discs as needed.

8. When the backup has finished, click **Close** to close the wizard.

Recover Your Data from Backup

To recover data from a backup, you restore the files:

1. Click **Start**, click **All Programs**, click **Maintenance**, and then click **Backup And Restore Center** to open the Backup And Restore Center window (shown in Figure 7-14, earlier in this chapter).

2. Click the **Restore Files** button to launch the Restore Files Wizard, which displays the What Do You Want To Restore? page.

3. Choose which files to restore:

   - If you want to restore your latest files (as is usually the case), select the **Files From The Latest Backup** option button. Click **Next** to display the Select The Files And Folders To Restore page.

   - If you want to restore older files (for example, because the latest backup files are lost, corrupted, or have a virus), select the **Files From An Older Backup** option button. Click **Next**, choose the backup on the Select The Date To Restore page, and then click **Next** to display the Select The Files And Folders To Restore page (see Figure 7-16).

4. Identify the files and folders you want to restore:

   - To add a file, click **Add Files**, select the files in the Add Files To Restore window, and then click **Add**.

   - To add one or more folders, click **Add Folders**, select the folders in the Add Folders To Restore window, and then click **Add**.

5. Click **Next** to display the Where Do You Want To Save The Restored Files? page.

6. Choose where to save the files:

   - If you want to overwrite the original files, select the **In The Original Location** option button.

   - If you want to use another folder (for example, so that you can compare the restored files with your current files and integrate change), select the **In The Following Location** option button. Click **Browse**, select the folder, and then click **OK**.

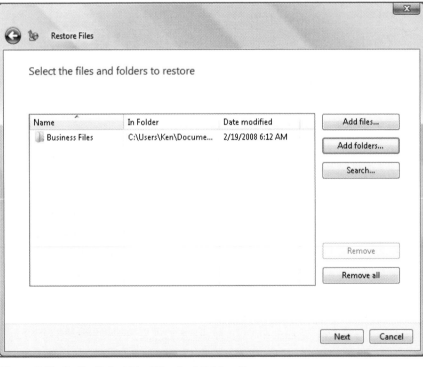

Figure 7-16: On the Select The Files And Folders To Restore page, assemble the list of files and folders you want to restore from backup. Adding folders is usually easier and faster than adding individual files.

7. Click **Start Restore**, and wait until the wizard has finished restoring the files.

8. Click **Finish** to close the wizard.

How to...

Chapter 8
Setting Up a Home Network

Networking is the sharing of resources and information between two or more connected computers—at home, within an organization, or around the world. A connection to the Internet (discussed in Chapter 3) is a form of networking known as a wide area network, or WAN.

Choose the Type of Network

The first step in setting up a home network is to decide the type of network you need. This section explains the several networking technologies that are available for home networks and helps you choose the technology best suited to your needs.

Understand Wired Ethernet

The most common way of connecting PCs is to use cables and equipment that conform to one of the wired Ethernet standards, which are based on speed and cable type. The three most common standards are

- **10BaseT**, which provides a network that operates at the regular Ethernet speed of 10Mbps (megabits, or millions of bits, per second).

WEIGHING THE PROS AND CONS OF WIRED ETHERNET

The advantages of wired Ethernet are

- It gives fast and reliable connections over distances of up to 100 meters per cable.

- The hardware is inexpensive. It usually costs less than $30 to network a PC via wired Ethernet.

- It offers good security. Unless someone can physically connect to the wires of your network or access your network across your Internet connection, he or she will not be able to break in without using fairly serious surveillance equipment.

The disadvantages of wired Ethernet are

- You must run the cables from one PC to another. Typically, this means drilling holes from room to room or leaving digital tripwires lying around.

- Each PC must be connected to the network via a cable. This works well for desktop PCs but makes it awkward to move a laptop PC around.

- **100BaseT**, or Fast Ethernet, which provides a network that operates at 100Mbps.

- **Gigabit Ethernet**, which provides a network that operates at speeds of 1Gbps (gigabit, or billion bits, per second).

Until recently, Gigabit Ethernet has been used mostly in corporate networks that needed extremely fast networks. However, prices of Gigabit Ethernet network equipment have fallen far enough to make Gigabit Ethernet the best choice if you're buying new equipment for a home, home-office, or small-office network. If you already have Fast Ethernet network equipment, you will probably find it plenty fast enough. For a modest network, even regular Ethernet may be adequate.

A wired network, shown in Figure 8-1, has three major components:

- The **network connection** on your PC connects it to the network.

- A **switch** or **router** joins several PCs together to form the network. This is a connection box into which you connect a cable for each PC or other networked device that is part of the network. The switch or router directs (routes) data around the network as needed.

- An **unshielded twisted pair (UTP)** cable with a simple RJ-45 connector (like a telephone connector, only bigger) joins the network connection to the hub, switch, or router.

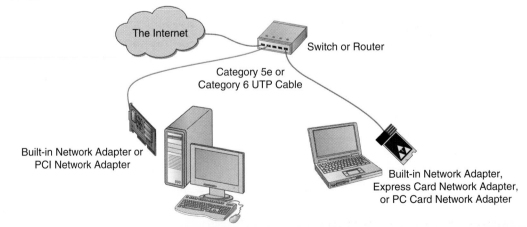

Figure 8-1: A wired Ethernet network consists of a network connection on your PC, a switch or router into which other PCs and devices are connected, and cables connecting each item to the switch or router.

Technically, a **router** joins two different networks—for example, joining a LAN to the Internet. However, a router often is combined with a switch in a single device to join several PCs to each other and to the Internet.

Instead of a switch or router, you can use a *hub*, an older style of connection box that doesn't work as efficiently. The only reason to use a hub nowadays is if you have an old one that you want to reuse to avoid buying new equipment. If not, buy a switch or router.

Ethernet networks are easy to set up (see "Set Up a Wired Ethernet Network," later in this chapter), have become pervasive throughout organizations, and typically cost less than $30 per PC on the network. Most PCs sold in the last few years include a network connection, either built into the system board (or motherboard) or installed separately.

Understand Wireless Ethernet

Wireless LANs (WLANs) replace the cable used in a wired network with small radio *transceivers* (combined transmitters and receivers) at the PC and at the switch or router. Several wireless standards are used at this writing, with further standards being developed to provide faster data transmission and greater security:

- **802.11n** is a standard that will support speeds of up to about 300Mbps. At this writing, 802.11n, also called Wireless-N, is a draft standard—it has not been ratified yet. However, manufacturers are releasing Draft-N wireless network equipment. Draft-N equipment from one manufacturer may not work at 802.11n speeds with Draft-N equipment from another manufacturer.

- **802.11g** is a standard that supports speeds of up to 54Mbps. Also called Wireless-G and generally referred to as *Wi-Fi*, 802.11g is widely used, and is backward compatible with 802.11b (discussed next).

- **802.11b** is a standard that supports speeds of up to 11Mbps. Generally referred to as *Wi-Fi*, 802.11b is still very widely used, especially in public wireless networks.

- **802.11a** is a standard that supports speeds of up to 54Mbps. However, 802.11a is not compatible with 802.11b or 802.11g and is not widely used.

NOTE

In the names for the Ethernet standards—10BaseT, 100BaseT, and 1000BaseT— the number indicates the operating speed in megabits per second; the "Base" stands for "baseband," a type of transmission; and the "T" indicates the type of cable required (twisted-pair cable).

QUICKFACTS

WEIGHING THE PROS AND CONS OF WIRELESS NETWORKS

The advantages of wireless networks are

- **No cables** Having no cables saves expense, effort, and the awkwardness of laying and maintaining cables.

- **Speed and flexibility** Wireless networks are great for temporary networks or for premises you can't change (for example, a rented apartment or office).

- **Simplicity** Adding users to and removing them from the network is extremely easy. Similarly, visitors can easily connect to the network if you grant them permission.

- **Movement and roaming** Users can move easily from office to office or roam within an area—for example, carrying their laptops to a meeting.

Continued . . .

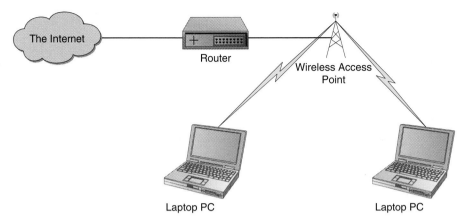

Figure 8-2: **A wireless network consists of a built-in wireless adapter or add-on wireless card in your PC and a wireless access point connected to a wired network, the Internet, or both.**

QUICK**FACTS**

WEIGHING THE PROS AND CONS OF WIRELESS NETWORKS *(Continued)*

The disadvantages of wireless networks are

- **Expense** Wireless network equipment is a bit expensive than wired network equipment.

- **Speed** Wireless networks are substantially slower than wired networks. The maximum speed of 802.11g networks is theoretically 54Mbps, compared to 100Mbps for Fast Ethernet, but the data rate drops when multiple users use the wireless network. The as-yet unratified 802.11n standard will provide maximum speeds of around 300Mbps.

- **Security** Because wireless network adapters and access points are essentially radios, wireless networking is inherently insecure. To make a wireless network adequately secure for moderately sensitive data, you must take several security measures, starting with encryption and passwords and progressing to more serious measures. Even so, a malefactor can attack your wireless network from a distance—even from several miles away, if he or she uses a high-gain antenna. By contrast, if you have a wired network, a malefactor must usually have direct access to the physical network to attack it.

NOTE

You can also create a wireless network without an access point. This is called a *computer-to-computer* wireless network or *ad hoc* wireless network.

A WLAN typically has two components (see Figure 8-2):

- An **access point** is connected to the wired Ethernet network via a switch or connected to the Internet via a router. It uses one or more transceivers to communicate wirelessly with cards installed in or attached to PCs using the WLAN.

- An **adapter** is installed in or plugs into your PC and has a transceiver built in to communicate wirelessly to an access point within its range. For laptop PCs, built-in adapters are increasingly common. For desktop PCs, adapters are typically either installed in the PC as a PCI card or attached to the PC via USB (Universal Serial Bus).

If the access point is connected to a switch or router on a wired network, the wireless PCs within the range of the access point operate on the network in exactly the same way as they would operate with a cable connection, only a little slower.

Understand Other Networking Technologies

If you're planning a home network, you should also know about the following networking options:

- **FireWire connections** enable you to create a small network of PCs equipped with FireWire ports. The advantages are high speed (up to 800Mbps) and easy setup.

QUICK**FACTS**

UNDERSTANDING WI-FI

The term "Wi-Fi" can be confusing, because it's used in different ways.

At this writing, it is widely used to mean either 802.11b or 802.11g. Technically, Wi-Fi means that a product has been certified by the Wi-Fi Alliance as conforming to Wi-Fi standards and thus is interoperable with other Wi-Fi–certified products.

In many airports, hotels, and coffee shops, you see signs for Wi-Fi *hotspots*, wireless networks that you can connect to using standard Wi-Fi equipment.

QUICK**FACTS**

SELECTING WIRED ETHERNET HARDWARE

To set up a wired Ethernet network, you'll need:

- A network connection in each PC
- A switch or router to form the link point in the network
- A cable to connect each PC to the switch or router

Many brands of network hardware are available. Having an unreliable network wastes time and effort, so buying bargain-basement network hardware tends to be a bad idea. To ensure that your network is reliable and that you can get support when you need it, stick with name-brand products from companies that are likely to be around for a while. Respected brands include 3Com, D-Link, Linksys (now a division of networking giant Cisco Systems), and NETGEAR.

SELECT A NETWORK ADAPTER

Many PCs come with a network connection built in, and if you buy a new PC to run Windows Vista, you'll almost

Continued . . .

The disadvantages are that the PCs must be close to each other, as the maximum cable length is 4.5 meters (about 15 feet), and preferably few in number. Many PCs don't have FireWire built in, so you may need to add it. Given that many current and recent PCs have either wired Ethernet or wireless Ethernet built in, you're not likely to want to use FireWire unless your PCs happen to have it already.

- **Powerline networks** enable your PCs to communicate across your home's electrical wiring using special adapters. The advantages are easy setup and not needing to run wires or drill holes. The disadvantages are higher costs than Ethernet networks, slower network speeds, and security concerns if your electric wiring is shared with neighbors.

- **Phone line networks** enable your PCs to communicate across your home's phone lines. The advantages are easy setup (provided you have phone jacks in suitable places) and not needing to run wires or drill holes. The disadvantages are higher costs and lower speeds than Ethernet networks.

- **USB networks** enable you to quickly connect two to four PCs together via their USB ports and a special cable. The advantages are easy setup and not needing to run wires or drill holes. The disadvantages are higher costs, lower speeds, and all PCs needing to be within a short cable's distance of the USB networking device.

- **Bluetooth connections** enable you to create cable-free networks between PCs within the same small area. The advantage is that you can set up a network without any infrastructure so that you can transfer files. The disadvantages are that Bluetooth is slow and short-range, so you probably won't want to use it for networking unless all the other networking options are unavailable. Bluetooth is primarily intended for transferring data among personal devices, such as mobile phones and PDAs, or between a personal device and a PC.

Set Up and Use the Network

When you installed Windows Vista, a basic set of networking services was installed and configured using the choices you made, some default settings, and the details of the hardware that Windows Vista found on your system. If Windows Vista found a network adapter (also called a *network card*), as is usually the case, networking should already be set up on your PC, and you will not need to perform any configuration.

SELECTING WIRED ETHERNET HARDWARE *(Continued)*

certainly have the option of having a network connection installed. If you're not sure whether your PC has a network connection, look on the back of the PC (or the side of some laptop PCs) for a connector that looks like an oversized phone connector marked with the symbol <...>.

If your PC doesn't have a network connection, you can add a network adapter via a PCI card (for a desktop PC), via a PC Card or ExpressCard (for a laptop PC), or via USB (for either a desktop PC or a laptop PC).

SELECT A SWITCH

To connect your wired Ethernet network, you need a switch. Switches run from under $50 for an 8-port switch to under $150 for a 24-port switch. You need a port for each PC or other network device, but you can plug one switch into another switch to increase the number of ports on your network. If you plan to do this, choose switches that are designed to stack one on top of the other for neatness and for speed (their interconnecting bus is faster than a wire connection).

SELECT CABLING

At this writing, Category 5 enhanced ("Cat 5e") cable is the best choice for your network. Cat 5e works for Gigabit Ethernet, Fast Ethernet, and regular Ethernet. If you want to future-proof your network, consider Category 6 cable instead, which will support even faster network speeds.

Cables come in various colors and in lengths of up to 100 feet with the connectors molded on. Alternatively, you can buy a spool of cable (typically 1,000 feet) and a crimping tool, cut the cables to the lengths you need, and crimp connectors on yourself. This takes more effort but works out to be much less expensive per cable.

Set Up the Network

This section walks you through creating a network using the three means you're most likely to use: wired Ethernet, wireless using an access point, and wireless without an access point. It then shows you how to check that your network configuration is working and how to make key changes to it.

If your PC doesn't have a network connection, you must physically connect or install the network adapter and install and configure it in Windows Vista. Windows Vista installs and configures many network adapters automatically, but if you have an unusual network adapter, you may need to configure it manually.

INSTALL A NETWORK ADAPTER

Install the network adapter in your PC or connect it to your PC.

- For a PCI network adapter, shut down the PC, disconnect the power supply, open the PC case (as discussed in Chapter 6), insert the adapter in a free PCI slot, close the case, reconnect the power, and restart the PC.

- For a PC Card or ExpressCard network adapter, insert the PC Card in a free slot while Windows Vista is running.

- For a USB network adapter, connect the USB cable to a USB port on your PC (or on a USB hub connected to your PC) while Windows Vista is running. You may be instructed to install the software before connecting the adapter to your PC. Follow the manufacturer's instructions to complete the installation.

When Windows Vista detects the network adapter, it displays a pop-up window above the notification area and then starts the Found New Hardware Wizard. If the wizard finds a suitable driver for the network adapter, it installs the driver without involving you. If the wizard doesn't find a suitable driver, it prompts you to supply one, as discussed in Chapter 6.

To verify that your network adapter is correctly configured:

1. Click the **Start** button, right-click **Network**, and then click **Properties** to open a Network And Sharing Center window.

2. In the Tasks list on the left, click **Manage Network Connections** to open the Network Connections window.

3. If the window contains an icon labeled Local Area Connection, the network adapter is properly installed.

SET UP A WIRED ETHERNET NETWORK

To create a wired Ethernet network, you need a Cat 5, Cat 5e, or Cat 6 cable for each computer that will be connected and a switch or router with enough ports for all computers or other devices that you will connect.

You can connect two PCs directly without a switch or router using a *crossover* cable, a special cable that reverses the wires in the cable from their standard arrangement. You can buy a crossover cable from most computer stores—or assemble one yourself if you have bought a reel of cable, RJ-45 connectors, and a crimping tool.

CONNECT THE PCS

To connect your PCs:

1. If the PCs are running, it's usually best to shut them down.

2. Plug one end of an Ethernet cable into your switch or router and the other end into the network adapter on your PC (see "Install a Network Adapter" earlier in this chapter).

3. Repeat the process for each of the other PCs that will be part of the network.

4. Turn on the power for the switch.

SET UP THE NETWORK CONNECTION ON EACH PC

After connecting your PCs, allow Windows Vista to detect the network and configure network settings:

1. Turn on each of the PCs, and log on to Windows Vista.

2. Windows Vista detects the Internet connection and configures network settings automatically, and then displays the Select Your Computer's Current Location dialog box (see Figure 8-3).

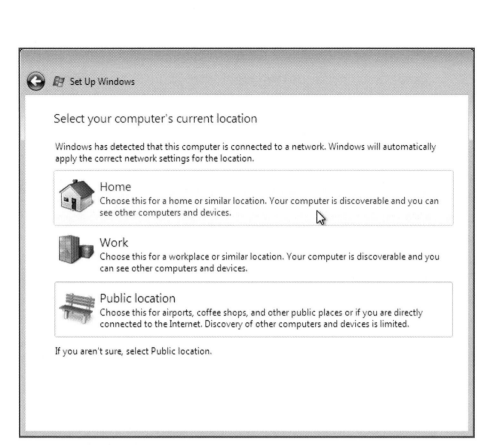

Select your computer's current location

Windows has detected that this computer is connected to a network. Windows will automatically apply the correct network settings for the location.

Home
Choose this for a home or similar location. Your computer is discoverable and you can see other computers and devices.

Work
Choose this for a workplace or similar location. Your computer is discoverable and you can see other computers and devices.

Public location
Choose this for airports, coffee shops, and other public places or if you are directly connected to the Internet. Discovery of other computers and devices is limited.

If you aren't sure, select Public location.

*Figure 8-3: **Once Windows Vista has detected and configured your network connection, it prompts you to decide whether the connection is Home, Work, or Public.***

CAUTION

When you mix wireless standards in a wireless network, you usually end up with the slowest speed for parts of the network or for all of it. For example, if you add a device using 802.11b to an otherwise 802.11g network, the whole network drops down to the 802.11b speed. However, some Draft-N equipment can maintain both Draft-N speeds with Draft-N equipment and 802.11g speeds with 802.11g equipment simultaneously.

3. Click the appropriate button:

- **Home** Click this button to designate this network a home network—one on which you want to be able to let computers "see" each other and share items. Normally, this is the best choice.

- **Work** Click this button if you're using a network at work. In most companies, an administrator will set up the network for you, so you may not need to do this.

- **Public Location** Click this button when you're connecting to a public network, such as a wireless hotspot at a coffee shop or airport.

SET UP A WIRELESS NETWORK USING AN ACCESS POINT

A wireless network is usually much easier to set up than a wired network because you don't have to run the cables among the items of network hardware. You can create a wireless network with an access point (as described in this section) or without an access point (as described in the next section).

To create a wireless network with an access point, you need a wireless adapter installed in or connected to each PC and a wireless access point. The wireless adapters and the wireless access point must be compatible with each other in one of the following ways:

- All Draft-N 802.11n products from the same manufacturer if you want Wireless-N speeds.

- All Wi-Fi–certified 802.11g products if you want 54Mbps speeds.

- Either a mixture of Wi-Fi–certified 802.11g products and Wi-Fi–certified 802.11b products or all Wi-Fi–certified 802.11b products if 11Mbps is good enough.

SELECTING WIRELESS HARDWARE

Hardware for a wireless network includes a wireless adapter and a wireless access point.

SELECT A WIRELESS SPEED

If you're buying hardware for a new wireless network, you have a tricky decision to make at this writing. You can buy draft 802.11n equipment to get the fastest data rate available (up to 300Mbps)—but because the standard is not yet final, the equipment may not be fully interoperable, so it is best to buy all your equipment from the same vendor. Alternatively, you can buy 802.11g equipment to get data rates of up to 54Mbps together with full compatibility.

Having a fast data rate is important if you're building a multiuser network, as each PC has to share the capacity with all the other PCs on the network at any given time. That said, 802.11g equipment is fast enough for most home uses.

If you'll need only to connect to public Wi-Fi networks, such as those in airports and coffee shops, 802.11g equipment—or even older 802.11b equipment—should be adequate. It is likely to be several years before public Wi-Fi networks upgrade to 802.11n.

SELECT A WIRELESS ADAPTER

These days, most laptop PCs come with wireless adapters built in. You can install wireless adapters in or on any other laptop or desktop PC.

- Plug a PC Card or ExpressCard wireless adapter into a laptop computer.
- Install a PCI wireless adapter inside a desktop computer.
- Plug a USB wireless adapter into a laptop or a desktop PC.

Continued . . .

SET UP THE WIRELESS ACCESS POINT

Most new and recent wireless access points can accept automatic configuration from a USB flash drive (a small memory device the size of a pack of gum that plugs into a USB port). If so, you can use the automated procedure described next. If your wireless access point has a USB port, it probably supports automatic configuration. Check the documentation to be sure.

If your wireless access point doesn't have a USB connector, you can be sure it doesn't support automatic configuration. Set up your access point by following the instructions that come with it. A typical manual setup process for an access point involves connecting your PC to it using an Ethernet cable so that you can communicate via a wired network in order to configure the wireless network. Configuration typically also includes the following:

- Specifying the name, or service set identifier (SSID), of the wireless network—often simply a descriptive text name (for example, Wireless1)—and choosing whether to broadcast it.
- Choosing whether to use encryption. If your access point offers a choice, choose Wi-Fi Protected Access (WPA) over Wired Equivalent Privacy (WEP), an older standard that includes known compromises; but even Wired Equivalent Privacy is better than no encryption at all.
- Choosing whether to restrict the network to a specified list of wireless adapters (identified by their Media Access Control number, or MAC number) or to leave it open to any wireless adapter within range. Specifying the wireless adapters that can connect is a good security measure, although it can be bypassed by a malefactor learning an approved MAC number and configuring a wireless adapter to use that number. The MAC address is usually printed on the wireless adapter. You can also learn it as follows:

1. Click **Start**, right-click **Network**, and then click **Properties** to display the Network And Sharing Center window.
2. In the upper-right corner of the window, click **View Full Map** to display the Network Map window.
3. Hover the mouse pointer over the computer in question, and then look at the MAC readout, as shown here.

SELECTING WIRELESS HARDWARE

(Continued)

For a desktop PC, a USB wireless adapter with a medium-length cable is usually a better choice than a PCI wireless adapter because you can not only connect and disconnect it easily, but can also position the antenna portion in the best place for connecting to the access point. By contrast, a PCI wireless adapter is harder to install but has the advantage of being mostly hidden inside the CPU box.

SELECT A WIRELESS ACCESS POINT

Wireless access points come in simple versions that plug into a wired Ethernet network and in more sophisticated versions, called "wireless broadband routers," that terminate a DSL or cable Internet connection. If you are about to buy broadband service, look at getting a wireless broadband router from the start, as it is easier to run your Internet connection and network using a single device than having multiple devices.

UNDERSTANDING NETWORKING PROTOCOLS

Networking protocols are sets of standards used to package and transmit data over a network. The protocol determines how the information is divided into packets for transmission, how it is addressed, and what is done to ensure it is transferred reliably.

To transmit data between your PC and other computers, Windows Vista by default uses a protocol called Transmission Control Protocol/Internet Protocol (TCP/IP), the networking protocol used on the Internet. TCP/IP is

Continued . . .

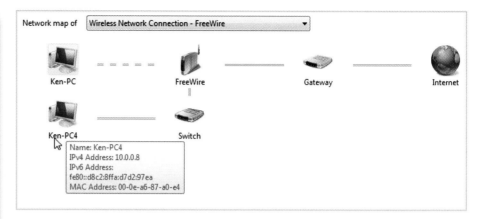

4. Click the Close button (the × button) to close the Network Map window and the Network And Sharing Center window.

INSTALL OR CONNECT THE WIRELESS ADAPTERS

If you haven't already installed the wireless adapters in (or connected them to) your PCs, do so now. For example, insert a PC Card or ExpressCard wireless adapter in a PC Card slot, or plug a USB wireless adapter into a USB port.

CONFIGURE THE WIRELESS ACCESS POINT

To set up your wireless access point:

1. Click **Start**, right-click **Network**, and then click **Properties** to display the Network And Sharing Center window.

2. In the left panel, click the **Set Up A Connection Or Network** link to launch the Set Up A Connection Or Network Wizard, which displays the Choose A Connection Option screen.

3. Click the **Set Up A Wireless Router Or Access Point** button, and then click **Next** to display the Set Up A Home Or Small Business Network screen.

4. Click the **Next** button, and then go through User Account Control for the Wireless Network Settings program. If the wizard displays the Network Discovery dialog box, shown here, click the **No, Make The Network That I Am Connected To A Private Network** button.

UNDERSTANDING NETWORKING PROTOCOLS *(Continued)*

a powerful and complex protocol. Windows Vista makes TCP/IP configuration as straightforward as possible, masking most of the ugly details from your sight, but it helps if you understand a few essentials about TCP/IP.

First, there are two main versions of the Internet Protocol: version 4 (usually called IPv4) and version 6 (usually called IPv6). IPv4 is still used most widely in North America and in much of the world, so this section discusses it. IPv6 is the new version, is widely used in China and other rapidly developing economies, and will eventually replace IPv4.

IP ADDRESSES

TCP/IP identifies different computers (technically, it identifies different network interfaces) on a network using addresses called *IP addresses*. In IPv4, an IP address takes the form of four groups of three decimal numbers separated by periods—for example, 192.168.0.1. The first group (192) defines the largest unit; the second group (168) defines the unit within that unit; the third defines another unit within the second unit; and the fourth defines another unit within the third. Roughly speaking, each of the numbers can go up to 255 (although there are exceptions to this).

For identification, each IP address must be unique on the network, so each network interface is assigned a different IP address. Many PCs come with several ways to connect to another computer or network: a wired network connection, a wireless network connection, a modem, and (rarely) a FireWire port. You can use two or more connections at the same time, so one PC can have two or more IP addresses at once. These IP addresses can be on the same network, but they'll typically be on different networks. For example, when your PC is connected directly to the Internet, it has one IP address on the Internet and another IP address on your local network.

Continued . . .

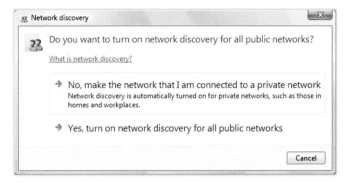

5. The wizard displays the Detecting Network Hardware And Settings screen while it attempts to detect your wireless network router. If the wizard can configure your router, it does so, but normally it cannot and so displays the Windows Detected Network Hardware But Cannot Configure It Automatically screen (see Figure 8-4).

Figure 8-4: **When the Set Up A Connection Or Network Wizard displays this screen, you will normally want to click the Create Wireless Network Settings And Save To USB Flash Drive button.**

UNDERSTANDING NETWORKING PROTOCOLS *(Continued)*

The Internet functions as a single huge TCP/IP network, so each computer on the Internet has to have a unique IP address. When you connect your broadband router or your PC to the Internet, your ISP (Internet service provider) assigns it an IP address from the block of IP addresses allocated to the ISP. For a typical dial-up connection, the IP address is *dynamic*, meaning that it is likely to be different each time you establish the connection: the ISP allocates one of the addresses assigned to its modem pool. For a typical broadband connection, the IP address is *static*, meaning that you keep the same IP address all the time (your ISP reserves the IP address for you).

NETWORK ADDRESS TRANSLATION

To reduce the number of computers directly connected to the Internet, many networks use a process called Network Address Translation (NAT). In NAT, either a computer or (more usually) a special-purpose device, such as a router, is connected to the Internet and has an IP address on the Internet. The NAT computer shares the Internet connection with the other computers on the internal network as required, funneling Internet requests and replies through its IP address.

OBTAIN AN IP ADDRESS

IP addresses can be allocated either manually or automatically. Manual allocation is handy for some situations (such as when you need a particular computer always to be reachable at the same IP address), but automatic allocation is the norm for most networks because it is more efficient. Most automatic allocation is performed by a DHCP (Dynamic Host Configuration Protocol) server, either at your ISP (for an Internet connection) or on your local network.

Continued . . .

If your access point doesn't support USB flash configuration, click the Configure This Device Manually button on the Windows Detected Network Hardware But Cannot Configure It Automatically screen. Windows opens Internet Explorer and displays the configuration screen for your wireless access point. (Normally, you will need to log in before setting the configuration screen.) Use the controls to configure the access point with the settings you have chosen. If the Set Up A Connection Or Network Wizard's manual configuration feature isn't able to deal with your access point, you will need to configure it using another tool. Consult the access point's documentation for details.

6. Click the **Create Wireless Network Settings And Save To USB Flash Drive** button to display the Give Your Network A Name screen.

7. Either accept the default name that Windows has chosen, or (preferably) type a distinctive name of your own. You can use up to 32 characters, including underscores and hyphens but not spaces.

8. Click **Next** to display the Help Make Your Network More Secure With A Passphrase screen (see Figure 8-5).

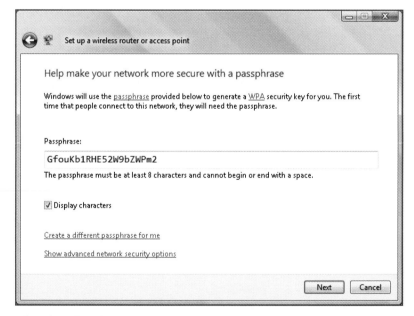

*Figure 8-5: **The wizard provides you with a highly secure passphrase for using WPA security to secure your wireless network. Change this passphrase only if you need to have a passphrase that you can remember.***

UNDERSTANDING NETWORKING PROTOCOLS *(Continued)*

When your PC detects that no DHCP server is available, it falls back on Automatic Private IP Addressing (APIPA). APIPA assigns an IP address in the address range 169.254.0.0 through 169.254.255.255 after checking that no other computer on the network is using that IP address.

TIP

If you want to choose a specific security type for your wireless network, click **Show Advanced Security Options**. On the Choose Advanced Network Security Options screen, choose the security method in the **Security Method** drop-down list, and then type the passphrase. Your choices of security methods are WPA-Personal (the default choice), WPA2-Personal (more secure; a good choice if all your wireless adapters support it), WEP (much less secure; use only if you have WEP equipment that cannot manage WPA), and No Security (which is never wise).

9. Either accept the default passphrase, or type a passphrase of your own if you need to be able to remember it (for example, so that you can enter it on devices that you cannot configure via USB).

10. Click **Next** to display the Choose File And Printer Sharing Options screen.

11. Select the appropriate option button:

   ● Select the **Do Not Allow Printer And File Sharing** option button if you do not want to use sharing or if you will configure it later.

   ● Select the **Allow Sharing With Anyone With A User Account And Password For This Computer** option button if you want other users of this PC to be able to access its Public folder and printers across the network.

   ● Select the **Allow Sharing With Anyone On The Same Network As This Computer** option button if you want all users of your network to be able to access its Public folder and printers across the network.

   ● Select the **Keep The Custom Settings I Currently Have** option button if you want to retain the settings you've already applied.

12. Click **Next** to display the Insert The USB Flash Drive Into This Computer screen.

13. Plug the USB flash drive into a USB port, and then choose the drive in the **Save Settings To** drop-down list.

14. Click **Next**. The wizard copies the wireless network settings to the drive and displays the To Add A Device Or Computer, Follow These Instructions screen.

15. Read the instructions, and then click **Close** to close the wizard.

16. In the notification area, click the **Safely Remove Hardware** icon to display the menu. Click the **Safely Remove USB Mass Storage** item for the USB drive you used. When Windows displays the Safe To Remove Hardware dialog box, click **OK**, and then disconnect the USB drive.

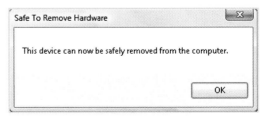

17. Plug the USB drive into the wireless access point. Allow 30 seconds for the wireless access point to apply the configuration information to itself, and then unplug the drive.

CONFIGURE A PC TO USE THE WIRELESS NETWORK

To configure a PC to use the wireless network:

1. Connect the USB flash drive with the configuration settings to the PC. Windows displays the AutoPlay dialog box.

2. Click **Wireless Network Setup Wizard** to launch the Wireless Network Setup Wizard, which prompts you to add the PC to the wireless network.

3. Click **OK**. The wizard adds the PC to the wireless network, and then tells you it has done so.

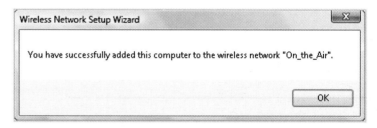

4. Click **OK** to close the message box.

5. In the notification area, click the **Safely Remove Hardware** icon to display the menu. Click the **Safely Remove USB Mass Storage** item for the USB drive you used. When Windows displays the Safe To Remove Hardware dialog box, click **OK**, and then disconnect the USB drive.

CONFIGURE A WIRELESS ADAPTER MANUALLY

If your wireless access point doesn't support automatic configuration, you'll need to configure the PCs in the wireless network manually.

1. Click **Start**, and then click **Connect To** to launch the Connect To A Network Wizard, which displays the Select A Network To Connect To screen (see Figure 8-6).

NOTE

If the Wireless Network Setup Wizard dialog box includes the Save This Network For All Users Of This Computer option button and the Save This Network For Me Only box, select the appropriate option button. The first option button is good for home situations, but you will need to go through User Account Control for the Manage Wireless Networks feature to apply it. The second option button is good for work networks that apply only to you; you will not need to go through User Account Control.

TIP

Disable SSID broadcasts if possible. This makes it harder for unauthorized people to connect to your wireless access point. A wireless network that broadcasts its SSID is described as *open*; one that doesn't is *closed*.

NOTE

Always use encryption on your wireless network. Encryption doesn't provide full security, but without it your network is open to anybody within broadcasting range of your wireless access point—up to several hundred yards in open surroundings or up to several miles if somebody aims an antenna toward your access point.

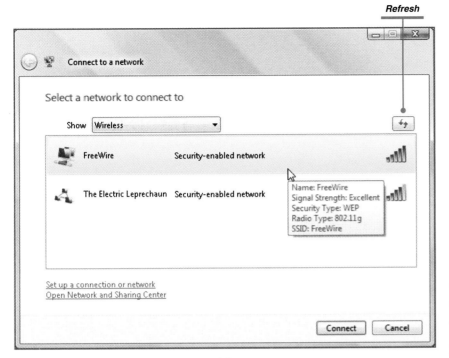

Refresh

Connect to a network

Select a network to connect to

Show Wireless ▾

FreeWire   Security-enabled network

The Electric Leprechaun   Security-enabled network

Name: FreeWire
Signal Strength: Excellent
Security Type: WEP
Radio Type: 802.11g
SSID: FreeWire

Set up a connection or network
Open Network and Sharing Center

Connect   Cancel

*Figure 8-6: **If the wireless network to which you want to connect doesn't appear on the Select A Network To Connect To screen, click the Refresh button. If the network still doesn't appear, it may be closed. See "Connect to a Closed Wireless Network," later in this chapter.***

TIP

When you plug the USB flash drive into each of the other PCs that you want to add to the wireless network, the Wireless Network Setup Wizard should start automatically. If it doesn't, click the **Start** button, and click **Computer**. A Computer window opens. Right-click the icon for the flash drive, and click **AutoPlay**. The Removable Disk dialog box appears. Click **Wireless Network Setup Wizard**, and click **OK**.

2. Click the network to which you want to connect, and then click **Connect**. The wizard displays the Type The Network Security Key Or Passphrase screen.

3. Type the passphrase or security key. Normally, it's a good idea to select the **Display Characters** check box so that you see the characters rather than security-conscious dots.

4. Click **Connect** to connect to the network. The wizard displays the Successfully Connected screen.

5. If you want to be able to use this network again, select the **Save This Network** check box. If you want Windows to connect automatically to this network when your PC is within range, select the **Start This Connection Automatically** check box.

6. Click **Close** to close the wizard.

CONNECT TO A CLOSED WIRELESS NETWORK

To connect to a closed wireless network (one that doesn't broadcast its SSID), you must know the SSID and password. Follow these steps:

1. Click **Start**, and then click **Connect To** to launch the Connect To A Network Wizard, which displays the Select A Network To Connect To screen.

2. In the lower-left corner, click **Set Up A Connection Or Network** to display the Choose A Connection Option screen.

3. Click **Manually Connect To A Wireless Network**, and then click **Next** to display the Enter Information For The Wireless Network You Want To Add screen (see Figure 8-7).

4. Type the network's name in the **Network Name** text box.

5. Choose the security in the **Security Type** drop-down list and the encryption in the **Encryption Type** drop-down list.

6. Type the passphrase in the **Security Key/Passphrase** text box. Select the **Display Characters** check box if you need to see what you're typing, as you often do with complex passphrases.

7. If you want Windows to connect automatically to this wireless network (as is often the case), select the **Start This Connection Automatically** check box.

8

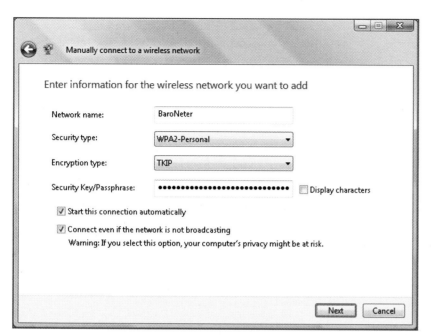

Figure 8-7: *Use the Manually Connect To A Wireless Network Wizard to connect to a closed wireless network.*

8. Select the **Connect Even If The Network Is Not Broadcasting** check box. (You need to select this check box because the network is closed.)

9. Click **Next**. The wizard adds the network to its list of wireless networks.

10. Click the **Connect To** button to display the Select A Network To Connect To screen.

11. Click the name of the network you just added, and then click **Connect** to connect to the network now.

MANAGE YOUR WIRELESS NETWORKS

If your PC connects to more than one wireless network, you may need to tell Windows which networks you prefer to use. Follow these steps:

1. Click **Start**, right-click **Network**, and then click **Properties** to display the Network And Sharing Center window.

2. In the left panel, click **Manage Wireless Networks** to display the Manage Wireless Networks window (see Figure 8-8).

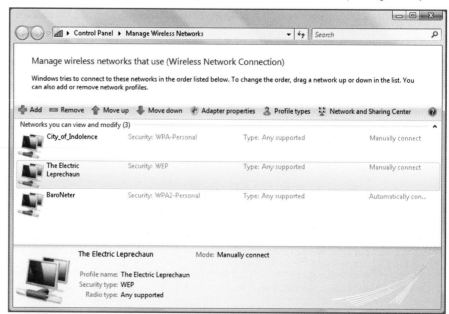

Figure 8-8: *Use the Move Up button and Move Down button in the Manage Wireless Networks window to shuffle the wireless networks into your preferred order.*

3. Click a network, and then click **Move Up** or **Move Down** to change its place in the list. Alternatively, drag the network up or down.

4. If you need to remove a network, click it, and then click **Remove**.

5. When you have finished rearranging the list, click the **Close** button (the × button) to close the Manage Networks window.

SET UP AN AD HOC WIRELESS NETWORK

If you don't have an access point, you can set up an *ad hoc* or *computer-to-computer* wireless network among two or more PCs. This capability means that one PC starts broadcasting an SSID and other PCs can join the network. Ad hoc computer networks work well for small numbers of computers, but if you plan to add more than half a dozen computers to your wireless network, an access point will give you better results.

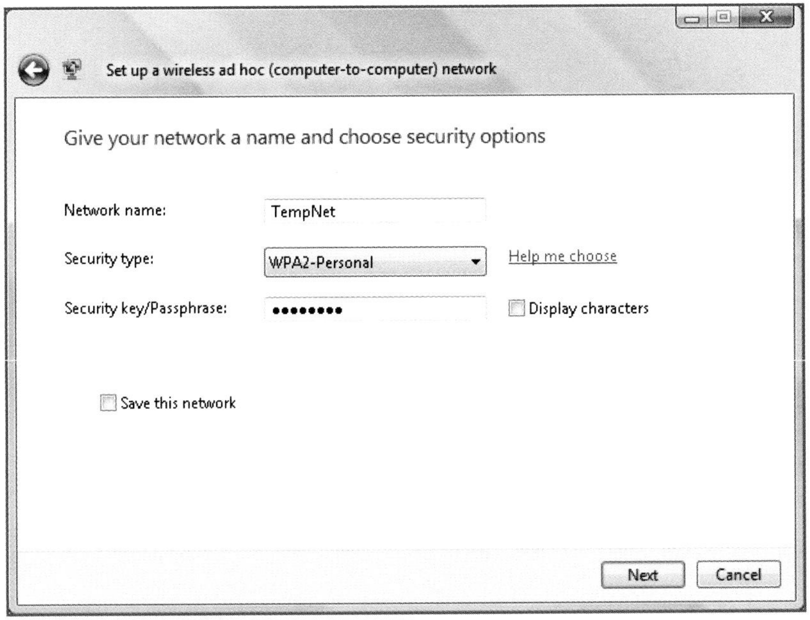

NOTE

You can't prevent an ad hoc wireless network from broadcasting its SSID. As a result, your wireless network can be seen by any wireless device within broadcasting range, so you must apply a password to keep it secure.

To set up an ad hoc wireless network:

1. Click **Start**, and then click **Connect To** to launch the Connect To A Network Wizard, which displays the Select A Network To Connect To screen.

2. In the lower-left corner, click **Set Up A Connection Or Network** to display the Choose A Connection Option screen.

3. Click **Set Up A Wireless Ad Hoc (Computer-To-Computer) Network**, and then click **Next** to display the Set Up A Wireless Ad Hoc Network screen.

4. Click **Next** to display the Give Your Network A Name And Choose Security Options screen (see Figure 8-9).

5. In the **Network Name** text box, type the name you want to give the network. You can use up to 32 characters.

6. Open the **Security Type** drop-down list and choose the security you want to use:

   - Use **No Authentication (Open)** in emergencies only.
   - Use **WEP** when you need to connect PCs that cannot use WPA2.
   - Use **WPA2-Personal** if all the PCs that will take part in the network support WPA2.

Set up a wireless ad hoc (computer-to-computer) network

Give your network a name and choose security options

Network name: TempNet

Security type: WPA2-Personal ▾   Help me choose

Security key/Passphrase: •••••••••   ☐ Display characters

☐ Save this network

[Next] [Cancel]

Figure 8-9: The Set Up A Wireless Ad Hoc (Computer-To-Computer) Network wizard lets you create a wireless network that uses a computer's connection rather than a wireless access point. Select the Save This Network check box if you want to be able to use the network again.

8

7. Type the passphrase in the **Security Key/Passphrase** text box. Select the **Display Characters** check box if you want to verify what you're typing.

- For WEP, you must use either alphanumeric characters (or 10 hexadecimal characters) for 40-bit encryption or 13 alphanumeric characters (or 26 hexadecimal characters) for 128-bit encryption.

- For WPA, you can choose a passphrase of any length.

8. Select the **Save This Network** check box if you want to use the network again. Clear this check box if you will use the network only once.

9. Click **Next**. The wizard creates the network connection and displays a screen saying that it is ready to use.

10. If you want to turn on Internet Connection Sharing for this network, click the **Turn On Internet Connection Sharing** button, and then go through User Account Control for the Ad Hoc Wireless Network program. Otherwise, simply click **Close** to close the wizard.

You can now join other PCs to the network as described in "Configure a PC to Use the Wireless Network," earlier in this chapter.

Access and Share Network Resources

Once you've established a connection to the network, either wired or wireless, you can access the resources on it. Typically, this means that you can use a shared Internet connection to connect to the network, access files and folders stored on shared drives on the network, and print to shared printers. Depending on the configuration of the network, you may also be able to use other resources, such as shared scanners, faxes, and other hardware. You can also share resources on your PC with users of other PCs.

EXPLORE THE NETWORK

To see what's available to you on the network, you can explore it. The best way to start is to use the Network window.

1. Click the **Start** button, and then click **Network**. The Network window opens.

2. If the top of the Network window shows a bar saying "Network discovery is turned off. Network computers and devices are not visible," click the bar, click **Turn On Network Discovery And File Sharing**, and then go through User Account Control for the Network And Sharing Center program. Windows turns on network discovery and file sharing.

NOTE

The shares (shared folders, disks, and other resources) that appear in the Network window are the result of your PC having searched your workgroup (or domain) for shares and other resources. When you first set up networking, you won't see any shares until they have been shared by other PCs and your PC has had time to find them.

3. The Network window displays the network *shares*—folders or disks on other computers that have been shared and are available to you. Figure 8-10 shows shares on a small network.

4. Double-click one of the computer shares to display the folders, printers, and other resources on that computer.

5. Double-click a folder to display its contents, or double-click a printer to connect to it.

6. Click **Close** to close the Network window.

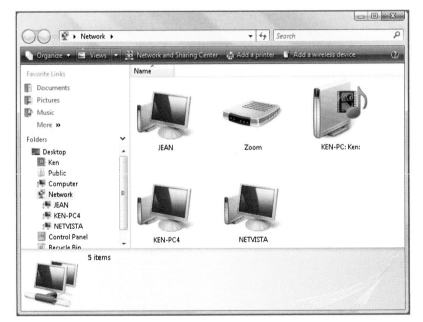

Figure 8-10: *Shares are drives, folders, and Windows Media Player libraries on other PCs that you can access via the network. Shares include devices, such as the Zoom Internet router shown here.*

PERMANENTLY CONNECT TO A NETWORK SHARE

If you use a specific network share frequently, you may want your PC to connect to it permanently so that you can use it as if it were a drive on your PC. You do this by mapping a network drive to the share. When you create such a mapping, Windows Vista reconnects to the share and represents it as a drive letter each time you log on until you disconnect the mapping from the share.

1. Click **Start**, and then click **Computer** to open a Computer window.

2. Click **Map Network Drive** on the toolbar to display the Map Network Drive dialog box (shown in Figure 8-11 with settings chosen).

3. If necessary, change the drive to use for the share. Windows Vista suggests the next unused letter working backward from the end of the alphabet.

4. Click **Browse**, use the Browse For Folder dialog box to select the folder you want to map, and then click **OK** to enter the folder in the Folder text box. (You can also type the path to the folder, but browsing is usually much easier.)

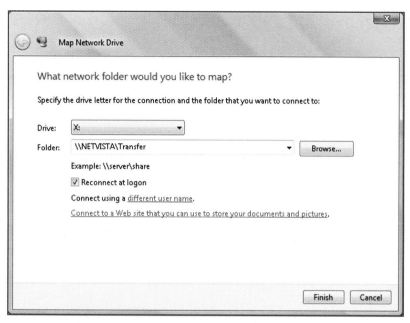

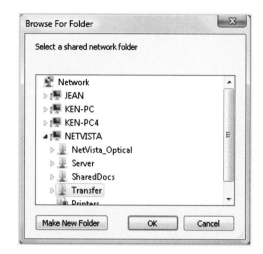

Figure 8-11: **Mapping a network drive gives you a permanent connection to that share.**

5. If you want to reconnect to the share every time you log on to your PC, make sure the **Reconnect At Logon** check box is selected.

6. Click **Finish**. The share opens in a separate window. Click the **Close** button to close that window.

7. Click **Close** to close the Network window.

DISCONNECT A MAPPED DRIVE

When you no longer want Windows Vista to map a drive to a network share, you disconnect the share.

1. Click the **Start** button, and click **Computer** to open a Computer window.

2. Right-click the mapped drive, and click **Disconnect**. The mapping disappears from the Computer window.

CONFIGURE YOUR PC'S SHARING SETTINGS

If you turn on Network Sharing And Discovery as described earlier in this chapter, Windows turns on all of the following items:

- **Network Discovery**   Allows your PC to "see" shared items on other PCs that have Network Discovery turned on. In turn, those PCs can see your PC's shared items.
- **File Sharing**   Allows other PCs to see files and printers your PC is sharing.
- **Public Folder Sharing**   Allows other PCs to see the contents of your Public folder.
- **Printer Sharing**   Allows other PCs to use any printer you're sharing.

QUICK**FACTS**

USING NETWORK ADDRESSES

Network addressing uses the *Uniform Naming Convention*, or *UNC*, to identify files, folders, and other resources on any computer on the network.

IDENTIFY A NETWORK SHARE

A network share, which is a folder or disk on a computer on the network, is identified by \\computername\pathname\folder or disk name. For example, a share named "2008 Budgets" in the Budgeting folder on the computer named "Server1" would have the UNC address of \\Server1\Budgeting\2008 Budgets.

IDENTIFY A NETWORK PRINTER

Identifying a network printer is similar to identifying a share. The printer's name takes the form \\computername\printername. For example, a printer named "HP4500" on Server1 would have the UNC \\Server1\HP4500.

TIP

To see which files and folders you're sharing, click **Show Me All The Files And Folders I Am Sharing** near the bottom of the Network And Sharing Center window. To see all the shared network folders, click **Show Me All The Shared Network Folders On This Computer**.

- **Password Protected Sharing**   When turned on, this feature allows only people with a user account and password on your PC to access your PC's shared folders, Public folder, and printers. When this feature is turned off, any network user can access these items.
- **Media Sharing**   Allows other PCs to see your Windows Media Player Library of songs, videos, and pictures.

If you want to set up more complex sharing, follow these steps:

1. Click **Start**, right-click **Network**, and then click **Properties** to display the Network And Sharing Center window.
2. Look at the Sharing And Discovery section to see which items you're sharing.

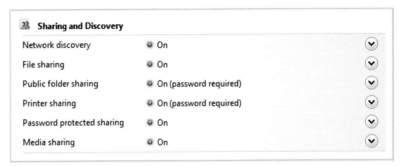

3. To change any of the first five items, click the down-arrow button at the right end of its bar to display the available options. The next illustration shows the Public Folder Sharing options. Choose the setting you want, and then click **Apply** and go through User Account Control for the Network And Sharing Center program to apply the change.

4. To change your media sharing settings, click the down-arrow button on the Media Sharing bar, and then click **Change**. Windows displays the Media Sharing dialog box (see Figure 8-12).

5. To turn off sharing, clear the **Share My Media To** check box, click **OK** to close the dialog box, and then skip the rest of this list. To turn sharing on, select the **Share My Media** check box and then click **OK** to display the full version of the Media Sharing dialog box.

6. If you want to share your media files with some users but not others, use the controls under Share My Media To. For example, click a PC with whom you do not want to share, click **Deny**, click **Yes** in the Deny dialog box (shown here) if you want to prevent other users of this PC from sharing media with the PC in question, and then go through User Account Control for the Windows Media Player Configuration program.

*Figure 8-12: **The Media Sharing dialog box appears in two different versions, depending on whether you're turning media sharing on or off, but the vital control is the Share My Media check box or Share My Media To check box.***

7. To control which media files you share, click **Settings**, use the Media Sharing Settings dialog box (see Figure 8-13) to customize the default sharing settings, and then click **OK**.

8. Click **OK** to close the Media Sharing dialog box, and then click **Close** to close the Network And Sharing Center window.

If you leave file and printer sharing turned on, you can control which folders and printers are shared manually.

SHARE A FOLDER MANUALLY

1. Open a Windows Explorer window, and browse to the folder that contains the folder you want to share. For example, click the **Start** button, click **Computer**, and then double-click the drive that contains the folder.

2. Right-click the folder, and click **Share** to launch the File Sharing Wizard (see Figure 8-14).

3. In the drop-down list box, select the person or group (for example, Everyone) with whom you want to share the folder, and then click **Add**.

TIP

To customize which media files you share with a particular PC or group of users (such as Other Users Of This PC), click the icon in the box, and then click **Customize**. Windows opens the Media Sharing – Customize dialog box, which is almost identical to the dialog box shown in Figure 8-13.

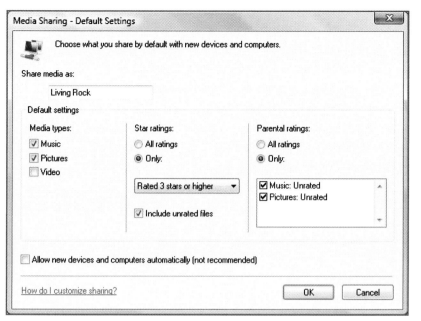

Figure 8-13: *You can use the Media Sharing – Default Settings dialog box to control which media files your PC shares by default. The Media Sharing – Customize dialog box contains most of the same settings but affects only the selected PC or group of users.*

4. In the list box, change the permission level as needed by clicking the drop-down list and choosing the appropriate item:

- **Reader**   Can open files and view them but cannot save changes or create new files in the folder.
- **Contributor**   Can open files, save changes, and create new files in the folder.
- **Co-Owner**   Can open files, save changes, create new files, and change permissions for other users of the folder.

5. Click **Share**, and then go through User Account Control for the Windows File Sharing program. The wizard displays the Your Folder Is Shared screen.

6. Click **Done** to close the wizard. Windows Explorer displays a graphic of other users on the folder to indicate that it is shared.

Figure 8-14: *For security, share as few folders as possible on your network. Even when you share a folder, you do not usually need to allow other users to change the files in the folder, so set the Reader permission level rather than Contributor or Co-owner permission.*

SHARE A PRINTER MANUALLY

1. Click **Start**, and then click **Printers** if it appears on the Start menu. If not, click **Control Panel**, click **Classic View** if a dot appears next to Control Panel Home in the left pane, and then double-click **Printers**. The Printers window opens.

2. Right-click the printer, and click **Sharing**. The Properties dialog box for the printer appears with the Sharing tab displayed.

3. If the sharing settings are unavailable, click **Change Sharing Options**, and then go through User Account Control for the Change Printing Settings program.

4. Select the **Share This Printer** check box.

5. Change the name in the Share Name text box if necessary.

6. Select the **Render Print Jobs On Client Computers** check box to make the other PCs process the print jobs they send to your printer (rather than having your PC process the jobs, which may slow it down).

7. Click **OK**.

Troubleshoot Home Network Problems

With new networking hardware and Windows Vista, you usually can set up a network easily using default settings and a minimum of effort—but not always. This section shows you essential techniques for configuring TCP/IP, checking that a network connection is working, and altering your sharing settings.

Configure TCP/IP for the Network Adapter

The network adapter in your PC not only needs a driver to tell Windows Vista how to communicate with it, it also needs networking software to tell it how to communicate with the networks to which your PC connects. When you successfully install a network adapter, Windows Vista automatically installs four components of networking software:

- **Client For Microsoft Networks** enables your PC to connect to Microsoft networks.

- **File And Printer Sharing For Microsoft Networks** enables your PC to share its files and printers with other PCs and use the files and printers that other PCs are sharing.

If you configure TCP/IP to obtain an IP address automatically and the server is not available, Automatic Private IP Addressing (APIPA) assigns an alternative IPv4 address automatically in the 169.254.0.0 through 169.254.255.255 range of numbers. APIPA is limited insofar as a PC using APIPA can communicate only with computers in the same range of numbers, but it can be effective in a pinch. The downside to APIPA is that each PC using it keeps checking for the server to reappear so that it can obtain a "proper" IP address, which reduces PC and network performance.

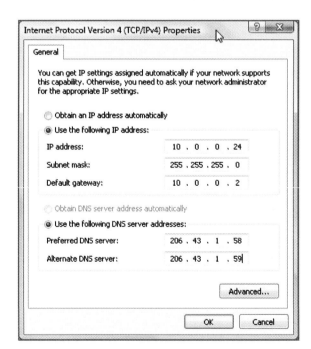

*Figure 8-15: **For most networks, you should use dynamic IP addresses so that your PC obtains an IP address automatically, but sometimes you will need to enter a fixed IP address, as shown here.***

- **QoS Packet Scheduler** prioritizes network traffic, giving time-dependent data priority over data that isn't time-dependent. (QoS is the abbreviation for Quality of Service.)
- **Internet Protocol Version 6 (TCP/IPv6)** tells your computer how to connect to networks using the new IPv6 protocol suite.
- **Internet Protocol Version 4 (TCP/IPv4)** tells your computer how to connect to networks using the widely used IPv4 protocol suite.
- **Link-Layer Topology Discovery Mapper I/O Driver** lets your PC discover other devices on the network.
- **Link-Layer Topology Discovery Responder** lets other PCs and devices discover your PC on the network.

Depending on how your PC connects to the network, you may need to configure Internet Protocol Version 4 (as described here). If your PC uses Internet Protocol Version 6 (which is much less likely), you may need to configure it. You will not need to configure any of the other components just discussed (in fact, most have no settings you can configure).

To configure Internet Protocol version 4:

1. Click **Start**, right-click **Network**, and then click **Properties** to display the Network And Sharing Center window.

2. In the left panel, click **Manage Network Connections** to display the Network Connections window.

3. Right-click the connection you want to configure, click **Properties**, and then go through User Account Control for the Network Connections program to display the dialog box for the connection.

4. Double-click **Internet Protocol Version 4 (TCP/IPv4)** in the This Connection Uses The Following Items list box. The Internet Protocol (TCP/IP) Properties dialog box appears (see Figure 8-15).

5. If your PC will obtain its IP address from a computer or device sharing an Internet connection (for example, a DSL or cable router), select the **Obtain An IP Address Automatically** option button and the **Obtain DNS Server Address Automatically** option button. If your ISP or an administrator has given you a static IP address and

a DNS (Domain Name Service) server address, select the **Use The Following IP Address** option button and the **Use The Following DNS Server Addresses** option button; and type the IP address, subnet mask, default gateway, and DNS server addresses in the text boxes.

6. Click **OK** to close the Internet Protocol Version 4 (TCP/IPv4) Properties dialog box, and click **OK** to close the Properties dialog box for the network connection.

Troubleshoot a Network Connection

Windows includes a tool for diagnosing and fixing problems with a network connection, but you may also need to troubleshoot network problems manually. This section shows you how to do both.

First, open the Network Connections window and check the status of the connection:

1. Click **Start**, right-click **Network**, and then click **Properties** to display the Network And Sharing Center window.

2. In the left panel, click **Manage Network Connections** to display the Network Connections window.

3. Double-click **Local Area Connection** to open the Local Area Connection Status dialog box (see Figure 8-16). You should see activity on both the Sent and Received sides. If you do see activity, all is well and you can stop troubleshooting; if you don't see activity on both sides, troubleshoot the problem as described next.

4. In either case, close the **Local Area Connection Status** dialog box.

TROUBLESHOOT A NETWORK CONNECTION AUTOMATICALLY

To troubleshoot problems with a network adapter and network connection automatically:

1. In the Network Connections window, click the network connection you want to troubleshoot, and then click **Diagnose This Connection** on the toolbar. Windows displays a diagnosis and (if it identifies a problem) usually suggests a means of fixing it, as shown here.

2. Click the link (such as the Enable The Network Adapter link shown in the illustration) to follow Windows' recommendation for fixing the problem.

Figure 8-16: Use the Status dialog box for a connection to check quickly that it is both sending and receiving data.

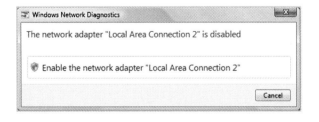

Ping (Packet Internet Groper) is used to query either the local computer or another computer on the network to see whether it responds to a simple TCP/IP request. *Ipconfig* is used to determine if a network configuration has been initialized and an IP address assigned.

TROUBLESHOOT A NETWORK CONNECTION MANUALLY

To verify that the network adapter is working and test a network connection manually:

1. Click **Start**, right-click **Network**, and then click **Properties** to display the Network And Sharing Center window.

2. In the left panel, click **Manage Network Connections** to display the Network Connections window.

3. Click the **Start** button, click **All Programs**, click **Accessories**, and then click **Command Prompt**. A Command Prompt window opens.

4. Type **ping loopback** and press **ENTER**. You should see replies from the network adapter, as shown here. If you don't, there is a problem with the network setup or the network adapter. The loopback address is a special address that refers to the computer on which it is entered. The loopback address is assigned the IP address 127.0.0.1.

5. Type **ipconfig** and press **ENTER**. You will see a readout of your network configuration, including the IP address, the subnet mask, and the default gateway (most likely your connection to the Internet), as shown here. (You may need to scroll back up the window to see some of the information.)

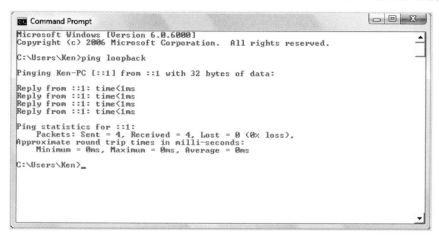

QUICK**FACTS**

UNDERSTANDING PRIVATE IP ADDRESS BLOCKS

Four blocks of IP addresses have been set aside and can be used by any organization for its private, internal needs without coordination with any other organization, but these blocks should not be used for directly connecting to the Internet. These private-use blocks of IP addresses are

- 10.0.0.0 through 10.255.255.255 (typically used for large networks)

- 169.254.0.0 through 169.254.255.255 (used for the Automatic Private IP Addressing protocol, or APIPA)

- 172.16.0.0 through 172.31.255.255 (typically used for medium-sized networks)

- 192.168.0.0 through 192.168.255.255 (widely used for small networks, used by Windows Vista's Internet Connection Sharing feature, and frequently automatically assigned by DSL routers for the local area network)

6. Type **ping** and the address of the default gateway (for example, **ping 192.168.0.1**). If you get four replies from the gateway, your network connection is working. If you don't, you will need to change your TCP/IP configuration to enable the PCs to communicate. The most likely problem is that the PCs' IP addresses are not in the same subnet (network segment), which prevents them from "seeing" each other. You should also check your network hardware for problems, such as disconnected cables or a switched-off access point.

```
Command Prompt

C:\Users\Ken>ping 10.0.0.2

Pinging 10.0.0.2 with 32 bytes of data:

Reply from 10.0.0.2: bytes=32 time=2ms TTL=64
Reply from 10.0.0.2: bytes=32 time=1ms TTL=64
Reply from 10.0.0.2: bytes=32 time=1ms TTL=64
Reply from 10.0.0.2: bytes=32 time=1ms TTL=64

Ping statistics for 10.0.0.2:
    Packets: Sent = 4, Received = 4, Lost = 0 (0% loss),
Approximate round trip times in milli-seconds:
    Minimum = 1ms, Maximum = 2ms, Average = 1ms

C:\Users\Ken>_
```

7. Click the Close button (the × button) to close the Command Prompt window.

8. If you do find a problem, review the earlier section on configuring TCP/IP to isolate and fix the problem.

How to...

Chapter 9
Getting Maximum Use out of Your Laptop PC

Laptop PCs are great because you can easily take them with you almost anywhere you go. They have disadvantages, however: you pay a higher price than desktop PCs (as discussed in Chapter 1), you sacrifice some flexibility in configuration (see Chapter 6), and you must guard more vigilantly against theft (see Chapter 7). All in all, though, most current laptop PCs offer impressive power and terrific convenience for their size.

To get the most out of your laptop PC, you'll need to put more work into configuring and managing it than you would for most desktop PCs. The main areas to focus on are power settings; network configurations; synchronizing files; using an external monitor, keyboard, and mouse; and deciding how you will use your laptop PC on the road.

CHOOSING LAPTOP PC BATTERIES

Lithium ion (Li-ion) batteries usually give longer battery life than do nickel metal hydride (NiMH) batteries, but they are more expensive. Most makes of laptop PC can take only one type of battery, so the only time you can choose between battery technologies is when buying a laptop PC.

Laptop PC batteries typically lose capacity after two or three years. To continue using your laptop PC on the road, you may need to replace the battery. Because capacity declines after the battery is manufactured regardless of use, you should buy the replacement battery only when you need it, not at the time you buy your laptop PC. If possible, check the replacement battery's date of manufacture to make sure you're not buying an old battery.

Manage Laptop PC Power Usage

Unlike desktop computers, laptop PCs have two sources of power: batteries and current from electrical outlets, converted by the laptop's power adapter. This means that you have several extra tasks with a laptop PC to manage how you use these two power sources and conserve limited battery power.

Maximize Your Battery Life

If you use your laptop computer extensively on the road, your first concern is likely to be maximizing your battery life so that you can get plenty of work (or play) done without having to plug in your computer. The main ways of maximizing battery life are

- **Decrease the screen brightness**   Your laptop PC's screen probably consumes the greatest proportion of battery power, so you can increase battery life by decreasing the screen brightness. Most laptop PCs have function keys for decreasing screen brightness. Some laptop PCs have hardware controls (for example, a slider). Otherwise, you can adjust the brightness by using the Display Brightness slider in Windows Mobility Center, which you'll meet later in this chapter.

- **Turn off unnecessary components**   Many laptop PCs let you disable components that you're not using in order to reduce power consumption. For example, when on the road, you might turn off your laptop PC's serial, parallel, and infrared ports if you don't need them. Consult your laptop PC's manual for details on what you can turn off and how to do so. In some laptop PCs, you must change these settings in the BIOS; other laptops provide graphical configuration utilities.

- **Get a high-capacity battery**   Some manufacturers make high-capacity batteries for certain laptop PC models. These almost always protrude beyond the standard battery compartment, usually doubling as a stand to elevate the back of the laptop PC, which improves the typing position and the airflow to the underside. Third-party companies make replacement batteries for popular laptop models. These batteries sometimes have somewhat higher capacity than the original battery (for example, because of improvements in battery technology).

- **Use an extra battery (or two)**   Some laptop PCs enable you to insert an extra battery in place of the optical drive or another component. If not, carry an extra battery separately. When the first battery runs out, shut down your laptop PC, replace the battery, and then start your PC again.

- **Get an external battery**   If your laptop PC can't take a high-capacity battery or an extra battery, consider getting an external battery for extra power. External batteries typically weigh several pounds and are around the size of a compact laptop PC, so they're an awkward solution—but they can deliver up to six or eight hours of extra battery life.

- **Use an auto adapter or air adapter**   To charge your laptop PC from your car battery, get an auto adapter; to charge your laptop PC in a plane, get an air adapter. Many different models are available, from custom models designed for specific laptop PCs to standard power inverters that deliver AC current that can power any device.

- **Buy a second power adapter**   If you commute with your laptop PC, get a second power adapter so that you can keep one at home and one at work, decreasing your laptop PC's travel weight and the chance of forgetting to take the adapter with you.

- **Get a portable solar panel**   If you need to use your laptop PC away from other sources of energy, consider a portable solar panel designed for powering a laptop PC. These are popular with computer-toting hikers as well as with those whose jobs require the use of a computer away from standard power sources.

- **Configure aggressive power management settings**   Reduce your laptop PC's power consumption by using aggressive power management settings. See "Configure Power Settings," later in this chapter.

- **Keep your battery fully charged**   Modern battery technologies don't need to be fully discharged before being recharged to avoid the "memory effect" that reduced the charge capacity of older batteries, so it's best to keep your laptop PC plugged in whenever you have a power source available. That way, the battery will remain as fully charged as possible.

Configure Power Settings

You should configure power management settings on your laptop PC so that it runs at full speed when the power adapter is delivering power but reduces its power consumption to a sensible minimum when running off the battery.

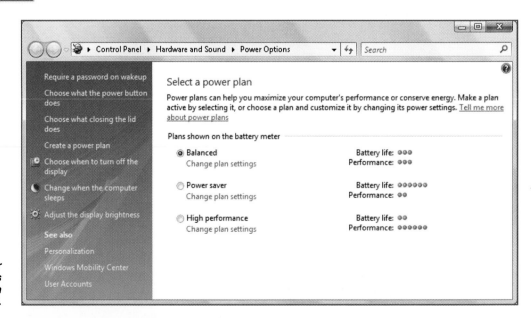

To configure power settings, open the Power Options window in either of these ways:

- Click the **Start** button, and click **Control Panel**. In Control Panel Home view, go to the **Mobile PC** heading, and then click **Change Battery Settings**. (In Classic View, double-click **Power Options**.)

  –Or–

- Click the Power icon in the notification area to display the Power Status panel, and then click the More Power Options link. (Depending on your laptop, you may see other options here.)

The Power Options window appears. Exactly which settings appear in the window depends on the capabilities that Windows Vista detects in your laptop PC and whether your PC manufacturer has installed any custom power management options. Figure 9-1 shows a fairly typical example of the Power Options window for a laptop PC.

*Figure 9-1: **The settings in the Power Options depend on your laptop PC's capabilities and whether any custom power management software is installed.***

TIP

To increase battery life in a power scheme, turn down the monitor brightness as far as you can bear, and set a short time in the **Turn Off The Display** drop-down list and the **Put The Computer To Sleep** drop-down list.

Set Up Power Schemes

To define the overall power settings Windows Vista uses, you configure a power scheme.

1. In the Power Options window (see "Configure Power Settings"), select the option button for the power scheme you want to use: **Balanced**, **Power Saver**, or **High Performance**.

2. Under the option button for the power scheme you've chosen, click the **Change Plan Settings** link to open the Edit Plan Settings window for the plan. Figure 9-2 shows an example.

3. Use the **Turn Off The Display**, **Put The Computer To Sleep**, and **Adjust Display Brightness** controls in the Plugged In column to choose settings for when the laptop PC is plugged in.

4. Use the **Turn Off The Display**, **Put The Computer To Sleep**, and **Adjust Display Brightness** controls in the On Battery column to choose settings for when the laptop PC is on battery power.

5. Click the **Save Changes** button to save the changes you've made to the power scheme.

Leave the Edit Plan Settings window open so that you can set battery alarms and alarm actions, as discussed next.

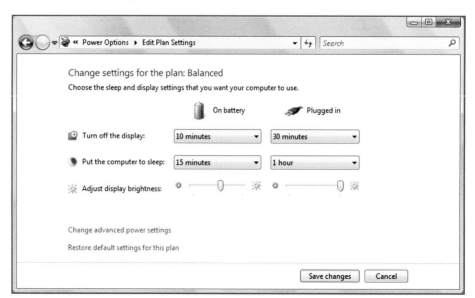

Figure 9-2: **The Edit Plan Settings window lets you adjust your chosen power scheme's settings to better suit your needs.**

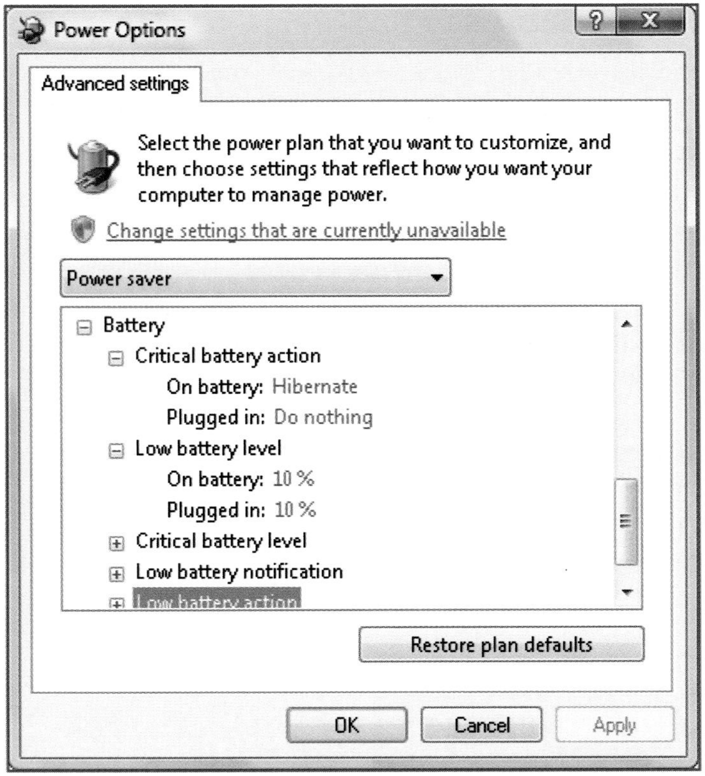

Power Options

Advanced settings

Select the power plan that you want to customize, and then choose settings that reflect how you want your computer to manage power.

Change settings that are currently unavailable

Power saver

- Battery
  - Critical battery action
    - On battery: Hibernate
    - Plugged in: Do nothing
  - Low battery level
    - On battery: 10 %
    - Plugged in: 10 %
  - Critical battery level
  - Low battery notification
  - Low battery action

Restore plan defaults

OK | Cancel | Apply

Figure 9-3: The Power Options dialog box includes settings that let you control what happens when your battery power reaches low and critical levels.

Set Battery Levels and Actions

Most laptop PCs automatically hibernate when the battery reaches a critically low level. This is normally the most convenient action, but you can configure your PC to shut down instead if you prefer. What you're more likely to need to do, however, is adjust the battery levels that Windows Vista considers to be "low" and "critically low."

1. In the Power Options window, click the **Change Advanced Power Settings** link to open the Power Options dialog box (see Figure 9-3).

2. The drop-down list above the main list box shows the power scheme from which you opened the Power Options dialog box. If necessary, choose another power scheme.

3. In the main list box, scroll down to the Battery category.

4. If the Battery category is collapsed, double-click it to expand it. (You can also click the + sign next to it.)

5. Expand the subcategory you want to adjust, and then choose the setting you want. For example:

   - To change the critical battery level, expand the Critical Battery Level category. Click the **On Battery** link to display a spin box, and then adjust it to the value you want. Repeat the process for the **Plugged In** link.

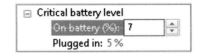

   - To change what Windows does when the battery reaches the critical battery level, expand the Critical Battery Action category. Click the **On Battery** link to display a drop-down list, and then choose the action you want—for example, **Hibernate** or **Shut Down**. Repeat the process for the **Plugged In** link if necessary.

6. Click the **OK** button to close the Power Options dialog box.

7. In the Edit Plan Settings window, click the **Save Changes** button to save the changes you've made. Windows displays the Power Options window once more.

Tell Windows What to Do When You Press the Power Button or Close the Lid

You can configure how Windows Vista interprets you pressing your laptop PC's power button or closing its lid.

1. In the Power Options window (see "Configure Power Settings"), click the **Choose What The Power Button Does** link in the left column. Windows displays the System Settings window (see Figure 9-4).

2. In the Power Button And Lid Settings area, use the **When I Press The Power Button** drop-down lists and the **When I Close The Lid** drop-down lists to tell Windows what to do: Sleep, Shut Down, or Do Nothing.

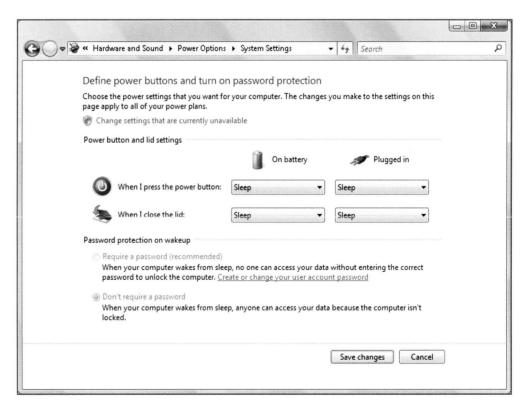

*Figure 9-4: **Tell Windows Vista how to respond when you push the power button or close the lid of your laptop PC. You can set different actions for when the laptop is running on battery power and when it is plugged in.***

TIP

For security reasons, it's a good idea to select the **Require A Password** option button in the Password Protection On Wakeup area of the System Settings window. If you don't, anyone who wakes your PC can access your data freely. However, if you normally leave your PC sleeping in a locked office (or home), you may prefer to select the **Don't Require A Password** option button so that you don't need to log back in when you wake the laptop again.

NOTE

Depending on your laptop's manufacturer, you may also see other options in Windows Mobility Center—for example, options for integrated wireless devices.

3. If you want to change the setting in the Password Protection On Wakeup area but find the options are dimmed, click the **Change Settings That Are Currently Unavailable** link, and then go through User Account Control for the Power Options Control Panel feature. You can then select the **Require A Password** option button or the **Don't Require A Password** option button, as needed.

4. Click the **Save Changes** button to save the changes you've made. Windows displays the Power Options window again.

Check Your Laptop PC's Battery Status

To check the status of your laptop PC's battery, hover the mouse pointer over the power icon in the notification area, as shown here.

Use Windows Mobility Center

Windows Vista's new Windows Mobility Center feature provides a one-stop shop for configuring laptops. From Windows Mobility Center (see Figure 9-5), you can configure the following:

● The brightness of the built-in display

● An external display that you've connected

● The volume

● Synchronization partnerships with devices or network drives

● The power plan

● Settings for giving a presentation

● Wireless network settings

Figure 9-5: *Windows Mobility Center lets you quickly configure essential components for easy and productive mobile computing.*

Open Windows Mobility Center

You can open Windows Mobility Center in various ways:

- Click the **Power** icon in the notification area, and then click the **Windows Mobility Center** link. This is usually the easiest way.

- Click the **Start** button, click **All Programs**, click **Accessories**, and then click **Windows Mobility Center**.

- Click the **Start** button, click **Control Panel**, click the **Classic View** link, and then double-click **Windows Mobility Center**.

Change the Display Brightness

To change the display brightness, simply drag the **Display Brightness** slider to the left (to decrease the brightness) or to the right (to increase it).

Connect an External Display to Your Laptop

You may want to connect an external display to your laptop for two reasons:

- So that you can use the laptop more comfortably at your desk—either replacing the laptop's screen with an external display or augmenting the built-in screen with another screen.

- To give a presentation (using either an external display or a projector).

TIP

If you find you need to change the display brightness often, change the brightness in your power scheme, as discussed earlier in this chapter.

NOTE

Windows may detect the new display without you needing to click the **Connect Display** button. If so, Windows displays the New Display Detected dialog box.

To connect and configure an external display, follow these steps:

1. With Windows running, connect the display to the PC, and connect its power supply.

2. Open Windows Mobility Center.

3. Click the **Connect Display** button. Windows displays the New Display Detected dialog box (see Figure 9-6).

4. Select the option button for the display arrangement you want:

   ● **Duplicate My Desktop On All Displays (Mirrored)**   Use this setting for presentations, when you need both your screen and the external display (or projector) to show the same image.

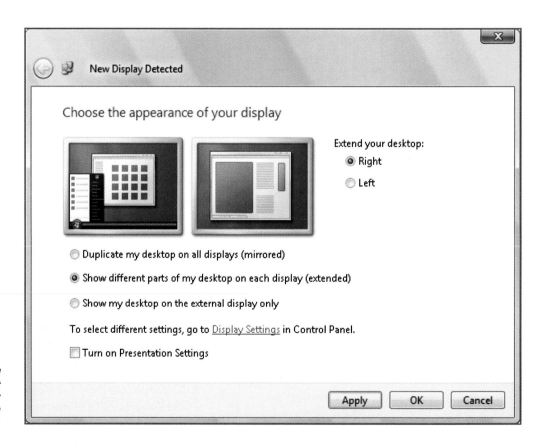

Figure 9-6: In the New Display Detected dialog box, choose the Show Different Parts Of My Desktop On Each Display (Extended) option button if you want to get the maximum desktop area possible.

NOTE

If the external display is above or below the laptop's display, click the **Display Settings** link to open the Display Settings dialog box. (Windows then closes the New Display Detected dialog box.) Drag the icon for the external display to above or below the icon for the laptop's monitor, as appropriate, and then click **OK**.

TIP

You may need to change the resolution or refresh rate for the external monitor. To do so, right-click the desktop, click **Personalize**, and then click **Display Settings**. Click the icon for the external monitor, and then drag the **Resolution** slider to change the resolution. To change the refresh rate, click the **Advanced Settings** button in the Display Settings dialog box, click the **Monitor** tab in the Properties dialog box, and then choose the refresh rate in the **Screen Refresh Rate** drop-down list.

- **Show Different Parts Of My Desktop On Each Display (Extended)** Use this setting when you want to use both your laptop's screen and an external display—for example, when working at home. In the Extend Your Desktop area, select the **Left** option button if the external display is positioned to the left of the laptop's display; select the **Right** option button if the external display is positioned to the right.

- **Show My Desktop On The External Display Only** Use this setting when you want to use only the external display (and not use the laptop's screen).

5. Select the **Turn On Presentation Settings** check box if you want to turn on presentation settings (discussed later in this chapter).

6. Click **Apply** to apply the settings you've chosen.

7. Verify that the effect is what you want. If it's not, change the settings and try again. If it is, click **OK**.

Change the Volume

Once you've opened Windows Mobility Center, you can drag the **Volume** slider to change the volume, or select the **Mute** check box to mute the sound.

But normally you'll find it easier to control the volume directly from the Volume icon in the notification area. Click the **Volume** icon to display the Volume pop-up window (shown here). You can then drag the slider up and down to control the volume, or click the Speaker icon at the bottom to toggle muting on or off.

Change the Battery Plan

You can change the battery plan quickly from Windows Mobility Center by using the drop-down list. However, you will probably find it easier to change power plan by clicking the **Power** icon in the notification area and then selecting the option button for the power plan in the panel that appears.

Figure 9-7: *The Presentation Settings dialog box lets you set up your laptop for giving a presentation. For example, you can turn off the screen saver, set the volume you want, and change the desktop background.*

Control Presentation Settings

If you use your laptop to give presentations, click the Presentation Settings icon (the icon of a projector) in Windows Mobility Center to display the Presentation Settings dialog box (see Figure 9-7).

PREPARE YOUR PC TO GIVE A PRESENTATION

Before you're due to give a presentation, choose settings in the When I Am Giving A Presentation area:

- **Turn Off The Screen Saver**   Select this check box to make sure the screen saver doesn't start during the presentation.

- **Set The Volume To**   Select this check box, and then drag the slider to set the volume you want to use for presentations. You will need to experiment to find a suitable volume.

- **Show This Background**   You can choose a different background just for presentations, without having to change your normal background. For example, you may need to use a corporate background for presentations that you prefer not to see in your everyday work.

If you always use the same displays for giving a presentation, you can tell Windows so:

1. Connect the external monitor or projector.

2. Open the Presentation Settings dialog box.

3. Click the **Connected Displays** button to open the Current Displays dialog box (shown here).

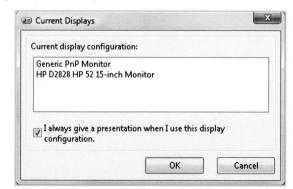

4. Make sure the Current Display Configuration list shows all the displays that are connected.

5. Select the **I Always Give A Presentation When I Use This Display Configuration** check box.

6. Click **OK**.

   If you're ready to start giving your presentation, select the **I Am Currently Giving A Presentation** check box.

   Click **OK** to close the Presentation Settings dialog box.

TURN ON PRESENTATION SETTINGS FOR THE PRESENTATION

When you're about to start a presentation, click the **Turn On** button in the Presentation Settings area of the Windows Mobility Center window. Windows applies the settings you've chosen for the screen saver, volume, or background image.

After you've finished giving the presentation, click the **Turn Off** button in the Presentation Settings area. Windows restores your normal setup.

Connect to a Wireless Network

To connect your laptop PC to a wireless network, click the Network Center button in the Wireless Network area of Windows Mobility Center. You can then use the Network And Sharing Center window to connect to a network as discussed in "Set Up a Wireless Network Using an Access Point" in Chapter 8.

The readout at the top of the Wireless Network area shows your current status: "Connected" or "Not Connected." Click the icon to open the Connect To A Network Wizard, which you can use to connect or disconnect.

Control Sync Partnerships

Windows Vista lets you synchronize data with either a device (for example, a handheld computer or phone using Windows Mobile) or with a network folder. Click the **Sync Settings** button to open the Sync Center window, which you use for setting up synchronization and managing it.

For details on synchronizing data with a network folder, see "Use Offline Files in Windows Vista Business, Ultimate, or Enterprise," later in this chapter.

Synchronize Your Laptop PC with Your Desktop PC

If you use both a laptop PC and a desktop PC, you'll often need to network the two and share files between them. You can do so in four ways:

- **Move or copy the files manually** Use the techniques discussed in Chapter 2 to move or copy the files from one computer to another. This works well for the occasional file but quickly becomes awkward with large numbers of files.

- **Keep all the files on the laptop PC** By keeping the files on the laptop PC and accessing them from the desktop PC when necessary, you can have all your files with you when you take your laptop PC on the road.

- **Use Windows Vista's Briefcase feature** All editions of Windows Vista include the Briefcase, a modest feature for synchronizing batches of files. See "Use the Briefcase Feature" later in this chapter.

- **Use the Offline Files feature** The Business, Ultimate, and Enterprise editions of Windows Vista have a feature named Offline Files. Offline Files lets you automatically store copies of files located on a network on your laptop PC so that you can work with them when the network isn't available. Neither of the Home editions of Windows Vista has this feature. See "Use Offline Files in Windows Vista Business, Ultimate, or Enterprise," later in this chapter.

Use the Briefcase Feature

The Briefcase feature enables you to create a special Briefcase folder for keeping files synchronized on two computers. This is how a Briefcase works:

1. Create a Briefcase on your laptop PC.
2. Copy the files from your desktop PC to your laptop PC.
3. Work on the files on the laptop PC.
4. Synchronize the files in the Briefcase with the files on your desktop PC when you return.

NOTE

You can create a Briefcase in any folder, but the desktop tends to be the most convenient location. You can also create a Briefcase on a removable disk (for example, a USB key drive) if you don't have a network. A floppy disk will work, but its capacity and performance are so poor that almost any other alternative is preferable.

To create and work with a Briefcase:

1. Connect your computers. For example, connect your laptop PC to your home network.

2. Right-click open space on the desktop, click **New**, and then click **Briefcase**. Windows Vista creates a Briefcase with the temporary name New Briefcase, and selects the name.

3. Type a descriptive name, and press **ENTER**.

4. Open **Windows Explorer**, navigate to the folder that contains the files you want, and drag the files to the Briefcase icon. The Updating Briefcase dialog box appears as the files are copied.

5. Disconnect your laptop PC, and work with the files in the Briefcase as usual. You can delete files from and create new files in the Briefcase.

6. Reconnect your laptop PC to your desktop PC.

7. Right-click the Briefcase, and click **Update All**. A dialog box appears, showing the files that need updating (see Figure 9-8).

8. Check the list of updates. To change an action, right-click the file, and click your preferred action in the shortcut menu.

9. Click **Update** to update your files with the changed versions.

TIP

If you want to update only some of the files in your Briefcase, double-click the Briefcase to display a Windows Explorer window of its contents. Select your desired files, open the **Briefcase** menu, and click **Update Selection**.

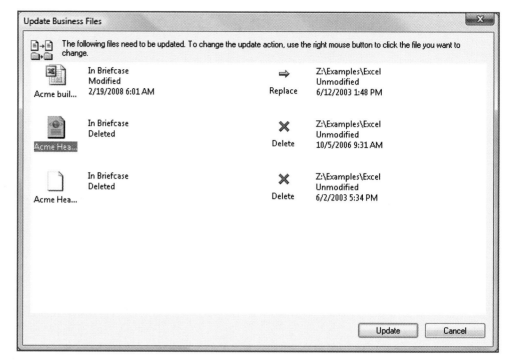

Figure 9-8: *Check the updates that Windows Vista intends to make to the Briefcase files and to the original files.*

NOTE

This book uses "Offline Files" (with initial capital letters) to refer to the Offline Files feature and "offline files" (lowercase) to refer to the files that are made available by using the Offline Files feature.

Use Offline Files in Windows Vista Business, Ultimate, or Enterprise

If your laptop PC has Windows Vista Business Edition, Windows Vista Ultimate Edition, or Windows Vista Enterprise Edition rather than one of the Home Editions, you can use the Offline Files feature for synchronizing files instead of the Briefcase feature. Offline Files is more powerful than the Briefcase feature, but it's more complicated to use.

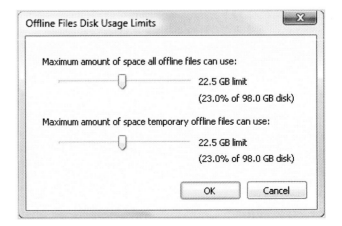

ENABLE AND CONFIGURE OFFLINE FILES

Before you can use Offline Files, check that the Offline Files feature is turned on, and make sure it's set to use only as much space as you can afford.

1. Click the **Start** button, and click **Control Panel** to open a Control Panel window.

2. If a dot appears next to Control Panel Home in the left pane, click **Classic View** to switch to Classic view.

3. Double-click the **Offline Files** item to open the Offline Files dialog box (see Figure 9-9).

4. If the Enable Offline Files button appears on the General tab, click it and then go through User Account Control for the Offline Files feature to turn on Offline Files. If the Disable Offline Files button appears, as in Figure 9-9, Windows Vista is already set to use Offline Files.

5. Click the **Disk Usage** tab to display its contents (see Figure 9-10).

6. Look at the All Offline Files readout and the Temporary Offline Files readout. If you need to adjust the amount of space, click the **Change Limits** button, go through User Account Control for the Offline Files feature, and then use the Offline Files Disk Usage Limits dialog box (shown here) to set how much space you want to make available for all offline files and temporary offline files. How much space you need depends on how many files you must take with you. Click **OK** when you've finished.

*Figure 9-9: **The Offline Files feature enables you to automatically make copies of network files on your laptop PC and then synchronize the copies with the network files when you reconnect.***

NOTE

Offline Files works with most file types (such as Microsoft Word documents, Excel workbooks, and PowerPoint presentations), but not with file types that cannot effectively be taken offline, such as Access databases (which can be accessed and changed by multiple users at the same time).

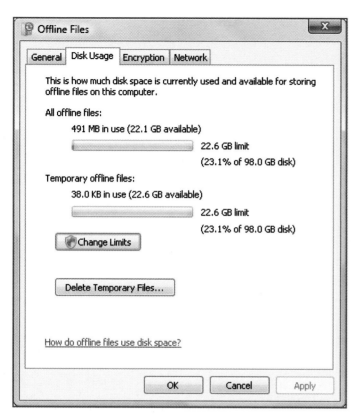

Figure 9-10: *The Disk Usage tab of the Offline Files dialog box lets you control how much space Offline Files can take up on your PC's hard drive.*

7. If you want to encrypt your offline files for security, click the **Encryption** tab, and then click the **Encrypt** button. This is a good idea for protecting important files in case your laptop PC is lost or stolen. (When you want to unencrypt encrypted offline files, you can click the **Unencrypt** button on this tab.)

8. If your PC sometimes connects to the network via a slow connection (such as dial-up using a modem), you can make Windows work offline automatically. To do so, click the **Network** tab, and then select the **On Slow Connections, Automatically Work Offline** check box. In the **Check For A Slow Connection Every NN Minutes** box, set a suitable number of minutes for Windows to check the connection speed. (If Windows finds a fast connection, it goes online.)

9. Click **OK** to close the Offline Files dialog box.

MAKE FILES AVAILABLE FOR OFFLINE USE

After enabling Offline Files, specify which files you want to make available.

1. Open **Windows Explorer** and navigate to the folder that contains the files you want.

2. Right-click the folder and click **Always Available Offline**. Windows displays the Always Available Offline dialog box (shown here) as it prepares the files for offline access.

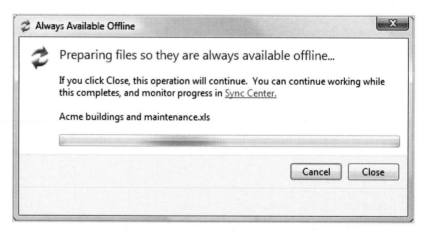

3. When the Always Available Offline dialog box tells you it has completed preparing files, click the **Close** button.

UNDERSTANDING SYNCHRONIZATION

Windows Vista synchronizes your offline files with the network files as follows:

- If the network file is unchanged and the offline file is changed, the offline file replaces the network file.

- If the network file is changed and the offline file is unchanged, the network file replaces the offline file.

- If both the network file and offline file are changed, Windows Vista prompts you to decide which one to keep.

- If the network file has been deleted and the offline file is unchanged, Windows Vista deletes the offline file.

- If the network file has been deleted, but the offline file is changed, Windows Vista prompts you to decide whether to delete the offline file or save it to the network.

- If the offline file has been deleted and the network file is unchanged, Windows Vista deletes the network file.

- If the offline file has been deleted, but the network file has changed, Windows Vista doesn't delete the network file.

- If there are new offline files, Windows Vista creates copies of them on the network.

- If there are new network files, Windows Vista creates offline copies of them.

Windows Vista displays a green Offline Folders icon containing two curving white arrows on each offline item, as shown here.

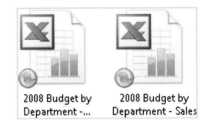

2008 Budget by Department -...   2008 Budget by Department - Sales

PREPARE TO WORK OFFLINE

Windows Vista synchronizes the files in the background while your PC is running, so normally, most of your offline files will be fully up to date at any moment. When you're ready to disconnect from the network, tell Windows to synchronize any offline files that contain fresh changes:

1. Open the **Start** menu and click **Computer**.

2. Open the drive that contains the offline files.

3. Click the **Work Offline** button on the toolbar. Windows synchronizes the files.

WORK WITH OFFLINE FILES

Once the synchronization is complete, you can disconnect your laptop PC from the network and work with the files. The files still appear to be in their network locations even though you are working with copies saved on your laptop PC's hard drive.

SYNCHRONIZE YOUR OFFLINE FILES

After you reconnect to your network, synchronize your offline files:

1. Connect your laptop PC to your network.

2. Open the **Start** menu, and click **Computer** to open a Computer window.

3. Open the drive that contains the offline files.

4. Click the **Work Online** button on the toolbar. Windows synchronizes the files that have changed, prompting you to resolve the conflicts for any files that have changed both on your laptop and in the original file.

Use Your Laptop PC at Home

If your laptop PC is your main (or only) PC, make sure it's as comfortable as possible for working with. Comfort and ergonomics should have played a major role in your choice of laptop PC, but you can increase both in several ways when using your PC in its main location.

- **External keyboard**   Plug in an external keyboard to use instead of the built-in keyboard. Even if you don't buy a special ergonomic keyboard, you'll probably benefit from having the numeric keypad (unless your laptop has one) and from being able to adjust the position of the keyboard relative to the laptop PC.

- **External mouse**   Plug in your favorite type of pointing device to use instead of, or in addition to, your laptop PC's touchpad or pointing stick. If your laptop PC has only one PS/2 connector (the round connector used for keyboards and mice), and you need to connect both a PS/2 keyboard and PS/2 mouse, get a splitter cable to provide two PS/2 connectors.

- **External monitor**   You can use an external monitor instead of—or in addition to—your laptop PC's monitor. If you have a large monitor, you may find it easier to use than your laptop PC's monitor. Otherwise, by adding even a modest-sized external monitor, you can substantially increase the size of your desktop and the amount of information you can see at once. See "Connect an External Display to Your Laptop," earlier in this chapter.

- **Laptop PC stand**   Consider getting a custom laptop PC stand to improve your laptop PC's work angle and increase ventilation to its underside. Alternatively, prop up the back of the laptop PC on a book or a stack of CD jewel cases.

- **Docking station**   If you need to connect a full suite of hardware to your laptop PC each time you bring it home, consider a docking station. A docking station is a component with connectors for keeping all the docked components (keyboard, mouse, monitor, printer, and so on) connected. You can then attach, or dock, your laptop PC to the docking station with a single connection. Docking stations are convenient but tend to be expensive because they're custom components for particular laptop PCs. You can find third-party "universal" docking stations (ones that work with many models of laptop PCs) from manufacturers such as Kensington Technology Group (www.kensington.com) and Belkin Corporation (www.belkin.com).

Use Your Laptop PC on the Road

When you need to take your laptop PC on the road:

1. Charge the main battery and any spare batteries.
2. Copy or synchronize all the files you need to the laptop PC.
3. Disconnect the laptop PC from whatever docking arrangement you've created.
4. Pack your laptop PC, power adapter, spare batteries, modem cable, wireless network adapter, and any other items you need.
5. Leave.

This section discusses two specific features that you may need to use while on the road: multiple configurations for dial-up networking and wireless networks.

Switch among Dial-Up Locations

If you use a dial-up Internet connection when you're on the road, you should create a separate network location for each place from which you connect rather than constantly change the phone number and other details of your main dial-up connection.

To create a new location:

1. Click the **Start** button, and click **Control Panel**. In Control Panel Home view, click the **Hardware And Sound** link, click **Printers And Other Hardware**, and then click **Phone And Modem Options**. (In Classic View, double-click **Phone And Modem Options**.) The Phone And Modem Options dialog box appears (see Figure 9-11).
2. Click **New** on the Dialing Rules tab to open the New Location dialog box (see Figure 9-12).
3. Type a descriptive name in the **Location Name** text box.
4. Specify the country and area code for the location.
5. Set up any dialing rules for the connection: the number to dial for an outside line for local or long-distance calls, the carrier code to use for long-distance and international calls, whether to disable call waiting (and which code to use), and whether to use tone or pulse dialing.
6. If necessary, use the options on the Area Code Rules tab to create rules for dialing in particular area codes, and use the options on the Calling Card tab to set up a credit card or calling card to use for making calls.

NOTE

The first time you ever click the Phone And Modem Options link, Windows Vista displays the Location Information dialog box. Choose your country or region (for example, United States), specify your area code and any carrier code or outside-line number needed, and then click **OK**. Windows displays the Phone And Modem Options dialog box.

NOTE

To switch to another location, display the **Phone And Modem Options** dialog box, select the location in the Location list, and click **OK**.

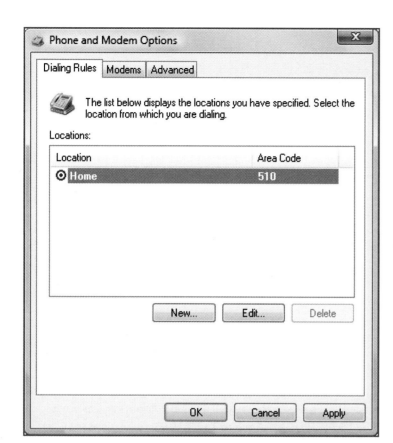

Figure 9-11: *From the Dialing Rules tab of the Phone And Modem Options dialog box, you can create new locations and switch among existing locations.*

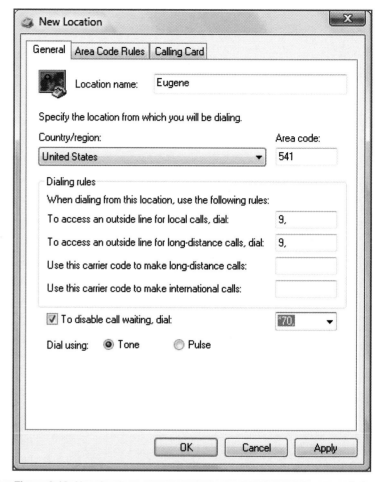

Figure 9-12: *Use the three tabs of the New Location dialog box to specify the details of the networking location.*

7. Click **OK** to close the New Location dialog box. Windows Vista adds the location to the list in the Phone And Modem Options dialog box.

8. If you want to use the new location immediately, select it in the **Location** list.

9. Click **OK** to close the Phone And Modem Options dialog box.

10. Click **Close** to close the Control Panel window.

Use Public Wireless Networks

Windows Vista's ability to switch quickly among dial-up locations simplifies the chore of connecting via modem while you're on the road, but dial-up connections remain slow and awkward. If your laptop PC has built-in Wi-Fi, or if you're prepared to buy a Wi-Fi adapter, you can often make a much faster connection by using a public wireless network, or Wi-Fi hotspot.

At this writing, many hotels, airports, and coffee shops offer wireless Internet access, some for free and the others for a modest fee. If you know you'll be somewhere that's short of hotspots, plan your access locations ahead of time by using a hotspot aggregator service, such as Boingo Wireless (www.boingo.com), T-Mobile (www.t-mobile.com), or iPass (www.ipass.com). Check the latest service plans from competing aggregators; use their online tools to find out whether they have hotspots where you need them; and establish which one will work best for your needs.

Beyond these formal public wireless networks, most cities contain many wireless networks that have been left open by their owners, some intentionally (so that other people can use them as needed), but most through ignorance or incompetence. Tools such as NetStumbler (www.netstumbler.com) can help you quickly locate open networks within range of your wireless-enabled device.

Chapter 10
Troubleshooting Hardware

PCs are notorious for giving their users trouble, and you may be one of the unlucky users who find that this reputation is wholly justified. This chapter shows you how to troubleshoot the hardware and software problems you're most likely to encounter: problems starting your PC, problems with Windows Vista running unstably, and problems that require you to get help from someone you know.

This chapter isn't exhaustive—large tomes have been written about troubleshooting PCs (if you're looking for a comprehensible and graphical treatment of this topic, see *PC Upgrading and Troubleshooting QuickSteps*, also published by McGraw-Hill)—but it will enable you to solve key problems and let you know when you must call in your local guru or get professional help.

Troubleshoot Problems Starting Your PC

Problems that occur when you start your PC can be tricky to deal with because you can't use most of Windows Vista's problem-solving tools. However, the Windows Vista installation DVD includes tools that will enable you to start your PC if vital system files get corrupted.

Deal with Startup Errors

This section discusses how to deal with the startup errors that you're most likely to see and that you stand a good chance of dealing with on your own. For other startup errors, you will probably want to consult a PC technician.

"NON-SYSTEM DISK OR DISK ERROR" MESSAGE

The message "Non-system disk or disk error" usually means that you have left a floppy disk in the floppy drive and your PC is trying to start from it. Remove the disk and press **CTRL+ALT+DELETE** to restart your PC.

If there's no floppy disk in the floppy drive, your PC probably has a disk error. Try restarting it a couple of times. If you get the same error, seek professional assistance.

"WINDOWS DID NOT SHUT DOWN SUCCESSFULLY"

If Windows Vista starts by announcing that "Windows did not shut down successfully" and suggesting that you start in Safe Mode (see Figure 10-1), it's usually best to attempt to start Windows Vista normally.

Press **DOWN ARROW** to move the selection to the **Start Windows Normally** option, and press **ENTER**. If Windows Vista then runs normally, all is probably well.

UICKSTEPS

CONFIGURING YOUR PC'S BOOT DRIVES

Most PCs can *boot*, or start, from the hard drive, from an optical drive, or from a floppy drive (if the PC has one); some can also start from a USB drive. You may sometimes need to change the list of drives from which your PC tries to boot and the order in which it tries those drives. For example, you may sometimes need to boot from a CD or DVD to perform tasks such as system recovery.

1. Start or restart your PC.

2. Press **DELETE**, **F2**, or another key during startup (following the onscreen prompt). The BIOS screen appears.

3. Choose the option for changing boot settings. These vary depending on the BIOS in your PC.

4. Choose the order in which you want the drives to be used.

5. Exit the BIOS settings, and choose the option for saving your changes. Your PC then restarts automatically using the drives and order you specified.

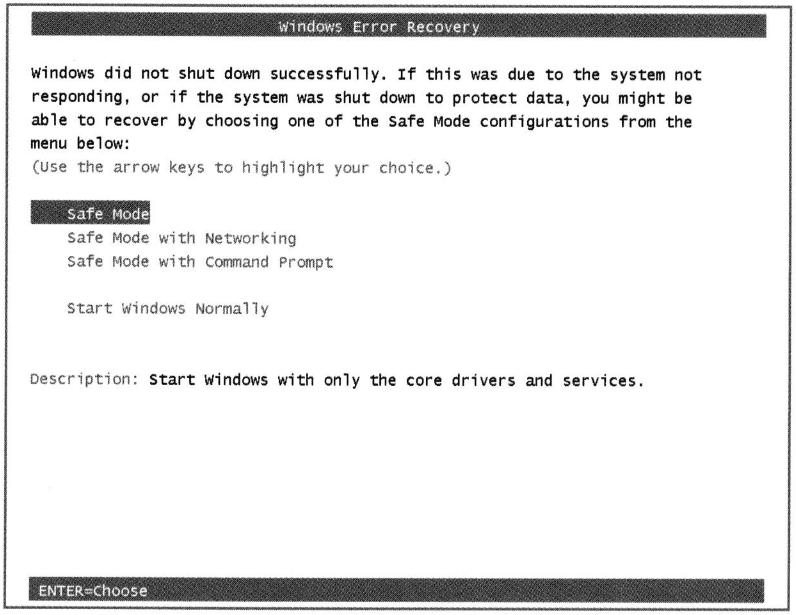

```
                    Windows Error Recovery

Windows did not shut down successfully. If this was due to the system not
responding, or if the system was shut down to protect data, you might be
able to recover by choosing one of the Safe Mode configurations from the
menu below:
(Use the arrow keys to highlight your choice.)

    Safe Mode
    Safe Mode with Networking
    Safe Mode with Command Prompt

    Start Windows Normally


Description: Start Windows with only the core drivers and services.




ENTER=Choose
```

Figure 10-1: You will see the first Windows Error Recovery screen if Windows suffered a severe error or your PC lost power suddenly.

If Windows Vista fails to start properly and hangs (stops responding) before the Welcome screen appears:

1. Press **CTRL+ALT+DELETE** to restart your PC. You'll see the Windows Error Recovery screen shown in Figure 10-2. This time, select the **Safe Mode** item, and then press **ENTER**.

2. At the Welcome screen, click your username, type your password, and press **ENTER**. Safe Mode appears (see Figure 10-3), using the 800×600 screen resolution (in case a higher resolution is making Windows Vista unstable or has prevented your monitor from displaying Windows correctly).

3. Troubleshoot the program or hardware that you think is causing the problem. See the next section, "Solve Problems When Windows Vista Is Running," for the tools you'll probably want to use.

4. After you finish working in Safe Mode, restart Windows Vista normally.

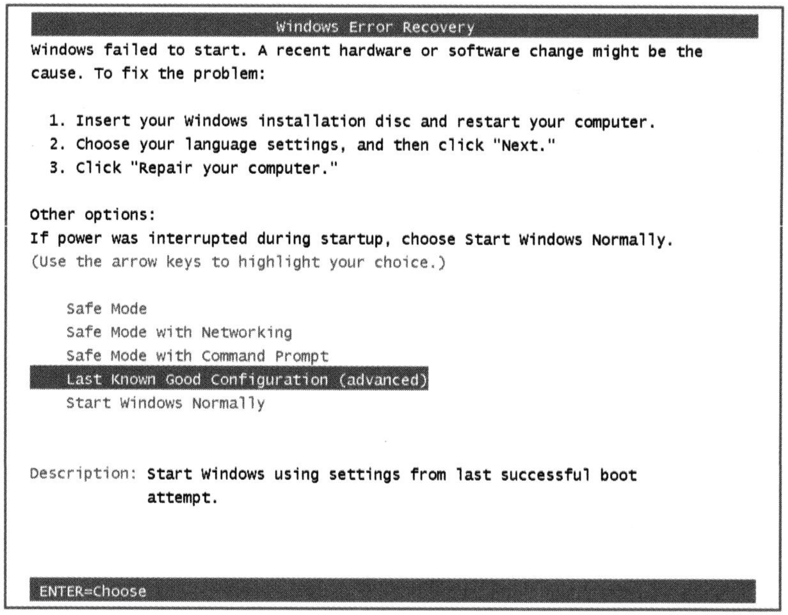

Figure 10-2: The second Windows Error Recovery screen includes instructions for repairing your Windows installation.

```
                    Windows Error Recovery

Windows failed to start. A recent hardware or software change might be the
cause. To fix the problem:

    1. Insert your Windows installation disc and restart your computer.
    2. Choose your language settings, and then click "Next."
    3. Click "Repair your computer."

Other options:
If power was interrupted during startup, choose Start Windows Normally.
(Use the arrow keys to highlight your choice.)

    Safe Mode
    Safe Mode with Networking
    Safe Mode with Command Prompt
    Last Known Good Configuration (advanced)
    Start Windows Normally


Description: Start Windows using settings from last successful boot
             attempt.



ENTER=Choose
```

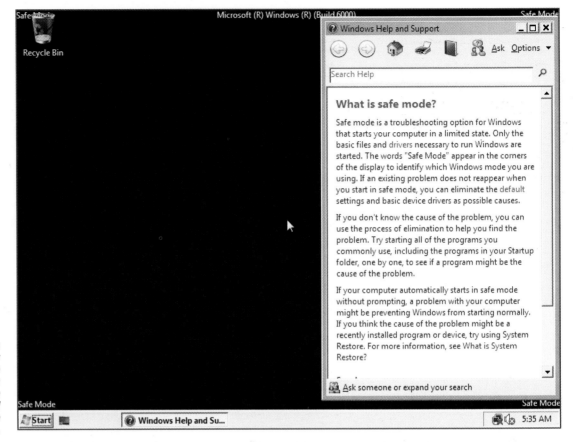

Figure 10-3: *Safe Mode simplifies Windows Vista by eliminating as many device drivers and services as possible so that you can troubleshoot problems without your PC crashing. Close or minimize the Windows Help And Support window to give yourself more screen space to work in.*

Solve Problems When Windows Vista Is Running

Problems that occur when Windows Vista is running (as opposed to when Windows Vista won't start) include a particular program or a hardware device making Windows Vista unstable, you deleting or losing files that you need, and you needing to restore Windows Vista to an earlier configuration to make it run stably again.

CAUTION

Unless Windows Vista is severely unstable and you are trying to troubleshoot it, you normally do not want to change the settings in System Configuration Utility.

Prevent Programs from Starting Automatically

If Windows Vista starts successfully, and you can log in as usual, but Windows Vista then becomes unstable before you open any programs or take any actions, the culprit may be a service (a system process) or a program that Windows Vista is starting automatically. You can control which services and programs start automatically using System Configuration Utility.

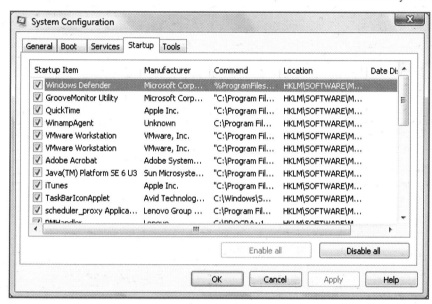

1. Press **WINDOWS KEY–R** to display the Run dialog box.

2. Type **msconfig**, press **ENTER**, and then go through User Account Control for the System Configuration Utility program. System Configuration Utility opens.

3. Click the **Startup** tab (see Figure 10-4). This tab lists all the programs that Windows Vista starts automatically.

4. Clear the check boxes for the programs you don't want to start the next time Windows Vista starts, and then click **OK** to close System Configuration Utility. Windows Vista displays the System Configuration dialog box, telling you that you may need to restart your PC.

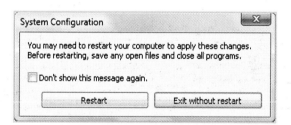

Figure 10-4: System Configuration Utility lets you see which programs Windows Vista is starting automatically and prevent specific programs from being started (in case they're causing problems).

5. Click **Restart** to restart your PC.

6. After your PC restarts and you log on to Windows, see if preventing these programs from running has cured the instability. If not, open System Configuration Utility again, and then try clearing the check boxes for other programs.

Remove a Problem Device

If a hardware device seems to be making Windows Vista unstable, remove the device. A device might be the culprit if the problems you're experiencing start just

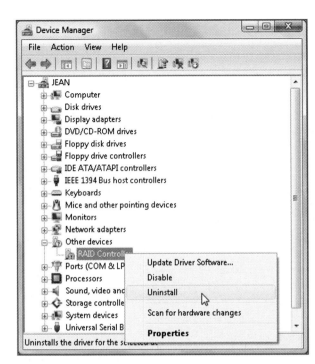

Figure 10-5: Use Device Manager to uninstall a hardware device that you think is making Windows Vista unstable. An exclamation point indicates that Windows has identified a problem with the device.

NOTE

If you are unable to locate a satisfactory driver for a device and you think the device is making Windows Vista unstable, uninstall the device as discussed in "Remove a Problem Device," earlier in this chapter.

after you install the device, Windows Vista displays error messages related to the device, or attempting to use the device causes Windows Vista to become unstable.

1. Press **WINDOWS KEY–BREAK** to display the System window.

2. In the left panel, click **Device Manager**, and then go through User Account Control for the Microsoft Management Console program to launch Device Manager (see Figure 10-5).

3. Right-click the offending device, and click **Uninstall**. Windows Vista removes the device's driver and stops using the device.

4. Shut down Windows, turn off your PC, and then physically remove the device from your PC. You should then be able to restart your PC without a problem.

Update a Driver for a Problem Device

If a device isn't working properly, you may be able to fix it by updating its driver.

1. Press **WINDOWS KEY–BREAK** to display the System window.

2. In the left panel, click **Device Manager**, and then go through User Account Control for the Microsoft Management Console program to launch Device Manager

3. Right-click the problem device, and click **Update Driver Software** to launch the Update Driver Software Wizard.

4. Choose where to search for the software:

   ● Usually, the best choice is to have Windows search your PC and the Internet for the driver software. To do so, click **Search Automatically For Updated Driver Software**. The wizard searches and, if it finds a suitable driver, installs it. On the final page of the wizard, click **Close**. If you see the Windows Was Unable To Install Your Hardware screen, and you have a driver you want to try, click **Back**; otherwise, click **Close** to leave the device with its existing, unsatisfactory driver, and go to step 5.

   ● If you have a file or disc containing the software, click **Browse My Computer For Driver Software**. On the Browse For Driver Software On Your Computer screen (see Figure 10-6), click **Browse**, use the Browse For Folder dialog box to locate the software, and then click **OK**. Make sure the **Include Subfolders** check box is selected, and then click **Next**. On the final screen of the wizard, click **Close**. Skip the rest of this list.

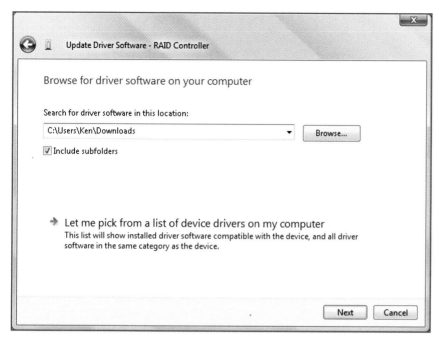

Figure 10-6: *If the Update Driver Software Wizard cannot find a suitable driver for a problem device, you can try to supply a driver manually. You can also click the Let Me Pick From A List Of Device Drivers On My Computer link to try using a different driver from Vista's store.*

5. If neither method produces a suitable driver, you can try using one of Windows Vista's drivers for similar hardware (consult the Internet for advice). Click the **Back** button in the upper-left corner of the wizard to return to the Browse For Driver Software On Your Computer screen.

6. Click **Let Me Pick From A List Of Device Drivers On My Computer** to display the Select Your Device's Type From The List Below page.

7. If the type of device appears in the Common Hardware Types list box, click it. Otherwise, click **Show All Devices**, and click **Next**. The wizard displays the Select The Device Driver You Want To Install For This Hardware page.

8. In the Manufacturer list box, click the manufacturer of the device you're installing (if the manufacturer is listed). In the Model list box, select the model (if it is listed). Click **Next**. On the The Wizard Is Ready To Install Your Hardware page, click **Next**. Skip to step 10.

9. If the manufacturer or model isn't listed, click **Have Disk**. The Install From Disk dialog box appears. Use the options in the Install From Disk dialog box to select the disk that contains the driver. If the driver is in a folder, browse to the folder, and then click **Open**. Click **OK**. The Select The Device Driver You Want To Install For This Hardware page appears.

10. Click the driver and then click **Next**. If the Update Driver Warning dialog box appears, and you're sure you want to proceed, click **Yes**. If the Hardware Installation dialog box appears, warning you that the driver has not passed Windows Logo testing to verify its compatibility with Windows Vista, click **Continue Anyway** if you want to proceed.

11. On the final page of the wizard, click **Finish** to close the wizard.

Restore Windows Vista to an Earlier Configuration

System Restore is a semiautomatic recovery tool that keeps track of the changes made to your PC's configuration, including the software you install and the settings you choose. If a hardware change, a software installation, or a driver

QUICKSTEPS

CREATING RESTORE POINTS

System Restore automatically creates restore points the first time you use Windows Vista and thereafter at roughly 24-hour intervals (the intervals vary if your PC happens to be switched off when System Restore is due to create a restore point).

System Restore automatically creates restore points when you install most programs and drivers in case the installation destabilizes your PC and you want to revert to your previous configuration. You can also create restore points manually when you feel the urge to perform some configuration of questionable wisdom.

1. Press **WINDOWS KEY+BREAK** to open the System window.

continued . . .

update causes the system not to run properly, you can use System Restore to return Windows Vista to how it was prior to that. System Restore works by creating *restore points* or *system checkpoints*, snapshots of your Windows Vista configuration, to which you can return if necessary.

CONFIGURE SYSTEM RESTORE

System Restore is automatically turned on in Windows Vista. You can turn System Restore on or off for each hard drive on your PC.

1. Press **WINDOWS KEY+BREAK** (or click **Start**, right-click **Computer**, and click **Properties**) to open the System window.

2. In the left pane, click **System Protection**, and then go through User Account Control for the System Protection program. The System Properties dialog box appears with the System Protection tab at the front (see Figure 10-7).

3. In the Automatic Restore Points list box, select the check box for each drive for which you want to create restore points automatically.

4. Click **OK** to close the System Properties dialog box.

RESTORE WINDOWS VISTA TO A RESTORE POINT

1. Close any program you're running, saving changes as necessary.

2. Click the **Start** button, click **All Programs**, click **Accessories**, click **System Tools**, click **System Restore**, and then go through User Account Control for the Microsoft Windows System Restore program. The System Restore Wizard opens.

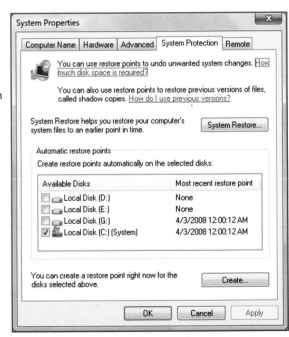

Figure 10-7: You can set up System Restore to monitor only your system drive or all the drives on your PC. Your system drive is the one that bears the Windows icon.

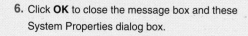

QUICKSTEPS

CREATING RESTORE POINTS

(*continued*)

2. In the left pane, click **System Protection**, and then go through User Account Control for the System Protection program. The System Properties dialog box appears with the System Protection tab at the front.

3. In the Automatic Restore Points list box, make sure that the check box is selected for each drive for which you want to create a restore point. If not, select the appropriate check boxes, and then click **Apply** to apply the change.

4. Click **Create** to display the System Protection: Create A Restore Point dialog box.

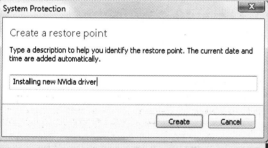

5. Type the description for the restore point (make clear what the restore point represents, but don't add the date and time because System Restore will add these automatically), and then click **Create**. System Restore creates the restore point and displays a message box telling you it has done so.

6. Click **OK** to close the message box and these System Properties dialog box.

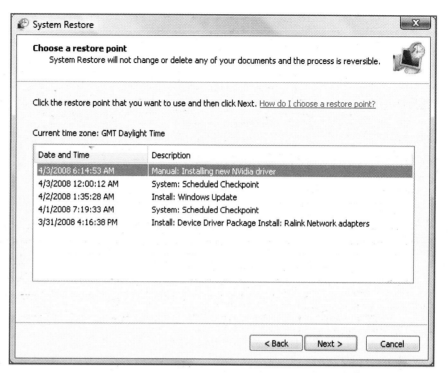

Figure 10-8: You can use System Restore to restore your PC's Windows configuration to how it was at any of the restore points saved on your PC. You can sort the restore points by clicking the Date And Time column heading or the Description column heading.

3. Click **Next** to display the Choose A Restore Point screen (see Figure 10-8).

4. Click the restore point you want to use, and then click **Next** to display the Confirm Disks To Restore screen.

5. Select the check box for each disk that you want to restore, and then click **Next** to display the Confirm Your Restore Point screen.

6. Verify the details and click **Finish** to perform the restoration. System Restore double-checks that you want to continue.

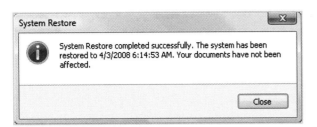

7. Click **Yes**.

8. After your PC restarts, log on as usual. System Restore displays a dialog box to indicate that it has completed successfully, as shown here. Click **Close**.

9. Check to ensure that Windows Vista is running properly. If it isn't, use System Restore to restore Windows Vista either to its previous state (undoing the restoration) or to an earlier restore point, depending on what the problem is.

RUN SYSTEM RESTORE FROM SAFE MODE

If Windows Vista is too unstable to run System Restore normally, you can start System Restore in Safe Mode to return Windows Vista to an earlier state.

1. Shut down Windows Vista, turn off your PC, and wait for at least two minutes to allow all of the components to discharge fully.

2. Turn your PC on. After the memory check, press and hold down **F8** to display the Windows Advanced Options Menu (see Figure 10-9).

3. Use the **ARROW** keys to move the highlight to the Safe Mode item, and then press **ENTER**. Windows Vista starts in Safe Mode.

4. At the Welcome screen, click your username, type your password, and press **ENTER**. Safe Mode appears.

5. Follow through the procedure for selecting a restore point and applying it, as described in "Restore Windows Vista to a Restore Point," earlier in this chapter.

RUN SYSTEM RESTORE FROM THE WINDOWS DVD

If you're not able to get your PC to start in Safe Mode, you can run System Restore from your Windows Vista DVD instead:

1. Insert the Windows Vista DVD in your PC's optical drive, and then restart your PC.

2. If your PC prompts you to press a key to start from the CD drive, press a key (for example, **SPACEBAR**).

3. On the first Install Windows screen of the DVD, choose your language and keyboard layout, and then click **Next** to display the next screen.

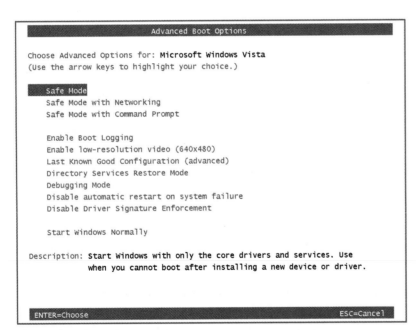

Figure 10-9: If Windows Vista is too unstable to run System Restore successfully, try starting Windows Vista in Safe Mode using the Windows Advanced Options menu.

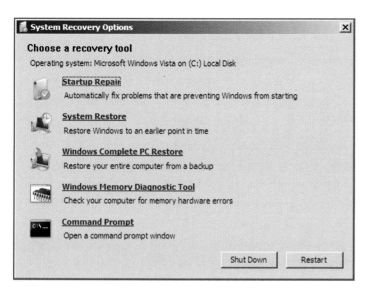

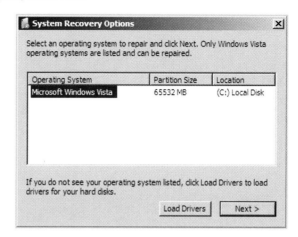

4. Click **Repair Your Computer** to display the first System Recovery Options dialog box, shown here.

5. Click **Microsoft Windows Vista** in the list box, and then click **Next** to display the second System Recovery Options dialog box (see Figure 10-10).

6. Click **System Restore** to launch the System Restore Wizard.

7. Follow through the procedure for selecting a restore point and applying it, as described in "Restore Windows Vista to a Restore Point," earlier in this chapter.

8. Back in the System Recovery Options window, click **Restart** to restart your PC.

RUN STARTUP REPAIR FROM THE WINDOWS DVD

If running System Restore from the Windows DVD doesn't get Windows Vista to start again, run Startup Repair from the Windows DVD:

1. Follow through steps 1 through 5 in the "Run System Restore from the Windows DVD" list to open the System Recovery Options dialog box.

2. Click **Startup Repair** to launch Startup Repair, which then runs automatically.

3. When Startup Repair has completed repairs (or not found any problems), click **Finish**.

4. Back in the System Recovery Options window, click **Restart** to restart your PC.

Figure 10-10: The System Recovery Options dialog box lets you run System Restore or Startup Repair.

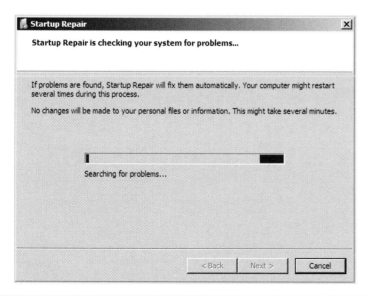

Receive and Give Help

If Windows Vista is running stably but you have a problem you can't fix, you may want to ask someone knowledgeable for help via Windows Vista's Remote Assistance feature. When the shoe is on the other foot, you can provide help to someone else who requests it.

Remote Assistance enables you to invite someone to connect to your PC from a remote PC so that this person can see what's happening, provide advice (via text or audio chat) on fixing problems, or even control your PC remotely to fix problems. The other person must be using Windows Vista, Windows XP, or Windows 2003 Server.

Set Up Remote Assistance

Before you can use Remote Assistance, you must set it up through the System Properties dialog box.

1. Press **WINDOWS KEY+BREAK** (or click the **Start** button, right-click **Computer**, and click **Properties**) to open the System window.

2. In the left panel, click **Remote Settings**, and then go through User Account Control for the System Remote Settings feature. Windows displays the System Properties dialog box with the Remote tab at the front.

3. Make sure the **Allow Remote Assistance Invitations To Be Sent From This Computer** check box is selected, and then click **Advanced**. The Remote Assistance Settings dialog box appears, as shown here.

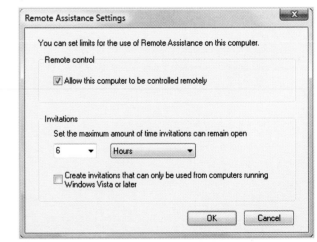

CAUTION

Allow your PC to be controlled remotely only if you absolutely trust the other person and his or her computer skills. If you decide to use this option, Windows Vista still prompts you to decide on each separate request from the other person to take control of your PC.

TIP

Chapter 3 discusses how to configure and use Windows Live Messenger.

4. If you want the other person to be able to help you actively rather than just providing suggestions via chat, select the **Allow This Computer To Be Controlled Remotely** check box.

5. Change the time period specified by the two **Set The Maximum Amount Of Time Invitations Can Remain Open** drop-down list boxes.

- If you'll issue invitations via Windows Live Messenger, set a short period—for example, 30 minutes.

- If you'll issue invitations via e-mail, allow several hours or even one or two days, depending on how quickly you expect the other person to respond.

6. If you want to increase security by limiting your helpers to using PCs running Windows Vista rather than earlier versions of Windows, select the **Create Invitations That Can Only Be Used From Computers Running Windows Vista Or Later** check box. Unless you're certain all your helpers will use Windows Vista, it is better to clear this check box.

7. Click **OK** twice to close the two open dialog boxes.

Request Remote Assistance

Windows Live Messenger is the fastest and easiest way to request Remote Assistance because you can see instantly whether your contact is online.

To request Remote Assistance using Windows Live Messenger:

1. Click the **Start** button, click **All Programs**, and then either click **Windows Live Messenger** (if it appears) or click **Windows Live** and then click **Windows Live Messenger**. Windows Live Messenger opens. If Windows Live Messenger doesn't automatically sign you in, sign in manually.

2. Begin a conversation with the contact as normal.

3. In the Conversation window, click the **Show Menu** button, click or highlight **Actions**, and then click **Request Remote Assistance**.

4. If the contact accepts the invitation, the Windows Remote Assistance dialog box shown here appears. Type a password of at least six characters, confirm it, and then click **OK**. You then need to communicate the password to your helper.

NOTE

To request Remote Assistance via e-mail, click the **Start** button, click **All Programs**, click Maintenance, and then click **Remote Assistance**. A Help And Support Center window opens to the Remote Assistance topic. Click **Invite Someone You Trust To Help You**, then click the Use E-mail To Send An Invitation button. On the Choose A Password For Connecting To Your Computer screen, type the password the other person must use, and then click Next. Windows then launches your e-mail program and starts a message with the invitation attached. Enter the e-mail address and send the message as you would any other message. You will then need to communicate the password to the other person securely—for example, by phone.

NOTE

Remote Assistance is relatively safe because nobody can connect to your PC via Remote Assistance without you sending them an invitation and then actively approving the connection. That said, you must keep your wits about you when receiving Remote Assistance. Even if you only chat with the other person and do not allow him or her to take control of your PC, implementing a poor suggestion can be every bit as destructive as letting somebody with poor computer skills take control of your PC.

5. After your helper enters the correct password, a Windows Remote Assistance confirmation dialog box appears, as shown here. Verify that it's the right person, and then click **Yes**. The Remote Assistance window opens (see Figure 10-11).

6. To communicate with the other person, click **Chat**, type a message in the text box that appears, and press **ENTER** or click **Send**. Your messages and the person's replies appear in the window.

7. If you have permitted remote control, the other person can request control of your PC. You'll see a dialog box such as the one shown here. Click **OK** if you trust the other person. (If you're going for broke, you can select the **Allow _Helper_ To Respond To User Account Control Prompts** check box, but normally it's better to respond to them yourself for security.) You can press **ESC** (or click **Stop Sharing**) at any time to cut off the other person's control.

8. To end a session, send a message to that effect, click **Disconnect**, and close the **Remote Assistance** window.

Figure 10-11: Remote Assistance is a fast and effective way to get help from a more experienced Windows user.

Provide Remote Assistance

If you're asked via Windows Live Messenger to provide Remote Assistance, proceed as follows:

1. Click the **Accept** link (or press **ALT+T**). Remote Assistance prompts the other person to create a password, and then prompts you for the password, as shown here.

When you receive a Remote Assistance invitation via e-mail, double-click the attached file, which is called rcBuddy.MsRcIncident. Verify that the invitation has not yet expired, type the password that the other person has given you, and click **Yes**. Windows Vista then establishes the connection.

2. Type the password, and then click **OK**.

3. If the other person confirms the connection, a Remote Assistance window opens on your screen (see Figure 10-12).

4. Provide advice, or take control to demonstrate what's needed.

   ● Click **Chat**, type a message in the text box, and press **ENTER** or click **Send** to transmit it.

   ● You can toggle the screen between actual size and scaled to fit on your screen by clicking **Fit To Screen**. (Which size is more convenient will depend on the size of the other person's screen, the size of your screen, and what you're trying to do.)

   ● Click **Request Control** to request control of the remote PC. Work on the remote PC without pressing **ESC** (the key to release control). To release control, press **ESC**.

   ● Click **Send File** if you need to send a file to the other PC to fix a problem. For example, you might need to download a driver and make it available to the other PC.

5. To end the Remote Assistance session, type a message telling the other person, send it, and then click **Disconnect**.

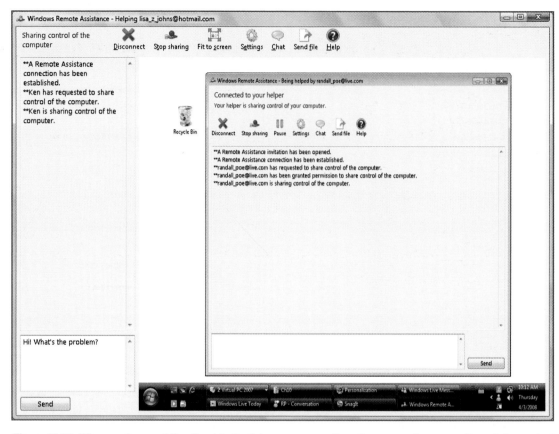

Figure 10-12: *When you're providing Remote Assistance, you see the other person's screen. If you take control (as shown here), you can show the other person how to perform the actions needed to remedy the problem.*

network adapters (cards) *(cont.)*
    installing, 168–169, 172
    selecting, 167–168
    wireless adapters, 7, 166, 170–172, 176–177
network addresses, 174, 183
Network Center button, 203
network drives, 39, 40, 41
network icon, 37
network shares, 180–186
networking protocols, 172–175, 187–188
networks
    Bluetooth connections, 167
    cables, 164–169, 172, 190
    choosing type of, 163–167
    connection options for, 166–167
    connection speed, 163–168, 170, 171
    Ethernet, 163–180
    hubs, 10, 164, 165, 168
    IP addresses, 173–175, 187–189
    LANs, 2, 54, 157, 190
    phone line, 167
    powerline, 167
    routers, 164–167, 169–171, 190
    security, 155–159, 164, 174–180, 185
    setting up, 167–180
    sharing over, 180–186
    switches, 164–169
    TCP/IP, 172–174, 186–188, 190
    troubleshooting, 186–190
    USB, 167
    wired. *See* wired networks
    wireless. *See* wireless networks
Notepad, 84, 85, 86
notification area, 15, 36, 37
NT File System (NTFS), 19, 41
NTFS (NT File System), 19, 41

O

Offline Files feature, 206–209
online chats. *See* instant messaging
operating systems, 10–13. *See also* Windows
    operating system; Windows Vista operating
    system
optical discs, 6, 8, 10, 120, 133
optical drives, 6, 8, 39, 40, 134
option buttons, 27, 28

P

Paint program, 85, 109–111, 112
parallel ports, 10
parental controls, 66, 151–154, 155
partitions, 18–19, 131–132
Passport, Microsoft, 75, 79
passwords
    boot, 140
    choosing, 19
    e-mail, 54, 56, 68
    entering at startup, 14
    resetting, 156–157
    sharing and, 175, 183
    user accounts, 19, 148–150
    Windows Live Messenger, 75, 79
PC Card, 10, 168
PCI cards, 10, 168
PCI/PCI Express cards, 134–135
PCs (personal computers)
    adding memory, 127, 128–129
    basics, 1–21
    components, 2, 3–10
    desktops. *See* desktop PCs
    laptops. *See* laptop PCs
    locking, 16, 20
    logging off (user session), 21

new vs. upgraded, 16
    overview, 1–2, 39
    restarting, 21
    setting up, 13
    sharing settings, 182–184
    shutdown alternatives, 20–21
    sleep mode, 21
    specifying current location, 20
    starting, 13–14
    supplying power to, 14
    uses for, 2
performance, 4, 6
peripheral devices. *See* devices
personal computers. *See* PCs
Personalization window, 31–35, 150
Phone And Modem Options dialog box, 55–56,
    211–212
pictures
    associated with account, 15
    capturing stills from webcam, 110
    choosing, 19
    converting to different format, 110–111
    copying from web pages, 65
    copying/pasting, 109
    creating with Paint, 109–111, 112
    as desktop background, 32
    formats, 110–112
    printing, 107–109
    scanning, 115–116
    viewing in Windows Photo Gallery, 111–116
Pictures folder, 42
Ping utility, 189, 190
"pinned" programs, 15, 86
pixels, 8
playback devices, 117
Plug and Play devices, 101
PNG format, 112

pointing devices, 8–9, 10, 15
pointing stick, 9
pop-up windows, 66–67, 158, 159
ports, 10, 13, 126, 169, 192
power, supplying to desktop PC, 14
power adapters, 14
power button, 13, 20
power cables, 14
Power icon, 21, 37, 194, 198, 199
power options, 15
power strip, 14
power supplies, 5, 14
power switch, 13
presentation programs, 90, 91
presentations, 90, 91, 202–203
preview windows, 37
Print dialog box, 107
print jobs, 106, 186
printers
    choosing, 102–103
    drivers, 103–105
    installing, 101–106
    network, 105–106
    sharing, 106–107, 156, 182, 184, 186
Printers window, 102
printing, 89, 107–109
privacy settings
    Internet, 65, 66, 158
    Windows Live Messenger, 79
processor benchmarks, 4
processor speeds, 4
processors, 3–5
product key, 18
programs
    business-related, 90–91
    configuring, 95–98
    described, 11

freeware/shareware, 88
frequently used, 15
included with Windows Vista, 84
installing/removing, 92–95
memory and, 38
older versions, 96
"pinned," 15, 86
recent, 36
running, 24, 82–83
searching for, 15
shortcuts, 98
starting at logon, 95, 219
stopping, 83
switching among, 83–85
toolbars in, 28
unsigned, 144–145
PS/2 ports, 13
Public Location button, 20, 170
public wireless networks, 213

Q

Quick Launch toolbar, 36, 37, 159

R

radio buttons, 27, 28
radio stations, 120–121
RAM. *See* memory
receiver, 7, 117, 121, 188
recordable discs, 50
recording audio, 121–122
recovering data, 45, 161
Recycle Bin, 15, 42, 46–47
refresh rate, 32
Remote Assistance, 225–230
removable drives, 41, 47–48, 50, 112, 177

resolution
    digital camera, 100
    monitor, 8, 31–32, 201
    screen, 8, 31–32
Restart option, 15
restarting PC, 21
restore points, 222–223
rewritable discs, 50
Ribbon interface, 30
root folders, 38
Run dialog box, 82

S

saving files, 38, 42
scanners, 101–102, 115–116
screen. *See also* monitor
    color quality, 31–32
    customizing, 31–33
    fonts, 35
    laptop PCs, 8, 199
    resolution, 8, 31–32
screen saver, 33, 150, 202
ScreenTip, 15, 29
scroll arrows, 25
scroll button, 25
Search feature, 44–47
searches. *See* finding items
security
    encryption, 132, 171, 176, 177, 180, 208
    firewalls, 140, 141, 155–157
    Internet, 64–67, 155–159
    networks, 155–159, 164, 174–180, 185
    recommended settings for, 20
    securing PC, 139–147
    sharing and, 185
    spyware, 159

USB 1.x standard, 10
USB 2.0 standard, 10, 130
USB connections, 10, 168, 172–176
USB networks, 167
USB ports, 10
USB (Universal Serial Bus) technology, 10
user accounts, 19, 148–150
user folders, 39
username, 14, 16, 19, 54, 68, 148
users
    logging off, 21
    passwords, 19, 148–150
    security for, 141, 147–154
    switching, 15, 21

V

video
    importing from camcorder, 116–117
    playing from Internet, 66
    watching on Windows Media Player, 122–123
    Windows Movie Maker, 42, 85, 116–117
video adapter (card), 7, 9, 38
video cameras, 100–101, 111–112
video/audio conversations, 80
Videos folder, 42
virtual memory, 42
virus protection, 142, 143–144
viruses, 80
Vista Basic user interface, 35
volume, adjusting, 37, 117, 118, 201

W

wallpapers, 32
Web, 57–67. *See also* Internet; networks

web browsers. *See also* Internet Explorer
    accessing Web, 57
    alternate browsers, 158
    favorite websites, 59–60
    navigation, 60, 61
    searching Web, 57–59
web pages
    copying entire page, 66
    copying pictures from, 65
    copying text from, 65–66
    displayed in tabs, 63
    displayed in windows, 63, 64
    history, 61–63
    home page, 61
    links on, 60
    opening multiple, 63–64
    pop-ups, 66–67, 158, 159
    recent, 61
webcams, 80, 100–101, 110
websites
    accessing directly, 60
    browsing, 60–61, 157–159
    categorizing, 64
    cookies, 64–65
    favorites, 59–60
    history, 61–63
    navigating, 60–61
Wi-Fi, 165, 167, 170, 171
window border, 25
windows
    activating, 27
    arranging multiple, 26
    changing appearance, 34
    changing state, 26
    closing, 27
    color, 34–35
    components of, 25–26
    dragging, 35

    illustrated, 24, 25
    positioning, 24, 25
    preview, 37
    size, 24, 25, 26
    states, 26
    switching between, 26
    title bar, 25
    web pages displayed in, 63, 64
    working with, 25–27
Windows Aero interface, 26, 34, 84
Windows Calendar, 71, 85
Windows Contacts, 69, 71–72, 85
Windows Explorer, 38–49
    Computer window, 38–41
    Favorite Links area, 39
    managing files/folders in, 38–49
    "old-style" menus, 29
    toolbars, 29
Windows interface, 23–30
    desktop. *See* desktop
    dialog boxes, 24, 25, 27–28
    menus, 25, 28–30, 35, 61
    toolbars. *See* toolbars
    windows. *See* windows
Windows Live ID, 75
Windows Live Messenger, 74–80, 226, 227–238
Windows Mail, 68–72, 85. *See also* e-mail
Windows Media Player, 85, 117–124, 157, 183
Windows Mobility Center, 198–203
Windows Movie Maker, 42, 85, 116–117
Windows operating system, 24, 34. *See also* operating systems; Windows Vista operating system
Windows Photo Gallery, 111–116
Windows Vista Business Edition, 11, 18
Windows Vista desktop. *See* desktop
Windows Vista Home Basic Edition, 11, 18, 34
Windows Vista Home Premium Edition, 11, 18